Redesigning Distribution

The Real Utopias Project

Series editor: Erik Olin Wright

The Real Utopias Project embraces a tension between dreams and practice. It is founded on the belief that what is pragmatically possible is not fixed independently of our imaginations, but is itself shaped by our visions. The fulfillment of such a belief involves 'real utopias': utopian ideals that are grounded in the real potentials for redesigning social institutions.

In its attempt at sustaining and deepening serious discussion of radical alternatives to existing social practices, the Real Utopias Project examines various basic institutions – property rights and the market, secondary associations, the family, the welfare state, among others – and focuses on specific proposals for their fundamental redesign. The books in the series are the result of workshop conferences, at which groups of scholars are invited to respond to provocative manuscripts.

Redesigning Distribution

Basic income and stakeholder grants as alternative
cornerstones for a more egalitarian capitalism

The Real Utopias Project
VOLUME V

BRUCE ACKERMAN
ANNE ALSTOTT
PHILIPPE VAN PARIJS

with contributions by
Barbara Bergmann
Irwin Garfinkel, Chien-Chung Huang and Wendy Naidich
Julian Le Grand
Carole Pateman
Guy Standing
Stuart White
Erik Olin Wright

Edited and Introduced by
Erik Olin Wright

2006

VERSO
London • New York

First published by Verso 2006

© in the collection, Verso 2006

© in the contributions, the individual contributors

1 3 5 7 9 10 8 6 4 2

Verso

UK: 6 Meard Street, London W1F 0EG

USA: 180 Varick Street, New York, NY 10014-4606

www.versobooks.com

Verso is the imprint of New Left Books

ISBN 1-84467-517-3 (paperback)

ISBN 1-84467-014-7 (hardback)

British Library Cataloguing in Publication Data

A catalogue record for this book is available from the British Library

Library of Congress Cataloging-in-Publication Data

A catalog record for this book is available from the Library of Congress

Typeset in Sabon by Andrea Stimpson

Printed in the USA

Contents

List of Tables and Figures

Tables

Figures

Introduction

Erik Olin Wright

The conference of the Real Utopias Project that generated the
original papers in this book was called "Rethinking Redistribution."
One of the interesting issues raised in the conference concerned the
use of the term "redistribution" in this title. The expression *re*distribution suggests that there is something called "distribution" which
exists prior to political interventions and is then transformed by deliberate political action. This corresponds to the conventional rhetoric
of economists and politicians: the income distribution generated by
markets is the result of voluntary exchanges by freely acting individuals; this spontaneous distribution is then altered by acts of states
that coercively take resources away from some people through taxes
and transfer them to others. Redistribution reflects coercion; market-
generated distribution reflects voluntary activity. This easily slides
into the libertarian view that all redistribution is a violation of fundamental freedoms: taxation is theft; people have an absolute moral
claim that whatever it is they can obtain from "voluntary exchange"
in markets.

There are several things wrong with this image. First of all, there is
plenty of coercion within markets themselves, ranging from the near
monopoly power of many large corporations to the coercion
embedded in inequalities of information of different actors in
markets, to the coercion that comes from some people facing very
limited alternatives in their market choices. Second, the state plays a
pivotal role in establishing the very possibility of markets through the
coercive enforcement of property rights that directly impact on the
nature of market-generated distributions. And third, in all sorts of
ways the state is involved in regulating aspects of market exchanges

and production – from health and safety rules, to credentialing requirements in many labor markets, to labor laws – which impact on the income distribution process. It is therefore misleading to talk about a clear distinction between some pure "distribution" of income and a process of politically shaped "redistribution".

We have thus decided to change the title of the book from the original "Rethinking Redistribution" to "Redesigning Distribution." Income and wealth distributions are the result of the simultaneous, joint operation of voluntary choices of interacting individuals and authoritative rule-making and enforcement by states. The problem is to figure what combination of voluntary choice and authoritative allocation generates the most desirable outcomes, in terms of both efficiency considerations and moral concerns.

There was a time, not so long ago, when the issue of the state's positive role in shaping income distribution was at the center of political debate. In Europe, Social Democratic parties argued for the desirability of an activist, affirmative state engaged in policies that would generate income distributions far more egalitarian than those produced through market forces and a passive state. Even in the United States, advocating such a role for the state was part of the spectrum of ordinary political debate. In the early 1970s in the United States, in the aftermath of the major expansion of welfare state programs of the previous decade, there was a lively political debate over whether or not a negative income tax should be adopted as a centerpiece of policies designed to alleviate poverty and reduce inequality. In the end the Family Assistance Program, as the proposal was known, was narrowly defeated in the U.S. Congress, and so the existing welfare mechanism of Aid to Families with Dependent Children remained intact. But still, in that debate of 30 years ago the issue was what sort of state intervention into patterns of income distribution would best serve broader social and economic goals, not whether the state should get out of the business of trying to affect distribution altogether.

The intervening three decades have witnessed a massive shift in the ideological coordinates of public policy discussions in the United States and elsewhere. By the early 1990s, particularly in the U.S., defenders of traditional income support policies of the affirmative state were on the defensive and virtually no one in the public debate argued that shaping the income distribution was a worthy political goal. Instead of a political ethos in which the basic well-being of all citizens was seen as part of a collective responsibility, the vision was one in which each person took full "personal responsibility" for their own well-being. The nearly universal call was to "end welfare as we know it", replacing it with a vestigial welfare state that at most would provide a minimal safety net only for those people clearly incapable of taking care of themselves. Times were indeed bleak for progressives committed to an egalitarian conception of social justice.

Given this ideological climate, it might seem like an unpropitious time to propose radical strategies for reducing inequality through new programs of income and wealth transfers. Government intervention to generate more egalitarian income distribution is now broadly regarded as antithetical to economic efficiency and thus ultimately self-defeating; there is no vocal political coalition demanding new efforts at egalitarian distribution; and talk of raising taxes and dramatically expanding the activities of the state are seen by most analysts as off the political agenda. The Real Utopias Project is based on the belief that it is important to engage in rigorous analysis of alternative visions of institutional change even when there seems to be little support for such ideas since posing clear designs for alternatives may contribute to creating the conditions in which such support can be built.

In this spirit, this volume in the Real Utopias Project examines two provocative proposals for radical redesigns of distributive institutions: universal basic income, as elaborated by Philippe Van Parijs, and stakeholder grants, as elaborated by Bruce Ackerman and Anne Alstott. While both of these proposals contain a range of complex details, as ideals they are both based on very simple principles:

Basic income. All citizens are given a monthly stipend sufficiently high to provide them with a standard of living above the poverty line. This monthly income is universal rather than means-tested – it is given automatically to all citizens regardless of their individual economic circumstances. And it is unconditional – receiving the basic income does not depend upon performing any labor services or satisfying other conditions. In this way basic income is like publicly-financed universal health insurance: in a universal health care system, medical care is provided both to citizens who exercise and eat healthy diets and to those who do not. It is not a condition of getting medical care that one be "responsible" with respect to one's health. Unconditional, universal basic income takes the same stance about basic needs: as a matter of basic rights, no one should live in poverty in an affluent society.

Stakeholder grants. All citizens, upon reaching the age of early adulthood – say 21 – receive a substantial one-time lump-sum grant sufficiently large that all young adults would be significant wealth holders. Ackerman and Alstott propose that this grant be in the vicinity of $80,000 and would be financed by an annual wealth tax of roughly 2 percent. In the absence of such grants, children of wealthy parents are able to get lump-sum stakes for education, housing, business start-ups, investments, and so on, whereas children of non-wealthy parents are not. This situation fundamentally violates values of equal opportunity. A system of stakeholder grants, they argue, "expresses a fundamental responsibility: every American has an obligation to contribute to a fair starting point for all."

In some ways, basic income and stakeholder grants are not completely different kinds of proposals. After all, if one invests a stakeholder grant in a relatively low-risk investment and waits a number of years, then it will eventually generate a permanent stream of income equivalent to an above-poverty basic income. Similarly, if one continues to work for earnings in the labor market while receiving a basic income and one saves the basic income, after a number of years it will become the equivalent of a stakeholder grant. Nevertheless, the two proposals reflect quite distinct visions of what kind of system of redistribution would be morally and pragmatically optimal in developed market economies. Stakeholder grants emphasize individual responsibility and what is sometimes called "starting gate equality of opportunity." Individuals get a stake, and if they blow it on conspicuous consumption rather than long-term plans, then this is their responsibility. Basic income envisions a system of distribution that permanently guarantees everyone freedom from poverty and a certain kind of lifetime equality of minimal opportunity: the opportunity to withdraw from the labor force to engage in non-remunerated activity.

There are, of course, many objections that can be raised against both of these proposals. Some of these objections are moral: basic income rewards people for being parasites; redistributions of wealth illegitimately takes assets away from people who have worked hard to build them up. Others are pragmatic: so many people would withdraw their labor from the labor market if there were a decent basic income that the economy would collapse; the rates of taxation required for basic income will undermine incentives; redistributions of wealth to create stakes will eliminate incentives to save and build up assets. The two core chapters in this book and the series of commentaries that follow attempt to clarify the arguments behind these two proposals and evaluate the cogency of the objections.

PART I

Proposals

Basic Income:
A simple and powerful idea for
the twenty-first century*

Philippe Van Parijs

Give all citizens a modest, yet unconditional income, and let them top it up at will with income from other sources.

This exceedingly simple idea has a surprisingly diverse pedigree. In the course of the last two centuries, it has been independently thought up under a variety of names – "territorial dividend" and "state bonus," for example, "demogrant" and "citizen's wage," "universal benefit" and "basic income" – in most cases without much success. In the late 1960s and early 1970s, it enjoyed a sudden popularity in the United States and was even put forward by a presidential candidate, but it was soon shelved and just about forgotten. In the last two decades, however, it has gradually become the subject of an unprecedented and fast expanding public discussion throughout the European Union. Some see it as a crucial remedy for many social ills, including unemployment and poverty. Others denounce it as a crazy, economically flawed, ethically objectionable proposal, to be forgotten as soon as possible, to be dumped once and for all into the dustbin of the history of ideas.

To shed light on this debate, I start off saying more about what basic income is and what it is not, and about what distinguishes it from existing guaranteed income schemes. On this background, it

---

* The first version of this chapter was prepared for the international seminar "Policies and Instruments to Fight Poverty in the European Union: A guaranteed minimum income" organized under the aegis of the Portuguese presidency of the European Union (Almancil, Portugal, February 2000). Later versions served as background papers for the VIIIth Congress of the Basic Income European Network (Berlin, Germany, October 2000) and, jointly with a paper by Bruce Ackerman and Anne Alstott, for the workshop "Rethinking Redistribution" (Madison, Wisconsin, May 2002).

will be easier to understand why basic income has recently been attracting so much attention, why resistance can be expected to be tough and how it will eventually be overcome. It is the author's firm conviction that basic income will not be forgotten, and that it must not be dumped. Basic income is one of those few simple ideas that must and will powerfully shape first the debate, and next the reality, of the new century.

WHAT BASIC INCOME IS AND WHAT IT IS NOT

A basic income is an income paid by a political community to all its members on an individual basis, without means test or work requirement. This is the definition I shall adopt. It does not fit all actual uses of the English expression "basic income," or of its most common translations into other European languages, such as "Bürgergeld," "allocation universelle," "renta básica," "reddito di cittadinanza," "basisinkomen," or "borgerlon." Some of these actual uses are broader: they also cover, for example, benefits whose level is affected by one's household situation or which are administered in the form of tax credits. Other uses are narrower: They also require, for example, that the level of the basic income should match what is required to satisfy basic needs or that it should replace all other transfers. The aim of the above definition is not to police usage but to clarify arguments. Let us briefly focus on each of its components in turn.

An income

Paid in cash, rather than in kind. One can conceive of a benefit that would have all other features of a basic income but be provided in kind, for example in the form of a standardized bundle of food, or the use of a plot of land. Or it could be provided in the form of a special currency with restricted uses, for example food stamps or housing grants, or more broadly consumption in the current period only without any possibility of saving it, as in Jacques Duboin's (1945) "distributive economy." A basic income, instead, is provided in cash, without any restriction as to the nature or timing of the consumption or investment it helps fund. In most variants, it supplements, rather than substitutes, existing in-kind transfers such as free education or basic health insurance.

Paid on a regular basis, rather than as a one-off endowment. A basic income consists in purchasing power provided at regular intervals, such as a week, a month, a term or a year, depending on the proposal. One can also conceive of a benefit that would have all other features of a basic income but be provided on a one-off basis, for example at the beginning of adult life. This has occasionally been proposed (see Cunliffe and Erreygers 2003), for example long ago by Thomas Paine (1796) and far more recently by Bruce Ackerman and Anne Alstott (1999). There is a significant difference between a regular basic income and such a basic endowment. Yet it should not be overstated. First, the basic endowment can be invested to generate an actuarially equivalent annual or monthly income up to the recipient's death, which would amount to a regular basic income. If left to the insurance market, the level of this annuity would be negatively affected by the length of a person's life expectancy. Women, for example, would receive a lower annuity than men. However, the advocates of a basic endowment (including Paine and Ackerman and Alstott) usually supplement it with a uniform basic pension from a certain age, which erases most of this difference. Second, while other uses can be made of a basic endowment than turning it into an annuity, the resulting difference with a basic income would be essentially annulled if the latter's recipients could freely borrow against their future basic income stream. Even if one wisely protects basic income against seizure by creditors, the security it provides will make it easier for its beneficiaries to take loans at every stage and will thereby reduce the gap between the ranges of options opened, respectively, by a one-off basic endowment and a regular basic income.

Paid by a political community

By definition, a basic income is paid by a government of some sort out of publicly controlled resources. But it need not be paid by a nation-state. Nor does it need to be paid out of redistributive taxation.

The nation-state, beneath and beyond. In most proposals, the basic income is supposed to be paid, and therefore funded, at the level of a nation-state, as sometimes indicated by the very choice of such labels as "state bonus," "national dividend" or "citizen's wage." However, it can in principle also be paid and funded at the level of a politically organized part of a nation-state, such as a province or a commune. Indeed, the only political unit which has ever introduced a genuine basic income, as defined, is the state of Alaska in the United States (see e.g. Palmer 1997). A basic income can also conceivably be paid by a supra-national political unit. Several proposals have been made at the level of the European Union (see Genet and Van Parijs 1992, Ferry 2000, Van Parijs and Vanderborght 2001) and some also, more speculatively, at the level of the United Nations (see e.g. Kooistra 1994, Barrez 1999, Frankman 2001).

Redistribution. The basic income may, but need not, be funded in a specific, ear-marked way. If it is not, it is simply funded along with all other government expenditures out of a common pool of revenues from a variety of sources. Among those who advocated ear-marked funding, most are thinking of a specific tax. Some want it funded out of a land tax or a tax on natural resources (from Thomas Paine (1796) and Joseph Charlier (1848) to Raymond Crotty (1987), Marc Davidson (1995) or James Robertson (1999) for example). Others prefer a specific levy on a very broadly defined income base (for example, Pelzer 1998, 1999) or a massively expanded value-added tax (for example, Duchatelet 1992, 1998). And some of those who are thinking of a worldwide basic income stress the potential of new tax instruments such as "Tobin taxes" on speculative capital movements (see Bresson 1999) or "bit taxes" on transfers of information (see Soete and Kamp 1996).

Distribution. Redistributive taxation, however, need not be the only source of funding. Alaska's dividend scheme (O'Brien and Olson 1990, Palmer 1997) is funded out of part of the return on a diversified investment fund which the state built up using the royalties on Alaska's vast oil fields. In the same vein, James Meade's (1989, 1993, 1994, 1995) blueprint of a fair and efficient economy comprises a social dividend funded out of the return on publicly owned productive assets. Finally, there has been a whole sequence of proposals to fund a basic income out of money creation, from Major Douglas's Social Credit movement (see Van Trier 1997) and Jacques and Marie-Louise Duboin's (1945, 1985) Mouvement français pour l'abondance to the more sophisticated (and more modest) proposals of Joseph Huber (1998, 1999, 2000 with J. Robertson).

To all its members

Non-citizens? There can be more or less inclusive conceptions of the membership of a political community. Some, especially among those who prefer the label "citizen's income," conceive of membership as restricted to nationals, or citizens in a legal sense. The right to a basic income is then of a piece with the whole package of rights and duties associated with full citizenship, as in the conception of the French philosopher Jean-Marc Ferry (1995, 2000). Most advocates of basic income, however, especially among those who view it as a policy against exclusion, do not want a restrictive entitlement to basic income to further deepen the dualization of the labor market. They therefore tend to conceive of membership in a broader sense that tends to include all legal permanent residents. The operational criterion may be, for non-citizens, a minimum length of past residence, or it may simply be provided by the conditions which currently define residence for tax purposes, or some combination of both.

Children? There can also be a more or less inclusive conception of membership along the age dimension. Some restrict basic income, by definition, to adult members of the population, but then tend to propose it side by side with a universal, that is, non-means-tested, child benefit system, with a level of benefit that may or may not be differentiated as a (positive or negative) function of the rank of the child or as a (positive) function of the child's age. Others conceive of basic income as an entitlement from the first to the last breath and therefore view it as a full substitute for the child benefit system. The level of the benefit then needs to be independent of the child's family situation, in particular of his or her rank. Some also want it to be the same as for adults, and hence independent of age, as is actually the case in the modest Alaskan dividend scheme and as would be the case under some more generous proposals (for example Miller 1983). But the majority of those who propose an integration of child benefits into the basic income scheme differentiate the latter's level according to age, with the maximum level not being granted until majority, or later.

Pensioners? Analogously, some restrict basic income to members of the population which have not reached retirement age and then see it as a natural complement to an individual, non-means-tested, non-contributory basic pension pitched at a higher level, of a sort that already exists in some European countries, like Sweden or the Netherlands. In most proposals, however, the basic income is granted beyond retirement age, either at the same level as for younger adults or at a somewhat higher level. In all cases, this basic income for the elderly can be supplemented by income from public or private contributory pension schemes, as well as from private savings and from employment.

Inmates? Even on the most inclusive definition of the relevant notion of membership, any population is still likely to contain some people who will not be paid a basic income. Detaining criminals in prison is far more expensive to the community than paying them a modest basic income, even if full account is taken of any productive work they may be made to perform. Unless the detention turns out to have been ill-founded, it is therefore obvious that prison inmates should lose the benefit of their basic income for the duration of their imprisonment. But they can get it back as soon as they are released. The same may apply to the long-term inmates of other institutions, such as mental hospitals or old people's homes, to the extent that the full cost of their stay is directly picked up by the community rather than paid for by the inmates themselves.

On an individual basis

Paid to each. The basic income is paid to each individual member of the community, rather than to each household taken as a whole, or to its head, as is the case under most existing guaranteed minimum schemes.

Uniform. Even if a benefit is paid to each individual, its level could still be affected by the composition of the household. To take account of the fact that the per capita cost of living decreases with the size of the household, existing guaranteed minimum income schemes grant a smaller per capita income to the members of a couple than to a person living alone. A fair and effective operation of such schemes therefore supposes that the administration should have the power to check the living arrangements of their beneficiaries. A basic income, instead, is paid on a strictly individual basis, not only in the sense that each individual member of the community is a recipient, but also in the sense that how much (s)he receives is independent of what type of household she belongs to. The operation of a basic income scheme therefore dispenses with any control over living arrangements, and it preserves the full advantages of reducing the cost of one's living by sharing one's accommodation with others. Precisely because of its strictly individualistic nature, a basic income tends to remove isolation traps and foster communal life.

Without means test

Irrespective of income. Relative to existing guaranteed minimum income schemes, the most striking feature of a basic income is no doubt that it is paid, indeed paid at the same level, to rich and poor alike, irrespective of their income level. Under the simplest variant of the existing schemes, a minimum level of income is specified for each type of household (single adult, childless couple, single parent of one child, and so on), the household's total income from other sources is assessed, and the difference between this income and the stipulated minimum is paid to each household as a cash benefit. In this sense, existing schemes operate *ex post*, on the basis of a prior assessment, be it provisional, of the beneficiaries' income. A basic income scheme, instead, operates *ex ante*, irrespective of any income test. The benefit is given in full to those whose income exceeds the stipulated minimum no less than to those whose income falls short of it. Nor are any other means taken into account when determining the level of benefit a person is entitled to: neither a person's informal income, nor the help she could claim from relatives, nor the value of her belongings. Taxable "means" may need to be taxed at a higher average rate in order to fund the basic income. But the tax-and-benefit system no longer rests on a dichotomy between two notions of "means": A broad one for the poor, by reference to which benefits are cut, and a narrow one for the better off, by reference to which income tax is levied.

Does not make the rich richer. From the fact that rich and poor receive the same basic income, it does not follow, however, that the introduction of a basic income would make both rich and poor richer than before. A basic income needs to be funded.

(1) If a basic income were simply added to existing tax-and-benefit systems, it is clear that the comparatively rich would need to pay both for their own basic income and for much of the basic income of the comparatively poor. This would clearly hold if the funding were through a progressive income tax, but would also hold under a flat tax or even a regressive consumption tax. For the *ex nihilo* introduction of a basic income to work to the financial advantage of the poor, the key condition is simply that, relative to their numbers (not necessarily to their incomes), the relatively rich should contribute more to its funding than the relatively poor.

(2) In most proposals, however, the introduction of a basic income is combined with a partial abolition of existing benefits and tax reductions. If the proposed reform simply consisted in spreading more thinly among all citizens the non-contributory benefits currently concentrated on the poor, the latter would clearly lose out. But no one is making such an absurd proposal. In most proposals that

rely on direct taxation, the basic income replaces only the bottom part of the non-contributory benefits, but also the exemptions or reduced tax rates on every taxpayer's lower income brackets. The immediate impact on the income distribution can then be kept within fairly narrow bounds for a modest basic income. But the higher its level, the higher the average rate of income tax and therefore the greater the redistribution from the comparatively rich to the comparatively poor.

Better for the poor to give to the rich? Thus, giving to all, rich and poor, is not meant to make things better for the rich. But, for a given level of minimum income, is there any reason to believe that it is better for the poor than a means-tested guaranteed income? Yes, for at least three interconnected reasons. First, the rate of take-up of benefits is likely to be higher under a universal scheme than if a means test is in place. Fewer among the poor will fail to be informed about their entitlements and to avail themselves of the benefits they have a right to. Second, there is nothing humiliating about benefits given to all as a matter of citizenship. This cannot be said, even with the least demeaning and intrusive procedures, about benefits reserved for the needy, the destitute, those identified as unable to fend for themselves. From the standpoint of the poor, this may count as an advantage in itself, because of the lesser stigma associated with a universal basic income. It also matters indirectly because of the effect of the stigma on the rate of take-up. Third, the regular, reliable payment of the benefit is not interrupted when accepting a job under a basic income scheme, whereas it would be under a standard means-tested scheme. Compared to means-tested schemes guaranteeing the same level of minimum income, this opens up real prospects for poor people who have good reasons not to take risks. This amounts to removing one aspect of the unemployment trap commonly associated with conventional benefit systems, an aspect to which social workers are usually far more sensitive than economists.

Makes work pay? The other aspect of the unemployment trap generated by means-tested guaranteed minimum schemes is the one most commonly stressed by economists. It consists in the lack of a significant positive income differential between no work and low-paid work. At the bottom end of the earnings distribution, if each euro of earnings is offset, or practically offset, or more than offset, by a loss of one euro in benefits, one does not need to be particularly lazy to turn down a job that would yield such earnings, or to actively look for such jobs. Given the additional costs, travelling time or child-care problems involved, one may not be able to afford to work under such circumstances. Moreover, it would generally not make much sense for employers to design and offer such jobs, as people who would be grateful for being sacked are unlikely to constitute a conscientious and reliable workforce. A minimum wage legislation may anyway prevent full-time jobs from being offered at a wage lower than the income guarantee, in which case the latter consideration only applies to part-time jobs. The replacement of a means-tested guaranteed income by a universal basic income is often presented as a way of tackling this second aspect of the unemployment trap too. If one gave everyone a universal basic income but taxed at 100 percent the portion of everyone's earnings that does not exceed the minimum guarantee (see for example Salverda 1984), the unemployment trap would be the same, in this respect, as under a means-tested guaranteed minimum income. (See Figure 1.1 and Figure 1.3 in the appendix.) But if one makes the mild assumption that the explicit tax rate applying to the lowest income brackets must remain noticeably lower than 100 percent, then the following statement holds. Since you can keep the full amount of your basic income, whether working or not, whether rich or poor, you are bound to be better off when working than out of work. (See Figure 1.2 in the appendix.)

Equivalent to a negative income tax? Note, however, that this second aspect of the unemployment trap can be removed just as effectively, it would seem, by a means-tested scheme that would phase out the benefit less steeply as earnings rise. This is achieved through the so-called negative income tax, a uniform and refundable tax credit. The notion of a negative income tax first appears in the writings of the French economist Augustin Cournot (1838). It was briefly proposed by Milton Friedman (1962) as a way of trimming down the welfare state, and explored in more depth by James Tobin (1965, 1966, 1967, 1968) and his associates as a way of fighting poverty while preserving work incentives. On the background of an explicit tax schedule which taxes no income at 100 percent and which can be, but need not by def-inition be, linear, a negative income tax amounts to reducing the income tax liability of every household (of a given composition) by the same fixed magnitude, while paying as a cash benefit the differ-ence between this magnitude and the tax liability whenever this difference is positive. (See Figure 1.3 below.) Suppose the fixed magni-tude of the tax credit is pitched at the same level as under some basic income scheme under consideration. Someone with no income, and hence no income tax liability, will then receive an amount equal to the basic income. As the income rises, the benefit will shrink, as in the case of conventional means-tested schemes, but at a slower rate, indeed at a rate that will keep post-and-transfer income at exactly the same level as under the corresponding basic income scheme. (See Figures 1.3 and 1.4.) The NIT variant simply consists in netting out taxes and benefits. Under a basic income scheme, the revenues needed to fund the NIT's universal tax credit are actually raised and paid back to all. Under NIT, transfers are all one-way only: positive transfers (or negative taxes) for households under the so-called break-even point, negative transfers (or positive taxes) for households above. (See Figure 1.3.)

Cheaper than a negative income tax? How much of a real difference there is between a basic income and a negative income tax depends on further specification of administrative procedures. It shrinks, for example, if taxes are levied at source on a pay-as-you-earn basis (rather than only after tax returns have been processed), or if tax liabilities are assessed on a weekly or monthly, rather than an annual basis, or if everyone is entitled, under a NIT scheme, to an advance payment of the presumptive tax credit (subject to subsequent correction), or if everyone is entitled, under a BI scheme, to get the BI as a tax discount rather than in cash. But even in the closest variant, there remains a difference between a system that operates, by default, "ex ante," and one that operates, by default, "ex post." Any remaining difference would count as an advantage for the basic income variant with respect to the first, uncertainty-linked dimension of the unemployment trap. Yet, with a rudimentary benefit payment technology (coins carried by the postman!) or with a tax collection administration plagued by corruption or inefficiency, the case for the NIT variant, which does away with the back-and-forth of tax money, may be overwhelming. In an era of technological transfers and with a reasonably well-run tax administration, on the other hand, the bulk of the administrative cost associated with an effective guaranteed minimum income scheme is the cost of information and control: The expenditure needed to inform all potential beneficiaries about what their entitlements are and to check whether those applying meet the eligibility conditions. In these respects, a universal system is bound to perform better than a means-tested one. As automaticity and reliability increase on both the payment and the collection side, it is therefore, in this administrative sense, increasingly likely to be the cheaper of the two, for a given degree of effectiveness at reaching all the poor. It is for this sort of reason that James Tobin (1997), for example, preferred a universal "demogrant" to its negative-income-tax variant.

Without work requirement

Irrespective of present work performance. The right to a guaranteed minimum income is by definition not restricted to those who have worked enough in the past, or paid in enough social security contributions to be entitled to some insurance benefits. From Juan Luis Vives (1526) onwards, however, its earliest variants were often linked to the obligation to perform some toil, whether in the old-fashioned and ill-famed workhouses or in a more varied gamut of contemporary private and public workfare settings. Being unconditional, a basic income sharply contrasts with these forms of guaranteed income intimately linked to guaranteed employment. It also diverges from in-work benefits restricted to households at least one member of which is in paid employment, such as the American Earned Income Tax Credit or the UK's more recent Working Families Tax Credit. By virtue of removing the unemployment trap – i.e. by providing its net beneficiaries with an incentive to work – a basic income (or a negative income tax) can be understood and used as an in-work benefit or a top-up on earnings. But it is not restricted to this role. Its unconditionality marks it off from any type of employment subsidy, however broadly conceived.

Irrespective of willingness to work. It also marks it off from conventional guaranteed minimum income schemes, which tend to restrict entitlement to those willing to work in some sense. The exact content of this restriction varies a great deal from country to country, indeed sometimes from one local authority to another within the same country. It may involve that one must accept a suitable job if offered, with significant administrative discretion as to what "suitable" may mean in terms of location or skill requirements; or that one must give proof of an active interest in finding a job; or that one must accept and respect an "insertion contract," whether connected to paid employment, to training or to some other useful activity. By contrast, a basic income is paid as a matter of right – and not under false pretences – to homemakers, students, break-takers and permanent tramps. Some intermediate proposals, such as Anthony Atkinson's (1993a, 1993b, 1996, 1998; Vanderborght and Van Parijs 2001) "participation income," impose a broad condition of social contribution, which can be fulfilled by full- or part-time waged employment or self-employment, by education, training or active job search, by home care for infant children or frail elderly people, or by regular voluntary work in a recognised association. The more broadly this condition is to be interpreted, the less of a difference there is with a basic income.

WHY DO WE NEED A BASIC INCOME?

If we want no means test, it is important to drop the work test. Bringing together the last two unconditionalities discussed – the absence of the means test and the absence of the work test – makes it possible to briefly formulate the core of what makes basic income particularly relevant under present circumstances. At first sight, there is total independence between these two unconditionalities, between the absence of an income test and the absence of a work test. But the strength of the basic income proposal crucially hinges on their being combined. The abolition of the means test, as we have seen, is intimately linked to the removal of the unemployment trap (in its two main dimensions), and hence to the creation of a potential for offering and accepting low-paid jobs that currently do not exist. But some of these jobs can be lousy, degrading dead-end jobs, which should not be promoted. Others are pleasant, enriching stepping-stone jobs, which are worth taking even at low pay because of their intrinsic value or the training they provide. Who can tell the difference? Not legislators or bureaucrats, but the individual workers who can be relied upon to know far more than what is known "at the top" about the countless facets of the job they do or consider taking. They have the knowledge that would enable them to be discriminating, but not always the power to do so, especially if they have poorly valued skills or limited mobility. A work-unconditional basic income endows the weakest with bargaining power in a way a work-conditional guaranteed income does not. Put differently, work-unconditionality is a key instrument to prevent means-unconditionality from leading to the expansion of lousy jobs.

If there is no means test, no work test is needed. At the same time the work incentives associated by means-unconditionality make work-conditionality less tempting as a way of alleviating the fear that benefits without a counterpart would nurture an idle underclass. In the absence of a means test, the tax and benefit structure can be expected to be such that beneficiaries can significantly increase their disposable incomes by working, even at a low rate and on a part-time basis, and without being trapped in such jobs once their skills improve or once they can improve their working time. Moving (back) into the work sphere will therefore be facilitated and encouraged, and, for those who fear a dualization of society into workers and non-workers, there will therefore be far less of a need to insist on coupling the right to the benefit to some obligation to (be available for) work. To put it (somewhat too) succinctly: Just as work-unconditionality prevents means-unconditionality from unacceptably supporting exploitation (which it would do by subsidizing unworthy low-paid jobs accepted under the threat of losing the benefit), similarly means-unconditionality prevents work-unconditionality from unacceptably fostering exclusion (which it would do by inviting one to no longer regard as problematic a system that durably disconnects the less productive from any labour participation by effectively killing off low-productive jobs). The two key unconditionalities of basic income are logically independent, but they are intrinsically linked as components of a strong proposal.

Activating while liberating. This solidarity between the two unconditionalities underlies the central case for basic income as a specific way of handling the joint challenge of poverty and unemployment. Compared to guaranteed income schemes of the conventional sort, the crucial argument in favor of the desirability of basic income rests on the widely shared view that social justice is not only a matter of right to an income, but also of access to (paid and unpaid) activity. The most effective way of taking care of both the income and the activity dimension consists in maintaining the income transfer (in gross terms) whatever the person's activity, thereby "activating" benefits, i.e. extending them, beyond forced inactivity, to low-paid activity. It can correctly be objected that there are other schemes – such as earned income tax credit or employment subsidies – that could serve better, or more cheaply, the objective of securing the viability of low-productive jobs and thereby providing a paid job to the worst off. However, if the concern is not to keep poor people busy at all cost, but rather to provide them with access to meaningful paid activity, the very unconditional nature of a basic income is a crucial advantage: It makes it possible to spread bargaining power so as to enable (as much as is sustainable) the less advantaged to discriminate between attractive or promising and lousy jobs.

Basic income and social justice. The preceding argument implicitly appeals to a conception of social justice as the fair distribution of the real freedom to pursue the realization of one's conception of the good life, whatever it is. It is such a conception that I have developed and defended in my *Real Freedom for All* (Van Parijs 1995). A handful of alternative principled justifications of basic income have been proposed (see Van Parijs 1992) and a large number of pragmatic justifications have been offered for it, as a simple handy second-best for a more complicated ideal package of policy instruments (see e.g. Goodin 1992, Barry 2003). However, I am convinced that any cogent case for basic income as a first-best must adopt some notion of "real freedom" (not only the right but also the means to do what one may wish) as the distribuendum of social justice and combine it with some strongly egalitarian criterion of distribution. The particular "real-libertarian" conception I offered gives a key role to the view that the substratum of our real freedom essentially consists in very unequal combinations of gifts we have received throughout our existences, among them the opportunities that enable us to hold our jobs. As a result there are massive "employment rents" incorporated in our jobs which can and must be (partly) captured through predictable and sustainable revenue-maximizing income taxation whose proceeds are to be used to fund a universal and unconditional basic income. The formulation I offer can no doubt be improved (see the critical essays collected in Elkin 1997, Krebs 2000 and Reeve and Williams 2003, followed by my replies), but I have no doubt that if a first-best case for basic income can be made, it must be some fairly close variant of what I propose.

IS A BASIC INCOME AFFORDABLE?

An underspecified question. Phrased in this very general way, the question makes no sense. Let us bear in mind that it is *not* part of the definition of a basic income that it should be sufficient to satisfy the beneficiaries' basic needs: Consistently with its definition, the level of the basic income could be more and it could be less. Nor is it part of the definition of a basic income that it should replace all other cash benefits: A universal benefit need not be a single benefit. A meaningful answer can only start being given to the question of affordability if one specifies the level at which the basic income is to be pitched and stipulates which benefits, if any, it is to replace. Under some specifications – for example "abolish all existing benefits and redistribute the corresponding revenues in the form of an equal low benefit for all" – the answer is trivially yes. Under other specifications – for example, "keep all existing benefits and supplement them with an equal benefit for all citizens at a level sufficient for a single person to live comfort-

ably" – the answer is obviously no. Each of these absurd extreme proposals is sometimes equated, by definition, with basic income. But
neither has, to my knowledge, been proposed by anyone. Every
serious proposal lies somewhere in between, and whether some basic
income proposal is affordable must therefore be assessed case by case.

More expensive because work-unconditional?

Are there, however, some general reasons why a basic income would
not be affordable at a level at which a conventional guaranteed income
would? One obvious reason might simply be that a basic income is
given to all, whether or not they are willing to work, whereas a conventional guaranteed minimum income is subordinated to a
willingness-to-work test. As a result, it is claimed, more poor people
will be receiving a basic income than a conventional guaranteed
income, or, if the number of beneficiaries is not much greater, they
will be doing less work than would be the case under a work-conditional benefit system. In net terms, therefore, a basic income scheme
is certain to cost more.

Job seeker's allowance versus state-sponsored workfare: A dilemma.
Closer scrutiny reveals that this expectation rests on feeble grounds
indeed. For suppose first that the work test is conceived as an obligation to accept work if offered by some (private or public) employer
concerned to get value for money. If the worker has no desire to take
or keep the job, her expected and actual productivity is unlikely to be
such that the employer will want to hire and keep her. But if the
worker is formally available for work, the fact that she is not hired or
that she is sacked (owing to too low a productivity, not to anything
identifiable as misconduct) cannot disqualify her from a work-tested
guaranteed income any more than from an unconditional basic
income. The only real difference between the former and the latter is
then simply that the former involves a waste of both the employer's
and the worker's time. Alternatively, suppose that the work test is
conceived as an obligation to accept a fall-back job provided by the
state for this very purpose. Rounding up the unemployable and unmo-
tivated is not exactly a recipe for high productivity, and even leaving
aside the long-term damage on the morale of the conscripted and on
the image of the public sector, the net cost of fitting this recalcitrant
human material into the workfare mold might just about manage to
remain lower than plain prison, with the cost of supervision and
blunder correction overshadowing the work-shy workers' contribution

to the national product. The economic case for the work test is just about as strong as the economic case for prisons.

Giving to the lazy is cheaper. Thus, as fully recognized by no-nonsense advocates of workfare (e.g. Kaus 1990), if a willingness-to-work condition is to be imposed, it must be justified on moral or political grounds, not on the basis of a flimsy cost argument inspired by the shaky presumption that a benefit coupled with work is necessarily cheaper than the same benefit taken alone. From the fact that workfare is likely to be costlier than welfare, it does not follow that the "unemployable" should be left to rot in their isolation and idleness. There can and must be a way of helping them out of it, namely by creating a suitable structure of incentives and opportunities of a sort a universal basic income aims to help create, whether or not a willingness-to-work test is coupled with it. Setting up such a structure is costly, as we shall shortly see, but adding a work test will not make it any cheaper – quite the contrary. And the absence of such a test, therefore, cannot be what jeopardizes basic income's affordability.

More expensive because income-unconditional?

The equivalence of means-tested and universal schemes. Instead of resting on the fact that a basic income is paid to all, whether or not they show any willingness to work, the claim that a basic income is unaffordable invokes even more often the fact that it is paid to rich and poor alike. The earlier discussion of the means test – in section 1(v) – should have made plain that this allegation is wrong, misled as it is by too superficial a notion of cost. As a comparison of Figure 1.1 and Figure 1.2 shows, it is in principle possible to achieve with a basic income exactly the same relationship between gross and net income as with a conventional guaranteed minimum income. If this relationship is the same, it means that the cost to those taxpayers who are net contributors to the scheme is the same in both cases. If one is politically affordable, therefore, the other should be too. If the relationship is the same, it also means that the marginal tax on earnings at any level of earnings is the same in both cases. If one of the two schemes is economically affordable, therefore, the other should be too.

Giving to the rich is cheaper. Of course, the budgetary cost is hugely different in the two cases, and if one could sensibly reason about transfers in the same way as about other public expenditures, there would indeed be a strong presumption that a basic income may be "unaffordable" when a conventional guaranteed minimum income is within our means. But transfers are not net expenditures. They are reallocations of purchasing power. This does not mean that they are costless. They do have a distributive cost to the net contributors, and they do have an economic cost through the disincentives they create. But both costs, we have seen, can be the same under either scheme. In addition, there are administrative costs. But, as also pointed out earlier, assuming a computerized and efficient tax-collection and transfer-payment technology, these are likely to be lower under a universal, *ex ante* scheme, than under a means-tested, *ex post* one, at least for a given level of effectiveness at reaching the poor. Paradoxically, therefore, giving to all is not more expensive but cheaper than giving only to the poor.

More expensive because creates work incentives at the bottom?

Marginal rates at the bottom and in the middle: The big trade off. To be fair, however, the fact that the basic income is not means-tested naturally combines with the mild requirement that the explicit rate of tax should fall short of 100 percent. Which means that the sort of basic income proposal we should be looking at is not represented by Figure 1.2, but rather by Figure 1.4, or at least by Figure 1.6. Relative to the conventional guaranteed minimum scheme represented by Figure 1.1, it can then no longer be said that there is not genuinely higher cost. True, it does not uniquely stick to the universal nature of the benefit, since the corresponding means-tested negative-income-tax variants share exactly the same feature. In particular, a linear tax combined with a uniform refundable tax credit at the current level of the minimum guaranteed income (Figure 1.3) would be very expensive in this sense. But that the problem should be entirely shared with negative income schemes does not make it less of a problem, which needs to be faced squarely. The basic fact is that the more material incentives one wishes to provide (for a given minimum income) to people earning at the bottom of the earnings scale, the more one needs to decrease the material incentives higher up. There is a sharp trade-off here, which can be spelled out as follows.

An example. To keep the reform budget-neutral while remaining able to pay for everyone's basic income, one must compensate the lowering of the rate at which the lowest layer of everyone's income is taxed by raising the rate at which higher layers are taxed. But while every earner has income in the lowest layer, not everyone earns income in higher layers, and the higher the layer, the fewer the tax payers involved. Suppose one starts from a basic income scheme of the sort depicted in Figure 1.2, i.e. with a tax rate of 100 percent on the lowest layer of income which mimics the effective rate of existing guaranteed minimum income schemes (Figure 1.1). Lowering by 20 percent the average rate of tax in the monthly income range comprising, say, between 0 and 500 euros will need to be offset by an increase in the rate of tax higher up. By how much? It depends on how many taxpayers have an income in the income bracket over which the tax increase is being considered. If it is in the 500–1,000 euros range, most incomes will still be affected by the rise, and budget neutrality may be achieved with, say, a 25 percent increase of the tax rate in that range. But if it is in the 2,000–2,500 range, a far smaller number of taxpayers will be affected, and the tax rate that balances the budget will need to rise by, say, over 50 percent. Once this is realized, the following conclusion is inescapable. If one is to finance a significant reduction of the effective marginal tax rate on the lowest earnings, one will have to significantly raise it on a broad range of rather modest earnings. Concentrating the increase on the higher brackets would quickly make them rocket towards 100 percent and make much of the corresponding incomes vanish (if only for domestic tax purposes).

Better for the poor that the poor be taxed more? This is not as terrible as it sounds. The modestly paid workers whose marginal tax rate would need to go up are also among the main beneficiaries of the introduction of a basic income, as the increased taxation of their wage falls short of the level of the basic income which they henceforth receive. The concern, therefore, need not be distributive. Even if one ends up, as in some proposals, with a linear income tax, i.e. if the lowest earnings are taxed at the same rate as the highest ones currently are, the reform would still redistribute downwards from the higher earners (whose tax increase on all income layers would exceed their basic income). However, there is some ground for a legitimate concern about the impact such a reform would have on incentives. As stressed by some opponents of basic income and negative income tax (e.g. the marginal rates would be lowered in a range in which there is a possibly growing, but still comparatively small proportion of the economy's marginal earnings, while being raised in a range in which far more workers would be affected. The incentive to work and train, to be conscientious and innovative would be increased in the very lowest range of incomes (say, between 0 and 500 euros per month), but it would be decreased upward of this threshold, where the bulk of society's work force, and particularly of its most productive work force, is concentrated. We would therefore be well advised not to rush too quickly to a system in which the effective marginal tax rate on the lowest incomes would not be higher than those higher up (see Piketty 1997).

Low earners' overcharge versus partial basic income. There are two ways of accommodating this advice in a basic income proposal. One consists in correcting a linear, or even a progressive system with an "overcharge" for the net beneficiaries of the basic income (Figure 1.6), as suggested for example by James Meade (1989). Another is a "partial basic income," as proposed for example by the Dutch Scientific Council for Government Policy (WRR 1985) and explored at length since, both in the Netherlands (Dekkers and Noteboom 1988, de Beer 1993, van der Veen and Pels 1995, Groot 1999) and in other European countries (Atkinson 1989, Parker 1991, Lahtinen 1992, Brittan 1995, Gilain and Van Parijs 1995, Clark and Healy 1997). A partial basic income would fall short of the level of income currently guaranteed to a single person, but it may approach or even exceed half the level currently guaranteed to a couple, and it would go hand in hand with the maintenance of a residual means-tested guaranteed income scheme. It would therefore imply the preservation of a 100 percent effective tax rate on a shrunk lower range (Figure 1.7). Under either variant, the earlier paradox becomes sharper: It is not only better for the poor that the rich should receive the same as the poor. It is also better for them that they should be taxed more than the rich.

More expensive because strictly individual?

The beauty of individualization. Thus, it cannot be denied that the lifting of the means test raises a genuine cost problem, not as such by virtue of the fact that the basic income is given to the rich as well as to the poor, but because (part of) its point is to provide the poor with stronger material incentives. It is not the only genuine cost problem intrinsic to basic income proposals. Another directly stems from the fact that, unlike most existing guaranteed minimum income schemes, basic income is meant to be strictly individual. These schemes typically provide a lower level of income support to each of the two members of a couple than to a single person, especially when account is taken of the housing subsidy, sometimes administered as a separate benefit. Why? Obviously because it is cheaper per capita to share a house, durable goods (cooker, washing machine, car, bed) and some services (child care) with one or more other people than to shoulder the cost

individually. The cheapest way of covering a given definition of fundamental needs therefore involves tracking the household composition
and modulating the per capita level of the income guarantee accordingly. Of course, the corollary of this household-conditionality is that
economies of scale are discouraged, fake domiciles rewarded and hence
checks on people's living arrangements required. One of the blatant
advantages of basic income is precisely that it would do away with all
that. People who put up with each other and thereby make society save
on accommodation and consumer durables would be entitled to the
benefits of the economies of scale they generate. There would therefore
also be no bonus for those pretending to live apart when they do not,
and no need to check who lives where and with whom.

Another dilemma: Inadequate or household-based? Great, but at what
level would the individual and unconditional basic income be pitched?
If it is at the level of the guaranteed income currently enjoyed by each
member of a couple, the amount is bound to fall far short of what is
needed by someone who has no option but to live alone. If it is at the
level currently awarded to a single person, the cost implications, in
some countries at any rate, are phenomenal. This is again not just a
matter of budgetary cost. There is an irreducible distributive cost in
the sense of a dramatic shift of purchasing power from one-adult to bi-
or multi-adult households. And there is also an irreducible economic
cost, owing mainly to a substantial increase in the marginal rates
required in order to fund the outlays for this enhanced basic income.
There is therefore, in the short term at any rate, a dilemma between
giving a fully individualized but inadequate basic income and giving a
sufficient but household-modulated one (see Brittan and Webb 1991,
Brittan 1995). Note, however, that this dilemma is not to be confused
with a dilemma between making some households unacceptably poor
(with too low an individual basic income) and subjecting all households for an indefinite period to a control of their living arrangements
(with an adequate, but household-dependent basic income). Even
under short-term cost constraints, the latter dilemma does not hold,
for it is possible to conceive of a strictly individual but inadequate
"partial" basic income for all, combined with a much shrunk residual
means-tested household-tested social assistance for the reduced
number of those who, despite the floor provided by the household's
basic income(s), do not earn enough to reach the income threshold as
from which means-tested assistance is switched off (see Figure 1.7).
Providing it is not conceived as an immediate full substitute for existing
social assistance, such a partial basic income thus provides an attrac-

tive way of handling both of the real cost problems – those stemming from incentives for low earners and individualization – which a full basic income would raise (see e.g. Gilain and Van Parijs 1995 for a microsimulation of the distributive impact of such a partial basic income in the case of Belgium).

WHICH WAY FORWARD?

An eye in the distance and an eye on the ground. For reasons explained at length elsewhere (Van Parijs 1995), a coherent and plausible conception of social justice requires us to aim, with some important qualifications, for an unconditional basic income at the highest level that is economically and ecologically sustainable, and on the highest scale that is politically imaginable. But while a defensible long-term vision is important, precise proposals for modest, immediately beneficial and politically feasible steps are no less essential. The sort of general but household-tested, means-tested and willingness-to-work-tested guaranteed minimum scheme that is now in place with many variants in most EU countries (including, most recently, Portugal) is a fundamental step in the right direction. But whatever the well-meaning "insertion" or "integration" conditions, it cannot avoid generating traps whose depth increases with the generosity of the scheme and whose threat increases as so-called "globalization" sharpens inequalities in market earning power. In countries in which guaranteed minimum schemes have been operating for a while, these traps and the dependency culture said to be associated with it risk triggering off a political backlash and the dismantling of what has been achieved. But they have also been prompting progressive moves in the form of basic income and related proposals. Like the fight for universal suffrage, the fight for basic income is not an all-or-nothing affair. This is no game for purists and fetishists, but for tinkerers and opportunists. Without going all the way to even a partial basic income, the following three types of proposals are plausible candidates – more or less plausible, depending on each country's institutions, and in particular its tax and social security context – as the most promising next step.

An individual tax credit. The Netherlands already have universal (i.e. non-means tested) systems of child benefits, of student grants and of non-contributory basic pensions, in addition to one of the world's most generous and comprehensive means-tested guaranteed income schemes. In January 2000, the Dutch Parliament approved the essentials of the government's plan for a comprehensive tax reform incorporating the replacement of the exemption on the lower income layer by a strictly individual tax credit at a level of about 140 euros per month for all families with at least one worker (see Boerlage 1999). Gradually increased and made individually refundable (so that a worker's non-working partner, for example, would be entitled to a cash payment equivalent to the credit rather than have the working partner doubly credited), this "negative income tax" for working families would provide the last missing element for the provision of a universal income floor. It could then be painlessly integrated into a low, but strictly individual, universal and unconditional basic income. Of course, even at a significantly increased level, this would remain a partial basic income, which would need to keep being supplemented, at any rate for single-adult households, with residual means-tested assistance. Similar, though more modest, schemes have since been approved by the Belgian and by the French governments (see Cantillon et al. 2000, Cohen 2001, Piketty 2001, Chaidron 2001, Vanderborght 2001).

A household-based regressive negative income tax. Despite the forbidding label, this would definitely be a major change in the right direction. Under the more enticing name of "Bürgergeld", it has been been advocated for many years in Germany by Joachim Mitschke (1985, 1995), professor of public finance at the University of Frankfurt. Ulrich Mückenberger, Claus Offe and Ilona Ostner (1989) argued for a less specific version of the same proposal, and Fritz Scharpf (1994, 2000), director of Cologne's Max Planck Institute, endorsed it as his preferred option. More recently, under the clumsier label "allocation compensatrice de revenu," a variant of it has been defended in France by Roger Godino (1999), former Dean of the management school INSEAD, and has been cautiously supported by sociologist Robert Castel (1999) and economists François Bourguignon (1999) and Laurent Caussat (2000). The idea is simply to take as given the household modulation of the current guaranteed minimum income and, instead of withdrawing the benefit at a 100 percent rate as earnings increase, to withdraw them at a somewhat lower rate, say 70 or even 50 percent, so as to create material incentives to work for any household, however low its earning power. In Godino's proposal for France, for example, the rate is calculated so that the benefit would be entirely phased out for single people as their earnings reached the level of the guaranteed minimum wage (seen Figure 1.3), as opposed to the much lower level of the guaranteed minimum income, as is currently the case (Figure 1.1). In the case of a larger household, the starting level is higher. If the same reduced rate of benefit withdrawal applies, the benefit is completely phased out only at a level of earnings that exceeds the minimum wage. One major political advantage of this formula is that it can be presented as taking the current guaranteed minimum income as its point of departure and strengthening it by getting rid of the absurd penalization of any effort to get out of the trap by taking on some low-paid activity. One major administrative disadvantage is that it implies not just that a much expanded number of households will be on benefit (admittedly at a far lower average rate), but, more awkwardly, that how high a benefit the households are entitled to receive depends on their living arrangements, which the administration must therefore be allowed to control.

A modest participation income. Finally, it is possible to build upon existing parental, study or care leave schemes and integrate them, jointly with tax credits for the employed, into a universal basic income subjected to a very broad condition of social contribution, as proposed for example by Anthony Atkinson (1993a, 1993b, 1996, 1998) under the label "participation income." "In order to secure political support," Atkinson (1993a) argues, "it may be necessary for the proponents of basic income to compromise. To compromise not on the principle that there is no means test, nor on the principle of independence [i.e., the idea that no one should be directly dependent on any particular person or group], but on the unconditional payment." A participation income would be a non-means-tested allowance paid to every person who actively participates in economic activity, whether paid or unpaid. Persons who care for young or elderly persons, undertake approved voluntary work or training, or are disabled due to sickness or handicap, would also be eligible for it. After a while, one may well realize that paying controllers to try to catch the few really work-shy would cost more, and create more resentment all over than just giving this modest floor income to all, no questions asked. But in the meanwhile the participation income will have politically bootstrapped a universal basic income into position. Compared to the income-tax-reform approach and the social-assistance-reform approach, this third approach would be particularly appropriate if some specific funding were set aside for basic income: A tax on energy consumption, or a dividend on some public asset, or simply some broadly based levy on the national product. But it could also be combined with either of the first two approaches.

Southern paths to basic income. In those countries which already have some sort of guaranteed minimum, there is much work to be done along each of these paths, both intellectually and politically. In less "advanced" countries, there is even more work to be done to build the first elements of a comprehensive scheme of social assistance (see Van Parijs 2002). However, two of these countries are particularly interesting in showing both how the basic income project can build on important existing achievements, and how it can mobilize and guide further progress on this basis. One is South Africa, which, since the final years of the apartheid regime, has a comprehensive non-contributory old-age pension scheme which distributes benefits to the overwhelming majority of black South African people in the relevant age category and no doubt constitutes the most powerful redistributive scheme in the whole of the African continent (see Case and Deaton 2000). On this background, a surprisingly vigorous campaign for a universal basic income has arisen, with support from the trade union movement, churches, and many other organizations (see Matisonn and Seekings 2002). The other country is Brazil, where Eduardo Suplicy, the Working Party's (PT) first senator, has been campaigning since the early 1990s for the introduction of a comprehensive negative-income-tax-type guaranteed minimum income (see Suplicy 1992), where countless schemes of family income support, coupled with compulsory school attendance have been introduced at the municipal level, after a while with federal support (see e.g. Suplicy and Buarque 1996; Sposati 1997), and where a number of people, not least Suplicy himself, have increasingly put present-day experiments and demands within the framework of a struggle for the eventual implementation of an unconditional basic income for all Brazilians (Suplicy 2002). In January 2004, President Lula promulgated a law previously adopted on Suplicy's initiative, by Brazil's federal congress, to the effect that a universal basic income for all Brazilians will be introduced gradually, as from 2005, starting with the most needy.

Fighting along these or other paths towards greater income security should of course not make one neglect the prior importance of providing every child with quality basic education and every person with quality basic health care. More important still, for the model advocated here ever to become a widespread reality, the most difficult and crucial struggles may well need to be fought on apparently very remote subjects: To ensure the efficiency and accountability of public administration, to regulate migration, to design appropriate electoral institutions, and to restructure the powers of supranational organizations. But these many struggles can gain direction and strength if they are guided by a clear and coherent picture of the core distributive institutions of a just, liberating society.

APPENDIX:
A stylised Presentation of Basic Income and Related Schemes

In order to get the concepts straight and to think clearly about the pros and cons of competing proposals, it is indispensable to keep in mind a stylized representation of the way in which each proposes to convert gross income – i.e. the income earned by people through their work or savings, prior to paying any taxes or social security contributions and to receiving any benefits – into net income – i.e. their disposable income taking taxes, contributions and benefits into account. In each of the following graphs, the horizontal and vertical axes correspond to gross and net income, respectively. Hence the dotted 45° line, which matches to each level of gross income an equal level of net income, represents what the net income would be if there were no redistribution whatever, while the bold curve indicates how a person's net income changes as her gross income increases when the tax-and-transfer scheme represented by the graph is in place.

To isolate the essential features of each scheme, it is convenient to abstract from any public expenditure other than the redistribution scheme under consideration and from the corresponding taxation. For the same reason, it is also useful to focus first on the case in which all households consist in one single adult.

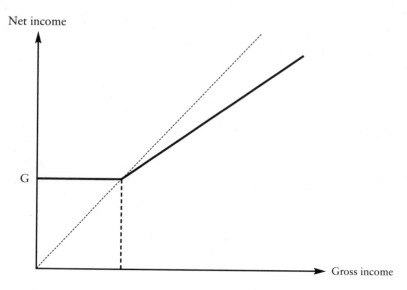

Figure 1.1. *Conventional minimum guaranteed income.*

Conventional minimum income schemes pick a particular level of income which they aim to secure for every household (G). They identify the households whose gross income is smaller than G and transfer to them a benefit equal to the difference between their gross income and G. Such schemes can therefore be said to be "income-tested" or "means-tested," in the sense that the size of the benefit they provide to a person is sensitive to some assessment of that person's income. The level of the benefit paid obviously reaches zero when the household's gross income reaches G. The benefits paid to households with a gross income lower than G are being funded by a tax on those with a gross income higher than G. This tax is here supposed to be linear, i.e. at the same rate on any gross income above G. How high this rate needs to be – and hence how depressed the slope of the right-hand portion of the bold line on the graph – depends on how many households have a gross income lower than G and on how much short of G their gross incomes fall. One feature of such a scheme – as represented by the flatness of the left-hand portion of the bold line – is that the effective marginal tax rate on all gross incomes below G is 100 percent. The effective marginal tax rate can be understood as 100 percent minus the rate of increase of net income relative to gross income. This rate of increase is here zero as any increase in gross income is exactly offset by a shrinking of the benefit. This feature of a guaranteed minimum scheme is often said to create an "unemployment trap" for people with a low earning power, as it kills any financial incentive to earn a gross income lower than G (or even somewhat higher, as being employed is likely to generate some costs), rather than nothing at all.

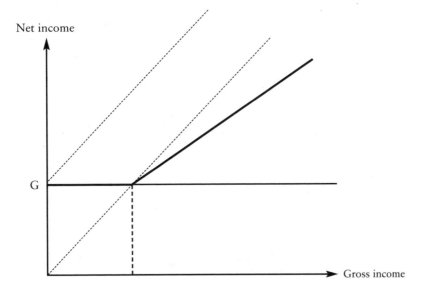

Figure 1.2. *Basic income with trap (e.g. Salverda 1984).*

Contrary to conventional schemes, a basic income is paid to all households, irrespective of their gross income. A basic income paid to all at level G lifts the initial 45° curve by a distance equal to G, which yields the higher dotted 45° line. A basic income at level G obviously involves an aggregate volume of benefits far larger than is the case with means-tested benefits paid only to households with gross incomes lower than G. One way – imaginable, though never actually proposed – of funding this larger volume consists in taxing all gross incomes below G at a 100 percent rate, and all gross incomes above G at whatever marginal rate is required to cover the costs of all benefits. What we end up with is a relationship between gross and net income (as represented by the bold line) identical, in both its flat left-hand portion and its sloping right-hand portion, to the one we had in the means-tested case (Figure 1.1). The slope needs to be the same as in the means-tested case because the net benefits paid to people with a gross income below G is the same in both cases, and hence also the tax revenue and tax rate needed to fund them. Considering this far-fetched case is important to clarify the conceptual distinction between means-tested schemes versus basic income on the one hand, and the presence versus the absence of an unemployment trap (or a 100 percent effective marginal tax rate on the lowest incomes) on the other.

Net income

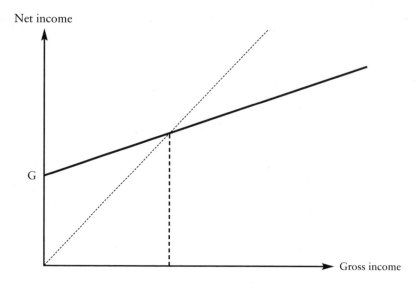

Gross income

Figure 1.3. *Linear negative income tax (e.g. Friedman 1962).*

A means-tested guaranteed minimum scheme can avoid creating an unemployment trap by maintaining the sensitiveness of the size of the benefit to a person's level of gross income, but by making the former fall less fast than the latter grows. When this is the case, the bold line that represents net income as a function of gross income no longer has a flat left-hand portion at level G, while the level of gross income from which people stop receiving benefits (called the "break-even point") rises. If we keep assuming (as in Figure 1.1) that all households who do not receive benefits pay tax at a uniform rate to finance the benefit, this rate obviously has to increase (relative to the situation of Figure 1.1) to fund the increase in the numbers and sizes of the benefits paid. With an unchanged minimum income fixed at G, the rate at which the benefit is withdrawn can be lowered below 100 percent (as it was in Figure 1.1) and the required rate of tax on higher incomes correspondingly adjusted upwards, until the rate of withdrawal of the benefit (below the break-even point) is the equal to the positive rate of taxation (above that point). This case corresponds to the linear negative income tax, which associates levels of negative tax (or benefit) and positive tax to gross income in such a way that net income increases at a same rate, relative to gross income, whatever a household's level of income.

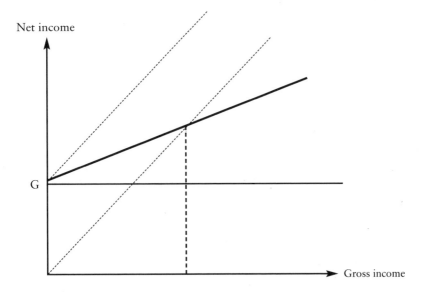

Figure 1.4. *Basic income combined with flat tax (e.g. Atkinson 1995).*

A basic income given to all at level G can conceivably be funded by a linear tax on all gross income, from 0 onwards. After people receive their basic income, their gross income, as represented by the 45° dotted line, shifts upward parallel to itself. The large amount of tax revenue required to fund this (tax-exempt) basic income determines the uniform rate at which all gross income in excess of the basic income needs to be taxed, and hence the slope of the bold line representing net income. The intersection between this bold line and the original 45° line determines the point below which people pay less in taxes than they receive as a basic income, and beyond which they pay more in taxes than they receive as a basic income. It is easy to understand that this point and the bold line that determines it must coincide with the break-even point and the corresponding bold line in Figure 1.3. For the slope of Figure 1.3 has been drawn so that the negative taxes collected by the relatively poor would exactly match the positive taxes paid by the relatively rich. Hence, if the slope in Figure 1.4 were flatter or steeper than the slope in Figure 1.3, the relatively poor would receive less or more net benefits (basic income minus tax) and hence fail to exhaust or overstretch the net contributions (tax minus basic income) of the relatively rich. In this sense, a basic income scheme funded by a flat tax can be said to be "equivalent" to a linear income tax with the same level of minimum income. And similar equivalences can be asserted for any matching pair of non-linear schemes.

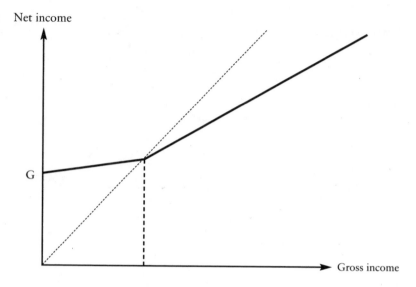

Figure 1.5. *Non-linear negative income tax (e.g. Mitschke 1985, Godino 1999).*

In order to abolish the unemployment trap without dropping the minimum income level nor raising too much the marginal rate of tax on the earnings of the bulk of the work force, various non-linear negative income tax proposals have been made. The rate of benefit withdrawal is then higher than the rate of positive tax, and the negative income tax scheme as a whole can be called regressive, in the sense that the effective marginal rate of tax is higher for the poor than for the rich. Such a scheme is of course nonetheless less regressive and more redistributive than conventional guaranteed minimum schemes of the type depicted in Figure 1.1.

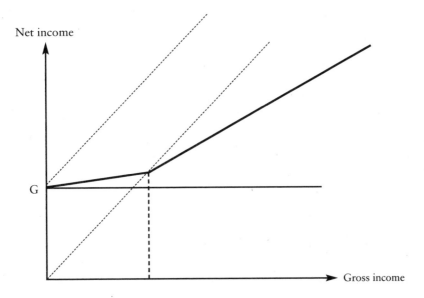

Figure 1.6. *Basic income with low earners' overcharge (e.g. Meade 1989).*

Just as some negative income tax proponents have proposed negative tax rates higher than positive tax rates (see Figure 1.5), some basic income advocates have recommended regressive taxation, for example in the form a "low earners' overcharge" on top of the standard rate of tax, as the best way of sustainably funding a relatively high basic income. The unemployment trap is abolished less vigorously than in the linear case, but the material incentives for skilled workers to supply labor, make efforts and improve their skills are eroded to a lesser extent. Even with this "tax on the poor," this sort of scheme is of course again less regressive and more redistributive towards the poor, than existing guaranteed income systems with the same level of minimum income (as in Figure 1.1). And this can remain the case even when the latter are funded by progressive positive taxation.

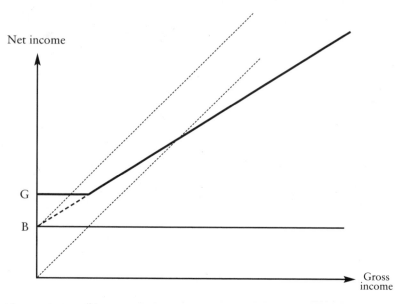

Figure 1.7. *Partial basic income (e.g. WRR 1985, Dekkers & Nooteboom 1988).*

Instead of funding a "full" basic income with a regressive income tax (as in Figure 1.6), one can try to combine a high minimum income, an improvement of the unemployment trap and a protection of incentives for the bulk of the work force by settling for a "partial" basic income combined with a partial preservation of a means-tested guaranteed minimum scheme. In this case, a universal basic income is introduced at level B, significantly less than the minimum income that needs to be guaranteed to a person living alone. This shifts the dotted 45° line upwards, parallel to itself at a distance of B. Any extra gross income is taxed at a uniform rate (which determines the flatter slope of the other discontinuous line starting from B), but supplemented in such a way that any post-tax income inferior to G is brought up to G thanks to a means-tested benefit. In this case, there remains a range of low earnings over which the effective marginal tax rate is 100 percent (the left-hand flat part of the bold line). But this range is significantly shortened relative to the conventional scheme depicted in Figure 1.1 (how significantly depends on how close B is to G). If most of the people stuck in the unemployment trap created by conventional schemes have potential earnings reasonably close to the minimum income, this low or "partial" but unconditional basic income, which people can combine at will with their earnings, will be enough to empty most of the trap. At the same time, maintaining a 100 percent rate on the first layer of everyone's income is precisely what makes it possible to tax higher layers at a far lower level than under the linear schemes of Figures 1.3 and 1.4.

BIBLIOGRAPHY

- http://www.basicincome.org contains a downloadable version of all contributions to the most recent congresses of the Basic Income European Network (BIEN), since 2004, Basic Income Earth Network, as well as comprehensive annotated bibliography of many publications in several languages.

- BIEN's electronic newsletter can be obtained free of charge by sending name and address + "subscribe BIEN" to bien@basicincome.org.

- http://www.usbig.net/, the web site of the US basic income guarantee network, contains a series of downloadable working papers.

- English-language book-length discussions of basic income include: van der Veen/Van Parijs et al. (1986), Walter (1989), Van Parijs (1992), Clark and Healy (1997), Fitzpatrick (1999), Lerner, Clark and Needham (1999), Van Parijs et al. (2001), Blais (2002).

- On the prehistory of the contemporary basic income discussion, see esp. Vanderborght and Van Parijs (2005, ch. 1), Cunliffe and Erreygers (2001, 2003), Van Trier (1995), Moynihan (1973), and the short history of basic income on http://www.basicincome.org.

REFERENCES

Ackerman, Bruce and Alstott, Anne. 1999. *The Stakeholder Society*. New Haven: Yale University Press.

Arneson, Richard, Fleurbaey, Marc, Melnyk, Andrew and Selznick, Philip. 1997. "A Symposium on Philippe Van Parijs' *Real Freedom for All*," *PEGS Bulletin* (Political Economy of the Good Society, University of Maryland), 38–51.

Atkinson, Anthony B. 1989. "Analysis of partial basic income schemes," in A.B. Atkinson, *Poverty and Social Security*. Hemel Hempstead: Harvester Wheatsheaf.

— 1993a. *Beveridge, the National Minimum, and its future in a European context*. STICERD Working Paper WSP/85, January 1993.

— 1993b. "Participation Income," *Citizen's Income Bulletin* 16, 7–11.

— 1995. *Public Economics in Action. The Basic Income/ Flat Tax Proposal*. Oxford: Oxford University Press.

— 1996. "The Case for a Participation Income," *Political Quarterly* (Oxford) 67 (1), January–March, 67–70.

— 1998. *Poverty in Europe*. Oxford: Blackwell.

Barrez, Dirk. 1999. "Tien frank per dag voor iedereen," *De Morgen* 22 December.

Barry, Brian. 2003. "Real Freedom and Basic Income," in *Real Libertarianism Assessed. Political Theory after Van Parijs* (Reeve, Andrew and Williams, Andrew, eds). Basingstoke: Palgrave-Macmillan, pp. 53–79.

BEIGEWUM ed. 1991. *Grundeinkommen: Zwischen Gesellschafts-veränderung, sozialpolitischer Resignation und Verteilungskonflikt*, special issue of *Kurswechsel* 1.

Blais, François 2002. *Ending Poverty. A Basic Income for All Canadians.* Halifax (Canada): Lorimer Paperback.

Boerlage, Saar. 1999. "Reactie op het belastingplan 2001," *Nieuwsbrief Basisinkomen* 29, December, 5–8.

Boulanger, Paul-Marie, Defeyt, Philippe and Van Parijs, Philippe, eds. 1985. *L'Allocation universelle. Une idée pour vivre autrement*, special issue of *La Revue nouvelle* (Brussels) 81 (4), April.

Bourguignon, François and Bureau, Dominique. 1999. *L'Architecture des prélèvements en France: Etat des lieux et voies de réforme.* Paris: La Documentation française.

Bovenberg, A.L. and van der Ploeg, F. 1995. "Het basisinkomen is een utopie," *Economisch-Statistische Berichten* 3995, 100–104.

Bresson, Yoland and Guilhaume, Philippe. 1986. *Le participat: réconcilier l'économique et le social.* Paris: Chotard et associés éditeurs.

Bresson, Yoland. 1994. *Le Partage du temps et des revenus.* Paris: Economica.
— 1999. "Il faut libérer le travail du carcan de l'emploi," *Le Monde* 16 March.

Brittan, Samuel and Webb, Steven. 1991. *Beyond the Welfare State. An examination of basic incomes in a market economy.* Aberdeen: Aberdeen University Press.

Brittan, Samuel. 1995. *Capitalism with a Human Face.* Aldershot: Edward Elgar.

Büchele, Herwig and Wohlgenannt, Lieselotte. 1985. *Grundeinkommen ohne Arbeit: Auf dem Weg zu einer kommunikativen Gesellschaft*, Vienna and Zürich: Europaverlag.

Caillé, Alain ed. 1987. *Du Revenu social: au-delà de l'aide, la citoyenneté?*, special issue of *Bulletin du M.A.U.S.S.* 23 September.
— 1996. *Vers un revenu minimum inconditionnel?* Paris: La Découverte.

Cantillon, Bea et al. 2000. "De verdelingseffecten van het ontwerp van fiscale hervorming. Microsimulatieresultaten." Antwen: UFSIA, Centrium voor sociaal beleid.

Case, Anne and Angus Deaton. 2000. "Large cash transfers to the elderly in South Africa," *Economic Journal* 108, 1330–61

Castel, Robert. 1999. "Minima sociaux, allocation compensatrice de revenu et RMI", in Castel, Robert, Godino, Roger, Jalmain, Michel and Piketty, Thomas. *Pour une réforme du RMI*, Paris: Notes de la Fondation Saint

Simon 104, February, pp. 39–48.

Caussat, Laurent. 2000. "Minima sociaux différentiels, allocation universelle, workfare: quels compromis dans la politique française de lutte contre la pauvreté?" Communication à la journée d'études "Quelle réforme des minima sociaux?," Marseille, 14 January.

Chaidron, Nicolas. 2001. *Les Réformes fiscales néerlandaise, française et belge au regard de l'équité*. Université catholique de Louvain, mémoire de licence en sciences économiques.

Charlier, Joseph. 1848. *Solution du problème social ou constitution humanitaire. Basée sur la loi naturelle, et précédée de l'exposé de motifs*. Brussels: "Chez tous les libraires du Royaume."

Charlier, Joseph. 1894. *La Question sociale résolue, précédée du testament philosophique d'un penseur*. Bruxelles: Weissenbruch.

Clark, Charles M.A. and Healy, John. 1997. *Pathways to a Basic Income*. The Justice Commission, Conference of Religious of Ireland.

Cohen, Daniel. 2001. "Impôt négatif: le mot et la chose," *Le Monde* 6 February.

Cournot, Augustin. 1838. *Recherches sur les principes mathématiques de la théorie des richesses*. Paris: Librairie Hachette (new edition Paris: Marcel Rivière, 1938).

Crotty, Raymond. 1986. *Ireland in Crisis. A study in capitalist colonial development*. Dingle (Ireland): Brandon.

Cunliffe John and Erreygers, Guido. 2001. "The Enigmatic Legacy of Charles Fourier: Joseph Charlier and Basic Income", *History of Political Economy* 33(3), 459–484.

— 2003. "Basic Income? Basic capital. Origins and issues of a debate," *Journal of Political Philosophy* 11 (1), 89–110.

Davidson, Marc. 1995. "Liberale grondrechten en milieu. Het recht op milieugebruiksruimte als grondslag van een basisinkomen", *Milieu* 5, 246–249.

de Beer, Paul. 1993. *Het verdiende inkomen*. Houten/ Zaventem: Bohn Stafleu Van Loghum and Amsterdam: Wiardi Beckman Stichting.

Dekkers, Jos M. and Nooteboom, Bart. 1988. *Het gedeeltelijk basisinkomen, de hervorming van de jaren negentig*. The Hague: Stichting Maatschappij en Onderneming.

den Hoed, P., ed. 1986. *Het gedeeltelijk basisinkomen*, special issue of *Bedrijf en Maatschapij*, 13 (5), September–October.

Duboin, Jacques. 1932. *La Grande relève des hommes par la machine*. Paris: Fustier.

— 1945. *L'Economie distributive de l'abondance*. Paris: OCIA.

Duboin, Marie-Louise. 1985. *L'économie libérée*. Paris: Syros.

— 1988. "Guaranteed income as an inheritance," *Proceedings of the First*

International Conference on Basic Income (A.G. Miller, ed.). London: BIRG and Antwerp: BIEN, 134–45.

Duchatelet, Roland. 1994. "An economic model for Europe based on consumption financing on the tax side and the basic income principle on the redistribution side," paper presented at the 5th BIEN Congress. London, September 8–10.

— 1998. *N.V. België. Verslag aan de aandeelhouders*. Gent: Globe.

Ferry, Jean-Marc. 1995. *L'Allocation universelle. Pour un revenu de citoyenneté*. Paris: Cerf.

— 2000. *La Question de l'Etat européen*. Paris: Gallimard.

Fitzpatrick, Tony. 1999. *Freedom and Security. An Introduction to the Basic Income Debate*. London: Macmillan and New York: St. Martin's Press.

Frankman, Myron. 2001. " From the Common Heritage of Mankind to a Planet-Wide Citizen's Income: Establishing the Basis for Solidarity," Montreal: McGill University, Department of Economics, May.

Friedman, Milton. 1962. *Capitalism and Freedom*. Chicago: University of Chicago Press.

— 1966. "The case for the negative income tax: a view from the right," *Issues of American Public Policy* (J.H. Bunzel, ed.), Englewood Cliffs (NJ): Prentice-Hall, 1968, pp. 111–120.

Fumagalli, Andrea and Lazzarotto, Maurizio eds. 1999. *Tutte bianche. Disoccupazione di massa e reddito di cittadinanza*. Roma: Derive Approdi.

Genet, Michel and Van Parijs, Philippe. 1992. "Eurogrant," in *BIRG Bulletin* 15, 4–7.

Gilain, Bruno and Van Parijs, Philippe. 1995. "L'allocation universelle: un scénario de court terme et de son impact distributif," *Revue belge de sécurité sociale* 38 (1), 5–80.

Godino, Roger. 1999. "Pour la création d'une allocation compensatrice de revenu," in Castel, Robert, Godino, Roger, Jalmain, Michel and Piketty, Thomas. *Pour une réforme du RMI*. Paris: Notes de la Fondation Saint Simon 104, February 1999, pp. 7–20.

Goodin, Robert E. 1992. "Toward a Minimally Presumptuous Social Policy," in *Arguing for Basic Income. Ethical foundations for a radical reform* (P. Van Parijs, ed.). London and New York: Verso, 195–214.

Groot, Loek F.M. 1999. *Basic Income and Unemployment*. Amsterdam: Netherlands School for Social and Economic Policy Research.

Heidsieck, Emmanuelle and Bresson, Yoland. *Bonne année! Manifeste pour un revenu d'existence*. Editions du Toit, 1999.

Huber, Joseph. 1998. *Vollgeld. Beschäftigung, Grundsicherung und weniger Staatsquote durch eine modernisierte Geldordnung*. Berlin: Duncker & Humbolt.

— 1999. *Plain Money. A Proposal for Supplying the Nations with the Necessary Means in a Modern Monetary System.* Martin-Luther-Universität Halle-Wittenberg: Forschungsberichte des Instituts für Soziologie.

Huber, Joseph and Robertson, James. 2000. *Creating New Money. A Monetary Reform of the Information Age.* London: New Economics Foundation.

Jordan, Bill, James, Simon, Kay, Helen and Redley, Marcus. 1992. *Trapped in Poverty? Labour-Market Decisions in Low-Income Households.* London and New York: Routledge.

Kooistra, Pieter. 1994. *Het ideale eigenbelang.* Kampen: Kok Agora.

Krause-Junk, Gerold. 1996. "Probleme einer Integration von Einkommens-besteuerung und steuerfinanzierten Sozialleistungen. Anmerkungen zum Gutachten der Experten-Kommission," *Wirtschaftsdienst* 7, 345–349.

Krebs, Angelika, ed. 2000. *Basic Income? A Symposium on Van Parijs,* special issue of *Analyse und Kritik* (Berlin) 22 (2).

Lahtinen, Ilpo. 1992. *Perustulo, kansalaisen palkka (Basic Income, the Citizen's Wage).* Helsinki: Hanki ja Jaeae.

Leleux, Claudine. 1998. *Travail ou revenu? Pour un revenu inconditionnel.* Paris: Cerf.

Lerner, Sally, Clark, Charles M.A. and Needham, W. Robert. 1999. *Basic Income: Economic Security for all Canadians.* Toronto: Between the Lines Press, 112 p.

Matisonn, Heidi and Seekings, Jeremy. 2002. "Welfare in Wonderland? The politics of the basic income grant in South Africa," paper presented at the IXth Congress of the Basic Income European Network. Geneva, ILO, September (available on http://www.basicincome.org).

Meade, James E. 1989. *Agathotopia: The Economics of Partnership.* Aberdeen: Aberdeen University Press.

— 1993. *Liberty, Equality and Efficiency.* London: Macmillan.

— 1994. *Full Employment Without Inflation.* London: The Employment Policy Institute.

— 1995. *Full Employment Regained? An Agathotopian Dream.* Cambridge: Cambridge University Press.

Miller, Anne. 1983. *In praise of social dividends.* Edinburgh: Heriot-Watt University, Department of Economics, Working Paper 1, December.

Mirabile, Maria Luisa, ed. 1991. *Il reddito minimo garantito. Il welfare tra nuovi e vecchi diritti.* Roma: Ediesse.

Mitschke, Joachim. 1985. *Steuer- und Transferordnung aus einem Guß.* Baden-Baden: Nomos.

— 1995. "Jenseits der Armenfürsorge," *Die Zeit* 50, 8 December, 30–31.

Moynihan, Daniel Patrick. 1973. *The Politics of a Guaranteed Income.* The

Nixon Administration and the Family Assistance Plan. New York: Random House.

Mückenberger, Ulrich, Offe, Claus and Ostner, Ilona. 1989. "Das staatlich garantierte Grundeinkommen – ein politisches Gebot der Stunde," in *Wege ins Reich der Freiheit. André Gorz zum 65. Geburtstag* (Hans Leo Krämer and Claus Leggewie, eds). Berlin: Rotbuch.

Murray, Michael L. 1997. *... And Economic Justice for All: Welfare Reform for the 21st Century.* Armonk, New York: M.E. Sharpe Publisher.

O'Brien, Patrick and Olson, Dennis O. 1990. "The Alaska permanent fund and dividend distribution program," *Public Finance Quarterly* 18(2), April, 139–156.

Opielka, Michael and Vobruba, Georg, eds. 1986. *Das garantierte Grundeinkommen: Entwicklung und Perspektiven einer Forderung.* Frankfurt am Main: Fischer Verlag.

Paine, Thomas. 1796. "Agrarian justice," in *The Life and Major Writings of Thomas Paine* (P.F. Foner, ed.). Secaucus (New Jersey): Citadel Press, 1974, pp. 605–623.

Palmer, Jim, ed. 1997. *Alaska's Permanent Fund. Remarkable Success at Age 20 ... but what now?*, special issue of *The Juneau Report*, Summer 1997.

Parker, Hermione. 1991. *Basic Income and the Labour Market.* London: Basic Income Research Group.

Pelzer, Helmut, ed. 1998. *Bürgergeld nach dem Ulmer Modell.* Ulm: RV-Verlag microedition, Reihe Wissenschaft, August 1998, 62p.

Pelzer, Helmut. 1999. *Finanzierung eines allgemeinen Basiseinkommens. Ansätze zu einer kombinierten Sozial- und Steuerreform.* Aachen: Shaker Verlag.

Piketty, Thomas. 1997. "La redistribution fiscale face au chômage," *Revue française d'économie* 12 (1), 157–201.

— 2001. "L'impôt négatif est né," *Libération* 29 January, 8.

Raventos, Daniel. 1999. *El derecho a la existencia.* Barcelona: Ariel.

Raventos, Daniel, ed. 2001. *La renta básica.* Barcelona: Ariel.

Reeve, Andrew and Williams, Andrew, eds. 2003. *Real Libertarianism Assessed. Political Theory after Van Parijs.* Basingstoke: Palgrave-Macmillan.

Robertson, James. 1999. *The New Economics of Sustainable Development. A Briefing for Policy Makers.* Luxembourg: Office for Official Publications of the European Communities and London: Kogan.

Roebroek, Joop and Hogenboom, Erik. 1990. *Basisinkomen: Alternatieve uitkering of nieuw paradigma?*, The Hague: Ministerie van Sociale Zaken en Werkgelegenheid (VUGA Uitgeverij), Report no. 24, May.

Salverda, Wim. 1984. "Basisinkomen en inkomensverdeling. De financiele uitvoerbaarheid van het basisinkomen," *Tijdschrift voor Politieke Ekonomie* 8, 9–41.

Scharpf, Fritz W. 1994. "Negative Einkommensteuer – ein Programm gegen Ausgrenzung," *Die Mitbestimmung* 40 (3), 27–32.

— 2000. "Basic Income and Social Europe", in *Basic Income on the Agenda. Policies and Politics* (Loek Groot and Robert J. van der Veen, eds). Amsterdam: Amsterdam University Press, forthcoming.

Schmid, Thomas ed. 1984. *Befreiung von falscher Arbeit: Thesen zum garantierten Mindesteinkommen*. Berlin: Wagenbachs Taschenbücherei.

Soete, Luc and Kamp, Karin. 1996. "The Bit Tax: Agenda for Further Research," Maastricht: MERIT, August.

Sposati, Aldaíza, ed. 1997. *Renda Mínima e Crise Mundial. Saída ou agravamento?*. São Paulo: Cortez editora.

Standing, Guy. 1999. *Global Labour Flexibility: Seeking Distributive Justice.* Basingstoke: Macmillan.

Suplicy, Eduardo ed. 1992. *Programa de garantia de renda mínima.* Brasilia: Senado Federal.

Suplicy, Eduardo M. and Buarque, Christovam. 1996. "A Guaranteed Minimum Income to eradicate poverty and help poor children go to school instead of being forced to work. The Brazilian debate and experience," paper presented at BIEN's 6th Congress, Vienna, 12–14 September.

Suplicy, Eduardo. 2002. *Renda de Cidadania: A saida é pela porta.* São Paulo: Cortez Editora.

Tobin, James. 1965. "On the Economic Status of the Negro," *Daedalus* 94 (4), Fall, 878–98.

— 1966. "The Case for an Income Guarantee," *The Public Interest* 4, 31–41.

— 1967. "It Can Be Done," *The New Republic* 3 June, 14–18.

Tobin, James, Pechman, Joseph A. and Mieszkowski, Peter M. 1967. "Is a Negative Income Tax Practical?," *Yale Law Journal* 77 (1), 1–27.

Tobin, James. 1968. "Raising the Incomes of the Poor," in *Agenda for the Nation* (Kermit Gordon, ed.), Washington, DC: The Brookings Institution, 77–116.

Vanderborght, Yannick. 2001. "La France sur la voie d'un 'revenu minimum inconditionnel'?", *Mouvements* (Paris) 15–16, 157–165.

Vanderborght, Yannick and Van Parijs, Philippe. 2001. "Assurance participation et revenu de participation. Deux manières d'élargir l'Etat social actif," *Reflets et perspectives de la vie économique* 40 (1–2), 183–96.

Vanderborght, Yannick. 2002. "Basic income in Belgium and the Netherlands. Implementation through the back door?," paper presented at the IXth Congress of the Basic Income European Network, Geneva: ILO, September (available on http://www.basicincome.org).

Vanderborght, Yannick and Van Parijs, Philippe. 2005. *L'Allocation universelle.* Paris: La Découverte.

van der Veen, Robert J. and Van Parijs, Philippe et al. 1986. *A Symposium on "A Capitalist Road to Communism,"* special issue of *Theory and Society* 15 (5). (Spanish translation as a special issue of *Zona Abierta*, (Madrid) 46–47, January–June 1988.)

van der Veen, Robert J. and Pels, Dick, eds. 1995. *Het basisinkomen. Sluitstuk van de verzorgingstaat?* Amsterdam: Van Gennep.

Van Parijs, Philippe ed. 1992. *Arguing for Basic Income: Ethical Foundations for a Radical Reform.* London: Verso.

Van Parijs, Philippe. 1995. *Real Freedom for All. What (if Anything) Can Justify Capitalism?* Oxford: Oxford University Press. (Spanish translation: *Libertad real para todos.* Barcelona: Paidos, 1996.)

Van Parijs, Philippe, Jacquet, Laurence and Salinas, Claudio. 2000. "Basic Income and its Cognates," in *Basic Income on the Agenda. Policies and Politics* (Loek Groot and Robert J. van der Veen, eds). Amsterdam: Amsterdam University Press, 53–84.

Van Parijs, Philippe et al. 2001. *What's Wrong with a Free Lunch?* Boston: Beacon Press.

Van Parijs, Philippe and Vanderborght, Yannick. 2001. "From Euro-stipendium to Euro-dividend. A Comment on Schmitter and Bauer," *Journal of European Social Policy* 11, 342–46.

Van Parijs, Philippe. 2002. "Does Basic Income Make Sense as a Worldwide Project?," paper presented at the IXth Congress of the Basic Income European Network, Geneva, ILO, September (available on http://www. basicincome.org).

Van Trier, Walter. 1995. *Everyone a King. An Investigation into the Meaning and Significance of the Debate on Basic Incomes with Special Reference to Three Episodes from the British Inter-War Experience.* Katholieke Universiteit Leuven: Fakulteit politieke en sociale wetenschappen, PhD thesis.

Vives, Juan Luis. 1526. *De Subventione Pauperum.* French translation: *De l'Assistance aux pauvres*, Brussels: Valero & fils, 1943. English translation: *On the Assistance to the Poor.* Toronto and London: University of Toronto Press, 1999.

Wetenschappelijke Raad voor het Regeringsbeleid (WRR). 1985. *Waarborgen voor Zekerheid. Een nieuw stelsel van sociale zekerheid in hoofdlijnen.* Den Haag: Staatsuitgeverij, Rapport 26. (English summary: WRR. 1985. *Safeguarding Social Security.* The Hague: Netherlands Scientific Council for Government Policy.)

Walter, Tony. 1989. *Basic Income. Freedom from Poverty, Freedom to Work.* London and New York: Marion Boyars.

Wohlgenannt, Lieselotte and Büchele, Herwig. 1990. *Den öko-sozialen Umbau beginnen: Grundeinkommen.* Vienna and Zürich: Europaverlag.

2

Why Stakeholding?

Bruce Ackerman and Anne Alstott

It is easy to view "liberty" and "equality" as if they were inexorably at war with one another. Easy, but a mistake. The great project of liberal political philosophy, over the last generation, has been to reject the false dichotomy between "leveling" equality and "free" markets that has had such a baleful influence over the modern mind.

The challenge has been to reconstruct the tradition of the liberal Enlightenment to achieve a deep reconciliation of these superficially competing ideals.[1] Modern liberalism is grounded in two affirmations. On the one hand, it affirms equality by insisting that each citizen has a fundamental right to a fair share of resources as he sets out in life. On the other hand, it affirms freedom by recognizing that different people will use their initial resources differently. The liberal state expects these differences to arise and refuses to suppress them. To the contrary, it systematically respects and facilitates individual choices – so long as they proceed from a background of fair initial entitlements.

The distribution of material resources crucially shapes this background. If citizens are to begin adult life under fair conditions, it is wrong to deprive them of their just share of the wealth created by prior generations. In a liberal society, this commitment should be cashed out in terms of private property – since property provides an essential tool for effective self-definition.

It follows that a grant of private property should be recognized as the birthright of every liberal citizen – not a scarce commodity to be doled out by the community as a reward for proper behavior.

Stakeholding and basic income both express this commitment – albeit in different ways. These differences are significant, but they should not conceal a common ambition. Both initiatives seek to use

43

the recent revival of liberal philosophy as a springboard for a new progressive agenda. Both respond to the same challenge: To transform the twenty-first century into a new age of liberal reform.

Contrast the libertarian and utilitarian philosophies that dominate political economy today. The libertarian trumpets her commitment to freedom. She opposes "social programs," seeks tax cuts to "return the people's money to them," and derides inheritance levies as "death taxes." But libertarian freedom is little more than a screen for inequality. By contrast, liberal freedom, to use Van Parijs' term, is *real* freedom: It requires society to give every individual the resources she needs to shape a life plan. Libertarianism offers individuals only the right to make the most of the circumstances into which they are born. Born to poor parents? "Too bad," says the libertarian. "Do the best you can." Competing in the marketplace with the sons and daughters of privilege? "Be content with your lot," she advises. "It would be wrong for the government to interfere." In place of these patronizing reassurances, stakeholding and basic income offer a social inheritance to every individual.

The utilitarian economist adopts a more progressive attitude toward redistribution but loses sight of individualism and freedom. In his enthusiasm for maximizing social welfare, he looks to paternalist schemes of social engineering. The utilitarian calculus favors transfers to the worst-off class, preferably in a form that directs them toward some "productive" activity like work or savings. Means-testing helps channel assistance to the needy. And restrictions like work requirements or vouchering prod the poor to take jobs and spend on approved items like food and shelter. The American welfare state, not coincidentally, comprises a collection of meager, means-tested programs directed at the very poor and designed to pull them into economic life.

We reject both the utilitarian philosophy and its mechanisms. We seek freedom for everyone, not charity for some. And we believe that respect for the individual requires respect for her choices – to work in the home, at a paid job, or not at all.

There are deep injustices in our nation's treatment of the poor, but we reject the idea that poverty relief is the only, or even the best, target for reform. Today, the very rich inherit from their parents the resources they need to shape a life plan. The government directs aid toward the top 25 percent of the population in the form of college subsidies, and toward the bottom 20 percent through means-tested social programs. But young adults in the vast middle group embark on their adult lives without the resources they need to make meaningful choices.

The basics of stakeholding reflect our philosophical commitments.

At age 21, as each liberal citizen steps forward to begin her adult life, she should receive a stake of $80,000 from the government.[2] The $80,000 is hers to spend, with just a few conditions intended to ensure that she has the capacity to make meaningful choices. First, she must graduate from high school. Without a high-school diploma, she receives a variation on basic income – interest on her stake each year.[3] Second, she must stay clear of crime.[4] Once a young citizen has met these requirements, she may collect her money in four annual installments of $20,000 each.[5] The money is hers to spend or invest. She may go to college, or not. She may save for a house or a rainy day – or blow her money in Las Vegas.

We will raise the necessary stakeholding fund in different ways as time marches on. During the "short term" – the first fifty years or so – we rely on a flat tax of 2 percent on each individual's wealth in excess of $230,000. This high exemption level means that 80 percent of Americans will pay no tax, and that the burden will be borne entirely by the big winners in a market society.[6] As the first generation of stakeholders begin to die out, we propose to shift the burden by means of a "payback requirement." Stakeholders who have done well with their $80,000 must pay back their stake, with interest, upon their death.[7] As the first generation of stakeholders recognize their responsibility to sustain the institution for their successors, it will be possible to reduce, or perhaps eliminate, the wealth tax.

Although stakeholding and basic income share a commitment to progressive redistribution, they challenge the identity politics and watered-down Marxism that have come to dominate conventional "left" thinking. Every citizen may claim her stake – or collect a basic income – simply because she is a human being, capable of shaping a life plan. She does not claim more – or less – by virtue of being female, or a minority, or possessing a disability. Stakeholding and basic income take a concrete step toward initial equality, recognizing the individual not the group. We do not deny the persistence of sex and race discrimination, or the importance of accommodations for severe handicaps – and wholeheartedly support special initiatives targeted at these problems. But stakeholding and basic income are universalistic programs, responding to the right of each individual citizen to his share in the achievements of past generations. They respond to other serious social problems only indirectly – by promoting women's economic independence, and alleviating African-Americans' striking disadvantage in family wealth.[8]

Stakeholding and basic income also reject the center-left's version of universalism: Social democracy.[9] Social democrats envision the paid workplace as the focus of social justice. In their utopia, everyone has a right to a job with good wages, short hours, and a pension that rewards years of diligent work. But stakeholding and basic income promise real freedom for all, rather than justice for the "working class." They offer every individual *un*conditional resources, and they refuse to make the moral judgment that paid work is the only proper focus of a good life. Van Parijs, famously, has defended the right of surfers – representing the nonconformist idlers – to a basic income.[10] And we defend the right of every young citizen to use her resources to shape her own life on her own terms.

Social democracy pushes far too many human beings off the center stage of social life. Van Parijs' defense of surfing is well-taken, but too limited. Social democracy demotes tens of millions of ordinary people to second-class citizenship. Begin with the caretakers: The great majority of women (and some men), who devote large portions of their lives to caring for children or elderly parents. For caretakers, justice linked to the workplace is too often no justice at all. Although the last generation of women has made remarkable gains in paid work, the average woman still has a far more interrupted work history, and earns far less, than the average man. Thus, when social democracy makes paid work and money wages the measure of "desert," caretakers lose out. In the United States, for example, the social security system links retirement security to paid work – or long-term marriage to a steady breadwinner. Divorced women, single women, and women married to low earners or intermittent workers may find themselves living in poverty despite a lifetime of real work on behalf of others.[11]

Workplace justice also offers far less freedom to workers at the bottom of the economic ladder. In a free market economy, less-skilled workers earn low wages for harsh and sometimes demeaning work. Liberals and social democrats agree that less-skilled workers are entitled to greater dignity than their market earnings alone will provide. But social democracy makes dignity conditional on paid work: mechanisms such as employment subsidies, the "earned income tax credit," and workfare offer the poor a bargain: Do the right thing by working, and society will take care of you. This bargain is surely better than the libertarian alternatives: Starve or steal.

But the work condition fails the test of liberal justice. No one else in a free society is required to make such a bargain. The middle- or upper-class person with a private inheritance need not prove to the bank manager that she is a productive citizen before drawing down her bank account. Basic income and stakeholding offer some of the same freedom to the less-skilled worker. She can work full-time, and use her stake or basic income as an income supplement or as a buffer against hard times. If she is willing to live frugally or with a partner, she can work less, or not at all, and devote herself to the matters that concern her most: Children, community, or perhaps some religious or artistic pursuit that engages her far more than fast-food jobs ever could.

But is there such a thing as too much freedom? Here is where stakeholding and basic income begin to part ways. Under basic income, citizens are not allowed to go to their neighborhood bank and capitalize their lifetime stream of basic income payments into a single stake. While Van Parijs prohibits citizens from switching to our program, we are more tolerant: Any stakeholder can switch to basic income simply by buying an annuity policy from an insurance company and asking it to send a monthly check.

To fix ideas, suppose that an insurance company would sell a young stakeholder a lifetime annuity of $400 a month in exchange for a stake of $80,000. The Ackerman–Alstott plan permits each citizen to arrange for her own basic income of $400 – but only if she wants to! Van Parijs would give her $400 a month, but forbids her to capitalize it into a single $80,000 payment.[12] Basic income, in short, is a fancy name for a *restraint on alienation*.

Anglo-American law contains a wonderfully evocative term to describe this particular restraint. Suppose you wanted to give $80,000 to your nephew when you die, but you didn't trust his judgment. Rather than providing him with a flat $80,000 in your will, the law permits you to create a *spendthrift trust* – which grants your nephew access to the money only with the permission of a trustee, who acts under the explicit instructions provided in your will. Van Parijs would extend this principle to the new liberal form of social inheritance. He would impose a *universal* spendthrift trust on all citizens as they rise to maturity.

We reject this extension as a matter of principle. Some citizens undoubtedly lack the capacity to make reasonable use of their economic freedom – and we do not oppose some broad sifting devices to identify them. This is why we have required all stakeholders to obtain a high school degree and refrain from criminal activity before gaining full access to their $80,000. But treating all young men and women as presumptive spendthrifts demeans their standing as autonomous citizens and radically constrains their real freedom.

A guaranteed income of $4,800 a year, every year, may be fine for surfers. But most young adults will find that basic income restricts their real freedom to shape their lives, often severely. Most obviously, the restraint sharply cuts into the freedom of people who want to invest their stakes in the development of their own "human capital." Consider a 21-year-old high school graduate aiming to become a first-rate auto mechanic. He needs $20,000 to learn the skills of this increasingly high-tech trade. Under basic income, he will have to wait four or five years to accumulate the money. Why?

Or consider newlyweds who want to have kids and share parenting responsibilities. In support of this decision, they would pour most of their joint stake of $160,000 into a small house and use the rest to reduce their work commitments out of the home and share child-rearing responsibilities. Suppose they can't do this on $8,800 a year. Why stop them?[13]

More broadly: Basic income encourages a short-term consumerist perspective, but stakeholding invites young adults to take the longer view. Most people in their twenties are crushed by the vast gap between adult responsibilities and small financial resources. Although their future is still ahead of them, they live lives of quiet desperation – trying to make ends meet from month to month.[14] Although $400 a month will ease short-term financial crises, it is too small a sum to give them real freedom to look decades ahead and appreciate the life-shaping choices they are making, often by default.

Stakeholding, by contrast, invites them to take charge of their lives. With $80,000 in the bank, young adults may pause and consider how their aims and abilities are likely to unfold over time, and whether a short-term perspective will lead them down paths that they will later bitterly regret.

Stakeholding's distinctive emphasis on the life-shaping perspective is dramatized by the way it treats the problem of premature death. If Jane Citizen dies at 35, she has received her full stake, but her stream of monthly payments has fallen far short of $80,000. On stakehold-ing's view, this is perfectly appropriate. Each young adult should have the precious opportunity to put meaning on the shape of her life as a whole. The only regret is that Jane probably hasn't had a decent opportunity to live out the commitments and investments she made in her twenties. Basic income proceeds on a different moral foundation. It presumes that Jane should get fewer payments because she will have fewer months to consume.

We reject this consumerist premise. Each citizen's claim to real freedom is independent of the number of months she will enjoy herself as an adult. It should depend instead on her status as a person capable of impressing a meaning on the shape of her life. If a young person uses her stake to pursue a risky but rewarding life, and this decision increases her chances of an early death, her claim to basic resources is worthy of no less respect than that made by risk-averse types.[15] "One person, one life, one stake" is the fundamental principle of the Stakeholder Society.[16]

Turn now from liberal ideals to some crucial real world matters of administration. Suppose that John Citizen is grimly determined to obtain his $20,000 course as an auto mechanic despite efforts to impose a spendthrift trust on his money. Here, some clever lawyering may suffice to convert basic income into stakeholding. Depending on how strictly the spendthrift provisions are written, John may be able to walk into a bank and take out a mortgage, pledging his basic income as security for the monthly repayments. To prevent this kind of transaction, the government would have to insulate John's basic income from creditors' claims. That rule would prevent advance borrowing, but it would also create a distasteful spectacle: Bankrupts would walk out of the bankruptcy court with basic income rights intact, no matter how high their debts. We propose to insulate young adults' stakes from creditors, but only to prevent advance borrowing before ages 21–24. After that, every citizen must take responsibility for his or her actions – and debts. In contrast, basic income runs the risk of underwriting adult irresponsibility: How to justify letting the *40-year-old* default on her credit-card debts while keeping her basic income intact?

And then there is the black market. Suppose that John, the would-be auto mechanic, is not deterred when legitimate banks refuse to deal with him on the ground that any loan which capitalizes his $400 monthly payments is illegal. He simply gets his neighborhood loan shark to lend him the $20,000, promising to use his $4,800 a year as collateral. Since this deal is illegal, Mr. Shark won't be able to go to court to enforce it – but he will hire thugs, at his own expense, if John refuses to cough up when the time comes. All this expense and uncertainty will greatly increase the interest that Shark will charge his customer. But John is willing to pay the price to begin executing his life plan.

How does basic income propose to respond? Putting the expense of an on-going campaign of criminal prosecution to one side, do we really want to transform John into a criminal – simply because he wants to make an investment in his future? What kind of crime is that?[17]

Sort of like making consensual sex into a crime. Only less sensible. After all, some people think that consensual sex outside of marriage is a mortal sin. But nobody thinks that it is a sin to become a trained mechanic. Whatever the law may say, it is virtually certain that it won't be enforced by draconian sanctions. The black-market option not only lets the loan sharks appropriate the lion's share of John's economic birthright, but it will also reorient his relationship to the entire program. Under stakeholding, John could proudly come forward and claim his stake as a free citizen; now the state's efforts to restrain his freedom has turned him into a devious thief. When John finally becomes a skilled mechanic, he will not remember the stakeholding experience with pride, and seek to reciprocate by acts of loyal citizenship. Instead, he will more probably reflect on the ways he cheated, and was cheated, in the process of turning his basic income into a capital grant.

The resulting demoralization is a matter of the first importance. We have thus far presented only one side of the case for stakeholding – emphasizing its function as a major new vehicle for the exercise of real freedom. But the initiative also discharges a second major function: We expect it to serve as the institutional focus for a dynamic culture of citizenship. From their earliest days, children will learn that stakeholding is part of their birthright as citizens: "When you grow up, you won't be casually left at the mercy of the market or the arbitrary will of wealthy friends and relations (if you have any). You will confront your future under economic conditions worthy of a citizen of a free society." Parents and schools will continually urge their charges to use their freedom in a responsible fashion, and as the stakeholding period draws near, each man and woman will be enmeshed in an ongoing and multilayered conversation about their stakes: "Did you hear how Jane spent her first payment $20,000 – what a fool! If she keeps this up, she'll never make anything of her life!" Stakeholding will provoke millions of such conversations – and they will forge a cultural bond that will make stakeholders' common citizenship into a central reality of social life. As they grow older, citizens will forever be returning to their youthful days, and reflecting on their choices, and what has become of them.

The dynamics of basic income would be different. Even if payments began on the eagerly awaited twenty-first birthday, the stream of small checks would not create a proud culture of free citizenship. Stakeholding creates a focal point at age 21 for young citizens and their elders alike, dramatizing the importance of the rise to maturity. Basic income makes its impact gradually and incrementally, adding a few thousand to the annual budget. Those sums would make a difference in day-to-day life, especially at the bottom of the income distribution. There is much to be said for replacing grudging handouts with a dignified income entitlement. But the power of stakeholding reaches well up the economic ladder, and offers everyone an opportunity to take their life-shaping decisions seriously.

To be sure, the stakeholding culture will have its dark side. Some stakeholders will curse the day they made such foolish, youthful choices. But all will recognize the fundamental role stakeholding played in their lives. And except for the most bitterly disappointed, these reflections will prompt a patriotic determination to pass on the heritage of stakeholding to the next generation.

This reciprocating sense of membership lies at the heart of liberal understandings of citizenship. The liberal state does not bind its citizens by an appeal to a common race or language or religion or other moral authority. It seeks to engage people in the common project of assuring equal freedom to all, and to take pride in a polity that guarantees everybody the resources needed to confront the mystery of life with dignity and responsibility. If this noble ideal is ever to become a reality, it must be embodied in social institutions that ordinary people find meaningful. Stakeholding promises to be such an institution, but basic income threatens to destroy the integrity of this message as millions predictably undermine its imposition of a universal spendthrift trust by countless deviations and obfuscations.

Van Parijs may respond by calling on us to face some harsh facts. Some young people *will* undoubtedly "blow" their stakes – going on a gambling spree, or crashing a fancy sports car. We agree, but is this a good reason for depriving millions of other people of the economic power over their own lives? After all, neither the auto mechanic nor the newlyweds are planning a trip to Las Vegas any time soon. Why should their claims to real freedom be sacrificed simply to prevent others from "abusing" their freedom?

We reject this utilitarian calculus. Each person is her own person. Each is entitled to real freedom to shape her own life. This precious freedom should be not be compromised merely to save others from the consequences of their own choices.

To be sure, this liberal commitment leaves us with an obvious problem: How to respond to somebody who goes directly from the Stakeholding Office to the nearest casino and loses everything?

Van Parijs doesn't have this problem, because he has imposed a spendthrift trust on everybody. Ms. Stakeblower is free to lose $400 a month at the casino, but can't go for broke. She must wait till next month for her next $400 check before she again spins the wheel of fortune.

But for us, stakeblowing raises a distinctive question: What to do when Ms. Stakeblower returns empty-handed and confronts the political community with her starving self?

We think it is a plus, not a minus, for stakeholding to place this question at the center of discussion surrounding the next reform agenda. The effort to provide answers will invite the polity to confront a question much in need of fundamental reappraisal. Call it the problem of *life-cycle distribution*.

Speaking broadly, welfare states of the twentieth century distributed different benefits during three different phases of life: youth, adulthood, and old age. During youth, the accent is on education; during adulthood, on need; during old age, on cash pensions. The average American, for example, has a fundamental right to a free high school education but is then left to fend for himself in the marketplace unless he demonstrates a dramatic "need" for assistance. Even then, he can expect the American government to respond in a miserly fashion until old age arrives, when more generous forms of cash (and medical) assistance are available.

Stakeholding suggests the importance of identifying a fourth moment in this distributional cycle – the moment of transition from youth to maturity. Just as all children receive an unconditional grant of educational resources, regardless of parental ability-to-pay, young adults should receive an unconditional grant of economic resources, regardless of parental ability-to-give. Just as liberal education provides each citizen with vital cultural resources for self-understanding, an economic stake provides them with the material resources for real freedom.

Within this life-cycle framework, stakeblowing is a special case of a much more general problem: How does the grant of a new right at an early stage of life (in this case, $80,000 to young adults) shape the collective response to claims of entitlement at later stages (in this case, Ms. Stakeblower's claim to "need" assistance)? Does the enhancement of entitlements early in the life cycle justify a reduction of entitlements at later stages? And if so, which ones, and on what principles?

The particular problem raised by stakeblowing seems pretty easy. *Of course* Ms. Stakeblower should be held responsible for her conduct in Las Vegas when she tries to collect a second time on the basis of her newly acquired financial "need." While a decent society shouldn't allow anybody to starve in the streets, her prior conduct disqualifies her from more than this minimum.[18] If she wants more out of life, let her work for it. (In other words, stakeblowers will be obliged to face a situation similar to that confronted by the overwhelming majority of people in any Western society.)

Other life-cycle issues are much harder: How should the earlier receipt of an $80,000 stake change government policy for the provision of unemployment benefits, or retraining assistance, or health insurance? What is the appropriate relationship between stakes to the young and government pensions to the elderly?

Our book proposes a few principles for confronting these life-cycle trade-offs.[19] Rather than revisiting these controversial matters, we focus on an important question of process. Given the likelihood of serious disagreement on life-cycle trade-offs, how to structure the ongoing process of political decision?

Begin with basic income, and consider the chaotic resolution that it will likely generate. If a political party seriously proposed a $400 monthly payment, this would *immediately* provoke a debate on basic income's ramifications on every other monthly payment provided by the modern welfare state – ranging from disability to unemployment to health care and beyond. Each affected group will predictably clamor to preserve its entire benefit while fiscal conservatives will be on the rampage for massive cut-backs to make room for the new fiscal requirements imposed by basic income.

This doesn't sounds like a recipe for deliberate attention to the demands of justice in particular contexts. Perhaps it is utopian to expect much from any scenario, but stakeholding does permit greater hope. Rather than proposing yet another monthly payment, it frames the key question in a different way: Are we making a big mistake ignoring the distinctive predicament of young adults as they start off in life with new responsibilities but without significant assets?

To answer this question responsibly, it isn't necessary to undertake a comprehensive scrutiny of every monthly payment made by the welfare state. Over time, the adoption of stakeholding will lead to reconsideration of other programs as they reach the top of the political agenda. But there is no compelling necessity to resolve all these loose ends at once.

And a good thing too. The effort to do so might readily defeat any serious progress on the basic income front. Once beneficiaries of all existing welfare programs are alerted to the danger, they may well join with conservatives to fight for the status quo. This right–left coalition would be tough to beat.

In contrast, the structure of stakeholding will predictably defuse potential opposition. Consider, for example, the clever way Tony Blair introduced stakeholding as the "big new idea" behind his successful campaign for reelection in 2001. Under the Labour Party initiative, each Briton would receive a "baby bond" of $750 or so at birth, which would accumulate compound interest until he received a stake at age 18.[20] Supplemental amounts would be added to each child's account on later birthdays – with the aim of providing him with as much as $7,500 when he reaches maturity.

From a dollars-and-cents view, Blair's initiative doesn't cost much in the near future. Surely it doesn't pose a clear and present danger to the monthly checks received by present beneficiaries of the welfare state. Indeed, even when payouts begin 18 years down the line, $7,500 isn't very much at all. Nevertheless, it is substantial enough to raise the question: Doesn't the next generation deserve something better than the indefinite extension of the present welfare state?

In framing his initiative, Blair copied a move out of Franklin Roosevelt's political playbook. When introducing Social Security in 1935, the President also took steps to minimize the short-run cost of his proposal. While he took immediate credit for pensions for the elderly, the first pay-out occurred five years later in 1940. The same political calculus is evident in the Prime Minister's program: every prospective parent breathes a bit easier today, even though payouts won't occur for a generation.

Similarly, the initial Social Security statute was a transparently inadequate response to the plight of the elderly. For example, Roosevelt secured the support of white Southern Congressmen by excluding agricultural and domestic workers from coverage, which immediately deprived most blacks of any benefits. So far as the President was concerned, it was far more important to secure public support for the principle of retirement pensions. Once this was accomplished, Roosevelt was confident that its success would generate pressure to expand coverage over time.

So too with the Prime Minister's "baby bonds." The important point at this stage is to gain public recognition of the imperative need to promote the real freedom of young adults at the threshold of life. It will then be time enough for activists to start campaigning for bigger stakes and quicker transitions.

It will be much harder to generate a similar political dynamic in the case of basic income. Within the context of stakeholding, it did not seem arbitrary for Blair to announce that only children born after the statutory date of enactment would qualify for a "baby bond." After all, the entire point of the program is to channel resources to the rising generation, and so it would have seemed bizarre for a 50-year-old, say, to demand that he be granted a "baby bond" retroactively.

In contrast, basic income does not focus on the particular predicament of the young, but spreads its concern to all citizens –

50-year-olds no less than 18-year-olds. Nobody would even think of proposing a "transitional scheme" that barred a particular age group as a cost-cutting measure. But this means, of course, that politicians will not find themselves in the delicious situation of granting immediate symbolic benefits to a large constituency while the financial costs only mount up later.

Which immediately leads to a second political problem. Since basic income's costs are immediate, and broadly distributed to the adult population, practical politicians won't be in a position to begin basic income with very generous monthly payments. Imagine, for example, that Tony Blair had taken the first year's budgetary cost of supplying "baby bonds" and had distributed this money to every adult Briton (of working age)[21] as a basic income. This would have amounted to the princely sum of $1.25 a month![22]

This simply doesn't have the same pizzazz as promising the next generation "baby bonds" that, upon maturity, will provide $4,500-$7,500 to each young adult.[23] While these sums are rather small, they are big enough to suggest a certain seriousness of purpose in aiming for a more just future for the next generation. In contrast, a monthly basic income of a dollar and twenty-five cents is just a joke.

Call this the "chump change" problem. To solve it, proponents of basic income must insist that, *from the very beginning*, budgetary expenditure be large enough to fund a significant-looking sum for every adult recipient. But this makes a Roosevelt–Blair gambit impossible. There is no prospect for gaining big symbolic gains at low short-term cost. Instead, the protagonist for basic income must immediately wrest big budgets away from competing programs, and somehow overcome the resistance of well-organized vested interests who will fight for their familiar share of the pie.

We do not say that victory is impossible. But the political calculus for basic income does suggest a certain utopianism that presently afflicts much liberal theorizing. It is one thing – and a great thing – to propose deep philosophical resolutions of the conflict between liberty and equality. But it is no less great to structure initiatives that have half-a-chance of enactment. We must rid ourselves, once and for all, of Marxist delusions that history will mysteriously work on behalf of the oppressed. The challenge is to design programs that promote justice *and* make political sense in real-world democracies.

This is where the taxation side of the equation becomes especially important. By casting itself as a form of *capital* endowment, stakeholding invites the construction of a symbolic tie to underutilized forms of taxation that focus on the present maldistribution of wealth.

Just as the promise of $80,000 at age 21 is readily comprehensible to ordinary citizens, so is the funding for the program: An annual wealth tax on everything above $230,000 and a payback from stakeholders at the time of their deaths. In an age of sound-bite journalism, it is no small virtue to convey the essence of a program in a sentence or two. More importantly, the link between stakeholding and its funding taps into the expressive power of taxation. The payback rule underlines the importance of intergenerational justice. To ensure a universal social inheritance, decedents must give back something from their estates. The old make way for the new – but in an egalitarian way. Regrettably, Democrats who opposed the 2001 repeal of the estate tax had no such symbolism on which to draw. Faced with Republican attacks on a macabre "death tax" that (ostensibly) forced family businesses into bankruptcy, Democrats managed only a muddled protest at "regressivity". Without any clear platform, their general commitment to progressive taxation met an easy defeat. Stakeholding, in contrast, makes the egalitarian debate vivid. Large inheritances for a few versus a meaningful inheritance for everyone.

The wealth tax weaves in a second symbolic message. By spotlighting the concentration of wealth in America, it both reveals a problem and, linked with stakeholding, suggests a remedy. The revenue potential of a 2 percent wealth tax is stunning – $406 billion using 1998 data.[24] And it speaks volumes about the vast gap in wealth. With a $230,000 exemption and a 2 percent rate, only the top 20 percent would pay any wealth tax at all.[25]

Our commitment to the wealth tax over an income or consumption tax reflects several considerations, both principled and pragmatic.[26] From a principled perspective, the extreme concentration of wealth reflects past injustice and perpetuates it. In an ideal setting, with true equal opportunity, differences in individual wealth-holdings would be untroubling; simply an indicator of one's life choices.[27] There would be no reason to penalize savers relative to spenders; or those with great material wealth over those with little, because (by hypothesis) everybody received a fair start. But today, the wealthy cannot plausibly claim that their fortunes were earned on a level playing field. It is impossible to know who would have prevailed in a fair competition, but lacking that information, the annual wealth tax is rough-cut justice.

The wealth tax also targets inequality in the next generation. Wealth buys advantages not merely for oneself, but, crucially, for one's children, who go to better schools, get into better colleges, and can rely on the security of the family bank account to get them out of future scrapes. Once again, a truly just state would remedy those inequalities directly, through education and the restriction of inheritance. But in the absence of such measures, it is fair to tax the wealthy to fund better opportunities for every child.

From a practical viewpoint, wealth taxation provides a useful backstop to the payback requirement, ensuring that wealthy market-winners who spend-down their assets before death will still contribute to stakeholding for the next generation. The wealth tax could even enhance the functioning of the income tax. The cumulation of administrative compromises and deliberate tax breaks has reduced the effective rate of income taxation on capital to very low levels.[28] By taxing capital directly, the wealth tax could do what the income tax, now hopelessly riddled with loopholes, cannot: Extract a fair contribution to the polity from capital owners. Although the wealth tax would require new administrative structures for valuing – and locating – assets, that technocratic challenge is also a virtue, because it offers the potential to broaden the capacity of the income tax as well.[29]

Basic income shares some of these virtues, but less clearly. Like stakeholding, it can be described in a sound bite that conveys its egalitarian character. But the tax side of Van Parijs' proposal is less expressive. In *Real Freedom for All*, Van Parijs proposes funding a basic income with an income tax and an inheritance tax.[30] The inheritance tax taps into the same symbolism we employ: the justice of social inheritance (or, more precisely for Van Parijs' plan, a social dividend) for all. The income tax reflects Van Parijs' conclusion that income from good jobs and investments are a scarce resource that should be considered to be owned collectively, and shared equally through basic income. There is a fine symmetry here: Unequal income streams transformed into an egalitarian minimum income. But the real-world income tax muddies that principled symmetry and may create harder political battles for the basic income idea. In the United States, as in most Western countries, the income tax is the workhorse of the fiscal system. Here, it accounts for 47 percent of revenue (compared to 28 percent in Germany, 34 percent in Italy, and 37 percent in Britain, though only 18 percent in France).[31] The result is a long line of political claimants for income tax revenue. Basic income is just one more. Given the already dismal record of the income tax in reaching income from capital, a hike in the income tax may amount, in effect, to yet another burden on wages, which are already heavily taxed for various social-insurance programs.

This brings us squarely back to politics in the most mundane sense – getting out the vote. Our ambition, like Van Parijs', is to bring modern liberal philosophy into the real world. We aim not merely for elegant principles but for practical programs with a realistic chance of adoption. But because liberal redistribution is costly in tax terms, it faces predictable political opposition. In the United States, proposals for "higher taxes" for "new welfare programs" have a predictably dismal fate. The challenge, then, is to frame the public debate in a new way.

We have already suggested how stakeholding allows for a Blairish mode of presentation – in which immediate symbolic gains can be won at small short-run costs. But suppose that we were dealing with a more adventurous political leader, who was not satisfied with the long transition contemplated by Blair's "baby bonds," and wished to move to a relatively rapid embrace of the full Ackerman–Alstott alternative. What would her political calculus look like?

Recall that our $230,000 exemption level means that only 20 percent of Americans will be paying any wealth tax. This gives our progressive politician lots of room for creative maneuver as she seeks to mobilize majority support. She is not, to be sure, proposing to put cash directly in the hands of the present generation of voters – who will not generally be young enough to qualify for stakeholding themselves. She is instead appealing to larger concerns, most notably, the concern to build a more just society for our posterity. We ourselves will never reach the promised land. But shouldn't we try to hand over a world that is moving in the right direction?

Call this the desire for progress, and consider the subtle way in which stakeholding elicits this progressive motivation. It does not plead with citizens to sacrifice for some large abstraction – Social Justice – that is projected onto the remote future and exists apart from their own concrete experience. It invites them to build on more proximate desires for human betterment. When confronting stakeholding, most voters will think of a favorite sister or son or granddaughter, and consider how much $80,000 would mean to these very particular people as they start off in life. They will reach more abstract principles through these more particular exercises in moral imagination: If stakeholding is good for my daughter, isn't it good for all other children as well?

John Stuart Mill often spoke of the interests of a "progressive being," and we propose to bring his talk down to earth to consider how progressive parents of young children might analyze their interest in stakeholding. Suppose that our family consists of two 35-year-old parents and two young children, and that the parents find themselves within the bottom 80 percent of the income distribution. These voters are "progressive beings" in two senses: First, they don't look upon their children as mere consumption goods, but care about their future development as autonomous human beings for their own sake; second, they are willing to look beyond their kin, and recognize a collective obligation, as citizens of a liberal state, to provide all of them with a fair start in life.

But needless to say, they are not willing to pay too big a price for progress – after all, they have lives to live as well, and they are unwilling utterly to sacrifice their own moral ambitions for themselves simply to provide more justice for the next generation.

Within this framework, stakeholding seems a very attractive proposition to our hypothetical 35-year-olds. As they look ahead a decade or so, they consider how much money they are likely to have in their bank account – and immediately recognize that they won't be in a position to stake their kids to $80,000 apiece as they start out in adult life. Better yet, they also figure that they won't be paying any extra taxes for stakeholding over the next decade or two. It is only as they contemplate the "longer run" that our couple may begin to have doubts. Perhaps when they reach 55 or 65, they may be accumulating sufficient wealth that they may have to pay a substantial wealth tax to finance the stakes for the next generation. But for the majority of citizens, even this is speculative: Isn't the chance of bearing this tax worth the certainty of giving one's children, and all other children, a solid head-start?[32]

It will take skill for progressive politicians to frame the issue in this way. But with the right kind of leadership, the AA package might generate a broad positive response. We foresee a tougher time for the VP package. As we have seen, income tax is already an overburdened instrument, and even if Van Parijs successfully uses it as primary funding source, the bottom 80 percent will be contributing a major share. While we would be happy if Van Parijs were persuaded to adopt a wealth tax, the marriage of basic income to a wealth tax lacks the same symbolic meaning generated by our proposal. The AA combination of universal stake and focused wealth tax speaks a language that everybody immediately understands: The time has come to create a world in which inheritance is not merely a function of family but of *citizenship* – where all members of the commonwealth have a right to inherit a fair share of the material endowment created by previous generations, and are not merely forced to rely on the luck of inheriting wealth from a rich family.

*

We close by sketching out some more common ground with Van Parijs – this time emphasizing our common diagnosis of the distinctive intellectual predicament confronting progressivism in the new century. From this perspective, we seem to be shadow-boxing against the same ghostly presences of the past.

Classical laissez faire provides a mirage of formal freedom that is a parody of liberal ideals. Contemporary political philosophy makes this point, but through thought-experiments too utopian for real-world implementation.

This is no news to old-time Marxists, who have disdained "bourgeois utopianism" and sought to displace it with a hard-headed analysis of class interests and historical dynamics. But these scientific pretensions have turned out to be pretentious: the "working class" isn't the locomotive of history. If classical liberalism gave us a bogus vision of liberal ideals, classical Marxism gave us a bogus understanding of historical causation. Worse yet, its emphasis on the causal agency of the working class tended to authorize much moralistic talk about the dignity of paid work, as if other activities were of lesser moral value.

We reject the labor theory of value – normatively as well as positively. But we do not reject the left's suspicion of liberal Utopianism as a feel-good mode of accommodation to the status quo. The liberal challenge is to make hard-headed appeals that channel politics toward the collective pursuit of real freedom in the real world.

Easier said than done. Both basic income and stakeholding suggest, however, that the effort may be worth making.

NOTES

1 See Rawls (1971), Ackerman (1980), Dworkin (1981a, 1981b), Walzer (1983), Sen (1992), Van Parijs (1995).

2 Only citizens may claim stakes. The citizenship restriction raises a number of moral quandaries, which we explore in Ackerman and Alstott (1999), pp. 46–49. We permit citizens not yet 21 to receive advance stake payments to fund higher education. Ibid., pp. 51–52.

3 Interest on a principal amount is not equivalent to the annuitized payment, which includes a partial return of principal, but especially for a long-term annuity, the numbers are close.

4 In many cases, commission of a crime should only lead to a postponement of a stake, not forfeiture. But we do support the selective use of forfeiture if the alternative is a lengthy term in prison. See Ackerman and Alstott (1999), pp. 49–51.

5   College-bound stakeholders may collect $20,000 each year beginning at 18. To equalize the present value of payments made to college-bound stake-holders and others, who wait until age 21, we provide for the accrual of interest. Ibid., p. 51.

6   Our book proposes a 2 percent wealth tax with an exemption of $80,000. Ibid., chapter 6. That proposal was based on 1995 Federal Reserve data, the most recent available at the time. As of 2001, we are able to draw on data from the 1998 Survey of Consumer Finances. Between 1995 and 1998, wealth in the middle and top of the distribution grew significantly. Wilhelm (2001), p. 1. These data show that a 2 percent tax on net worth in excess of $80,000 would raise $547 billion, far more than the cost of stakeholding, and far more than the $402 billion (in 1998 dollars; $378 billion in 1995 dollars) we originally proposed to raise. Ibid. We estimate that the 1998 cost of stake-holding would be $268 billion. Authors' calculations, updating the calculation in Ackerman and Alstott (1999), pp. 219–220.

We propose to take advantage of the nation's increasing prosperity by retaining the 2 percent rate but increasing the exemption level to increase the progressivity of the tax. With an exemption of $230,000 per individual, we could raise $406 billion from the top 20 percent of individual wealth-holders. Wilhelm (2001), p. 10 (Table 3). Alternatively, a tax rate of 1.5 percent with an exemption of $80,000 would raise $410 billion (in 1998 dollars).

Although 1998 numbers are the most recent available, they are outdated today. Nevertheless, there is no reason to suppose, a priori, that they system-atically understate wealth tax revenues compared to 2001. As of June 2001, the S&P500, the broadest major stock index, is higher than or flat relative to 1998; the Dow Jones Industrials are higher than in 1998, and the NASDAQ is flat compared to that year. See http://host.businessweek.com/businessweek/Corporate_Snapshot.html, (viewed 22 June, 2001).

7   Of course, those who have not done well financially will not be able to contribute to the stakeholding fund at death. Ackerman and Alstott, ch. 5.

8   For feminist support of basic income, see, e.g., Pateman (1988). For data on African-American wealth, see Keister (2000), who notes that in 1992, median black income was 60 percent of whites', but median black wealth was only 8 percent of whites'. In the same year. 25 percent of white families but 60 percent of black families had zero net wealth.

9   One of us has praised basic income for this reason. See Alstott (1999).

10   Van Parijs (1991).

11   See Ackerman and Alstott (1999), pp. 145–148.

12   Throughout our discussion of basic income, we assume that a basic income would be paid to adults from, say, age 21 to retirement age. We do this because we advocate stakeholding in lieu of basic income only for this group. We favor children's allowances and other initiatives for children, and

a flat-rate pension for old age. See Ackerman and Alstott (1999), ch. 8. It is only for the group rising to maturity that we believe stakeholding is the right idea.

13 Or will Van Parijs allow them, covertly, to capitalize their stake by taking out a mortgage on their home, pledging their basic income as security? If so, he is well on the way to the stakeholder society. We will return to this point shortly.

14 In 1998, the median wealth for all U.S. households was $60,700. 30 percent of U.S. households had net worth of less than $10,000. Wolff (2000), table 1. Wolff does not provide data on median wealth by age, but he does show that *mean* wealth of households headed by adults under age 35 was just 22 percent of mean wealth. Ibid., table 10.

15 This point, unfortunately, has great salience for minorities, who live with multiple injustices, including greater poverty rates, poorer health, and greater exposure to violence. African-American men, for example, have an average life expectancy of just 66 years at birth, compared to 74 for white men. Statistical Abstract (1999), table 127. Black men are far more likely to die from criminal violence than are white men. Ibid., table 145.

16 See Ackerman (1980), pp. 49–53.

17 To respond to these difficulties, some have suggested a more elaborate form of "spendthrift" trust under which young adults receive $80,000 but can only obtain access to their money by convincing a bureaucrat of the merits of their proposed expenditures. See, e.g., Nissan (2000) pp. 12–13. But bureaucrats will inevitably import their own value judgments into the process, and claimants will be made to feel like supplicants. A standard list of worthy projects would avoid egregious forms of caseworker paternalism but would encourage legalistic manipulation and downright cheating. In purely practical terms, it would be impossible to design a process that is flexible and fair. Think of the borderline cases, which would quickly discredit the system. Amy may use her stake to open a hair salon, because that is entrepreneurship, but Ben may not become a street musician, because it is not a "business." Chris can enroll in divinity school and become an ordained minister because that is "education," but Dana may not travel to Asia to live in Buddhist monasteries because that is merely "travel." Extra procedural protections – like agency adjudication or judicial review – may worsen the situation. See generally Mashaw (1983); Lipsky (1980).

More fundamentally, stakeholders are free men and women, not claimants on state charity. They should not be required to bend the knee to some caseworker before moving on with their lives. The entire ritual smacks of a welfare state mentality inconsistent with the liberal spirit of stakeholding.

18 In fact, Ms. Stakeblower would be lucky to get a half-decent hand-out in America today. So much the worse for America.

19 See Ackerman and Alstott (1999), pp. 129–180.

20 For details, see U.K. Treasury (2001). Contributions would be based on a sliding scale – $750 to children born to poor families, reduced to a minimum of $450 for children in better-off circumstances. See ibid.; see also Broder (2001).

21 As noted above, we focus on a basic income for working-age adults; we have endorsed a basic-income-type scheme of our own for the elderly, in addition to stakeholding. Ackerman and Alstott (1999), ch. 8.

22 Translated into dollars, the baby bond proposal would pay up to $750 to each of the 750,000 infants born in Britain annually, or a total of $563 million. That estimate overstates the first-year cost of the program, because a means-testing rule would limit to $450 the grant to babies born to higher-income parents. But the first-year estimate also understates the steady-state program cost, because in future years the Blair plan would make deposits into each child's account of $75–$150 at ages 5, 11, and 16. For purposes of a rough estimate, we have settled on $750 per newborn. According to Downing Street statisticians, there are 37 million Britons between the ages of 16 and retirement age. See http://www.number-10.gov.uk/default.asp?PageID=3396, visited June 22, 2001. Thus, a basic income costing $563 million and paid only to working-age adults would yield $15 per year, or $1.25 per month.

23 For the particular details surrounding the Blair plan, see U.K. Treasury Consultative Document (2001); for a discussion in U.S. terms, see Broder (2001).

24 Wilhelm (2001), p. 10.

25 See note 6.

26 For a more detailed discussion of the ideas in this paragraph and the next, see Ackerman and Alstott (1998), pp. 96–101. For additional arguments on behalf of wealth taxation, see Shakow and Shuldiner (2000).

27 We emphasize that stakeholding alone will not guarantee anything like true equality of opportunity. Aggressive steps are also required to assure liberal education for all, to fight racial and other forms of invidious discrimination, and to remedy serious handicaps. See Ackerman (1980), parts 1 and 2.

28 Slemrod and Bakija (1996), p. 179.

29 For a detailed consideration, see Ackerman and Alstott, ch. 5.

30 Van Parijs (1995), pp. 100–102, 113–119.

31 Statistical Abstract (1999), table 1373 (1996 data). France collects a larger percentage of its revenue in social security wage taxes and in consumption taxes. Ibid.

32 The age distribution of wealth is heavily skewed toward the middle-aged and elderly. In 1998, households headed by someone under age 35 had average wealth of just 22 percent of mean wealth, while those 35–44 had 68 percent of the mean. Wealth is highest in the 55–74-year-old age group.

64   REDESIGNING DISTRIBUTION

Wolff (2000), table 10. Younger voters, then, are likely to appraise their future wealth tax prospects in probabilistic terms. Some, with secure jobs and good retirement plans, may count on being in the wealthy group burdened by the tax. But others will take the security of a good start for their children against the gamble of future wealth.

REFERENCES

Ackerman, Bruce. 1980. *Social Justice in the Liberal State*. New Haven, CT: Yale University Press.

Ackerman, Bruce, and Anne Alstott. 1999. *The Stakeholder Society*. New Haven: Yale University Press.

Alstott, Anne. 1999. "Work Versus Freedom: A Liberal Challenge to Employment Subsidies," *Yale Law Journal* 108, 967.

Broder, David. 2001. "Tony Blair's Eye-Catchers," *Washington Post*, A21 May 2.

Dworkin, Ronald. 1981a. "What Is Equality? Part I: Equality of Welfare," 10 *Phil. and Pub. Aff.* 185.

— 1981b. "What Is Equality? Part 2: Equality of Resources," 10 *Phil. and Pub. Aff.* 283.

Keister, Lisa. 2000. "Family Structure, Race, and Wealth Ownership: A Longitudinal Exploration of Wealth Accumulation Processes," Jerome Levy Economics Institute, No. 304, May 2000.

Lipsky, Michael. 1980. *Street-Level Bureaucracy*. New York: Russell Sage.

Mashaw, Jerry L. 1983. *Bureaucratic Justice*. New Haven, CT: Yale University Press.

Nissan, David, and Julian Le Grand. 2000. *A Capital Idea: Start-Up Grants for Young People*. London: Fabian Society.

Pateman, Carole. 1998. "The Patriarchal Welfare State," in *Democracy and the Welfare State* (Amy Gutmann, ed., 1988). Princeton, NJ: Princeton University Press.

Rawls, John. 1971. *A Theory of Justice*. New Haven, CT: Harvard University Press.

Sen, Amartya. 1992. *Inequality Reexamined*. Oxford: Oxford University Press.

Shakow, David, and Reed Shuldiner. 2000. "A Comprehensive Wealth Tax," Oxford: Oxford University Press. *Tax. L. Rev.*, 53, 499.

Slemrod, Joel, and Jon Bakija. 1996. *Taxing Ourselves*. Cambridge, MA: MIT Press.

Statistical Abstract of the United States, U.S. Census Bureau. 1999.

Van Parijs, Philippe. 1995. *Real Freedom for All: What (if Anything) Can Justify Capitalism?* Oxford: Oxford University Press.

— 1991. "Why Surfers Should Be Fed: The Liberal Case for an

Unconditional Basic Income," 20 *Philo. and Public Affairs* 101.

U.K. (HM) Treasury Consultative Document, *Saving and Assets for All, The Modernisation of Britain's Tax and Benefit System*, No. 8, downloaded from http://www.hm-treasury.gov.uk (2001).

Walzer, Michael. 1983. *Spheres of Justice*. Oxford: Robertson.

Wilhelm, Mark. 2001. "A Proposed Wealth Tax: Revenue Estimates and Distributional Analysis Using the 1998 Survey of Consumer Finances" (unpublished paper on file with authors).

Wolff, Edward N.. 2000. "Recent Trends in Wealth Ownership, 1983–1998," Jerome Levy Economics Institute, Working Paper No. 300, April.

PART II
Commentaries

3

The Citizen's Stake and Paternalism

Stuart White

"It was not the quantity of what I had which was striking, but the quality of what I could do and be by virtue of having a little. The difference between having twenty thousand a year and three hundred is as nothing compared with that between having three hundred and none."

– Stephen Spender, 1951

"It is not freedom to be allowed to alienate [one's] freedom."

– John Stuart Mill, 1859

INTRODUCTION: TWO OBJECTIONS

The first of these two remarks appears in Stephen Spender's autobiography, *World Within World*. Spender is commenting on how even a modest financial inheritance meant that he had the freedom to think and act independently and creatively at the start of his working life: "... although I had comparatively little money, my whole position of independence depended on it."[1] All those who inherit at least a certain modest amount have this independence, he implies, while those who inherit little or nothing do not. This division between the independent and the dependent is more striking and significant, Spender suggests, than inequalities within the class of fortunate independents. Spender's insight leads directly to the question: Why not guarantee every citizen an inheritance sufficient to have this independence? Why not socialize the inheritance process so that, as a right of citizenship, everybody receives a modest, but not trivial, economic stake – a *citizen's stake*, as we might call it? The proposals of Bruce Ackerman

and Anne Alstott and of Philippe Van Parijs offer us two different
models of how the citizen's stake idea might be implemented.
Ackerman and Alstott propose to implement the stake (largely) as a
one-off, lump-sum capital grant on maturity, with no restrictions as
to how people may use this grant.[2] I shall refer to this as the capital
grant (CG) proposal. Van Parijs proposes to implement the stake as a
periodic, but non-mortgageable income grant. I shall refer to this as
the citizen's income (CI) proposal.

At least two kinds of objection appear in the literature on these proposals. One objection, which is salient in the literature on CI, is that
such policies will allow citizens to establish a morally troubling, para-
sitical relationship to their fellow citizens. A generous CI, it is argued,
would allow citizens to free-ride on the productive efforts of other
citizens, by guaranteeing them a share of the social product without
demanding a productive contribution in return. A second objection,
which applies more specifically to the CG proposal, is that the
freedom secured by citizen's stake policies is too easily alienated, too
easily lost through careless employment of the stake. I have considered the former, exploitation objection at length in earlier work. In
this short chapter, I intend to switch focus to the second, alienation
objection.

Specifically, I consider three responses to the objection. The first
response, putting great emphasis on the distinction between disadvantage attributable to brute luck and that attributable to choice, denies
that there really is an objection here at all. I argue that this response
is unpersuasive. The second response emphasizes the need to complement citizen's stake policies with an appropriate kind of education in
asset management. The third response is to propose, on paternalistic
grounds, some kind of restriction on how stakes can be used. One
direction this response points us in is CI as opposed to CG. But there
are other directions it points us in that also warrant exploration,
notably the proposal for enacting the stake as a development grant: A
capital grant that may be used only for approved investment purposes
such as education, training, house purchases, or establishing a new
business. In concluding the chapter, I defend this option as one that
should inform the development of a citizen's stake policy.

The alienation objection briefly stated

As suggested, a primary rationale for a generous citizen's stake policy,
and the one I shall focus on for purposes of this chapter, is to help
secure for each citizen (at least) a minimally decent degree of

freedom.[3] To understand and respond to the alienation objection it will help to begin by clarifying this claim.

We are familiar with the view that someone is free when she is able to act as she wishes without being subject to interference by others. Many people claim that freedom in this sense is not diminished by poverty, by limited command over resources. But this appears to be mistaken. There is no action that can be performed without laying claim to some resource. All efforts to act thus involve claims on resources. If resources are privately owned, and one happens to lack property rights in resources, then there will be many actions one wishes to perform that one will not be able to perform without being subject to the legally sanctioned interference of others. Imagine, for example, that one is homeless and wishes to sleep. One identifies an area in which one would like to sleep. But this area is owned by Jones, and if you move on to it to sleep, Jones will call the police and move you off. If you turn to Smith's land, she will do the same. And so on, for every landowner in the vicinity. Propertylessness directly affects the degree to which you are free to do as you wish without being subject to interference by others.[4]

In reply, it might be argued that someone in the position of the homeless person we have imagined is not necessarily unfree, even if all the land is privately owned, because a given landowner might give her permission to use his land to sleep. The homeless person is certainly *vulnerable to* interference, but this vulnerability need not translate into *actual* interference. However, this does not seem to be a very forceful reply. Even if the homeless person is allowed to enter a given landowner's territory to sleep, she can be woken up in the middle of the night and moved on if the landowner so chooses. She sleeps at his discretion, and it can be plausibly argued that to live under another's power of discretionary interference like this is itself a significant curtailment of one's freedom. Philip Pettit explains that to live subject to the will of another in this way "is to suffer an extra malaise over and beyond that of having your choices intentionally curtailed. It is to have to endure a high level of uncertainty [that] makes planning much more difficult ... and [it] is to have strategic deference and anticipation forced upon you at every point ..."[5] I shall refer to relationships like that just depicted between the homeless person and the landowner as relationships of *dependency*. As the example of the homeless person illustrates, poverty can readily produce dependency of this kind, and, as Pettit suggests, thereby reduces freedom in a significant way.[6] Of course, such dependency may be considered a bad thing not simply because in itself it represents a diminution of personal freedom, but because people who are dependent in this way tend also to be vulnerable to various kinds of exploitation and abuse.[7]

Citizen's stake policies offer a form of protection against freedom-reducing dependency. Of course, a simple welfare safety-net will offer some protection of this kind. But conventional welfare policies often come with strings attached that may make it difficult to access resources at critical moments. CI and CG policies remove these strings and might therefore be thought to offer better protection.

At this point, however, the objection I wish to consider looms into view. Imagine that we could enact a truly radical citizen's stake policy in which all existing wealth holdings are taxed at 100 percent and redistributed as lump-sum capital grants to individuals on a completely egalitarian basis. Critics will object, quite plausibly, that substantial wealth inequality will quickly re-emerge, with some people dissipating their endowments and, thereby, the material basis of their freedom. In short, the objection is that citizens will be able quite readily to "blow" their stakes and thus *alienate* the material basis of their freedom so that, under even the most radical citizen's stake regime, we will still end up with a society divided between the free and the dependent. How might the proponent of the citizen's stake reply to this alienation objection?

The "So what?" response

The first response we must consider can be summed up in the phrase "So what"? If a division between free and unfree arises as a result of the choices people have made, starting from a sufficiently equal place, then perhaps, morally speaking, there is nothing to worry about. What should concern us, it might be said, is disadvantage that is due to bad "brute luck" rather than that due to choice.[8] I find this response to the alienation objection inadequate for two reasons.

First, I think we have reason to worry about situations of dependency even if they result unambiguously from choice rather than initial brute luck inequality. Consider the case of Rosa. Rosa lives in a society where all that citizens receive on maturity is a hefty capital grant. A few days after her eighteenth birthday she takes her stake and sets out to start her adult life in a new and fascinating city. However, within a few weeks of arriving in the city, she has spent her stake, losing most of it in foolish bets at a casino. Her immediate options are now such that she has no acceptable alternative but to take a job that one particular employer, Brian, a dodgy night-club owner, offers to her. Brian is well aware of her desperation and takes advantage of her resulting vulnerability to pay a very low wage (compared to the typical wage for the job). He also conditions her retention of the job on accepting a range of interferences in her life that she would not otherwise entertain. Surely Rosa suffers exploitation and a kind of unfreedom, and this is a proper matter of moral concern. Even if it is not intrinsically unjust for her to be relatively impoverished as a result of her foolish stakeblowing, Brian takes unfair advantage of her impoverishment. It seems implausible to say that Brian's exploitation and domination of Rosa are somehow acceptable – somehow not really exploitation or domination – because Rosa is responsible for getting herself into a state where she is vulnerable to apparently exploitative and oppressive treatment.[9]

Second, the argument that the loss of freedom following stakeblowing reflects choice rather than brute luck is anyway more problematic than we have thus far assumed. Choices are affected by a range of personal characteristics, some of which are, in the circumstances of societies such as our own, inheritances of social class. In the case of the utopian citizen's stake policy we have just imagined, people who come from families with little wealth, and thus little experience of managing wealth, will be more likely to blow their generous stakes than those who come from wealthy families that have transmitted the attitudes and skills relevant to wealth accumulation. One of the ways in which social class affects outcomes, including wealth outcomes, is through the transmission of what we might call *asset management capacity*: The ability to manage assets effectively with a view to the maintenance of the material basis of one's freedom (intuitively, the ability to manage assets so that one at least retains the equivalent of Spender's "three hundred a year"). This capacity is in part a matter of knowing about and understanding investment options. It is also in part attitudinal: A matter of seeing the future as something for which plans can and should be made, and of being willing to defer immediate consumption in the interests of long-term security. It is both about having a certain kind of time preference and about having the knowledge and understanding necessary to act on this preference.

However, the fact that stakeblowing can frequently be seen as a matter of brute luck, grounded in class-based inequalities in asset management capacity, rather than as a simple matter of choice, does not necessarily rescue the citizen's stake idea from the objection we started with. On the face of it, it seems in fact to add force to this objection: Not only are some people going to end up unfree under the citizen's stake regime, but many of them will be unfree due to accidents of birth for which they are not responsible. It is precisely this consideration that leads some radical egalitarians to reject citizen's stake ideas. In this vein, for example, John Roemer has argued that we should reject what he terms people's capitalist approaches to overcoming class inequality based on the simple redistribution of assets.[10] As Roemer says:

> Some people have learned to save under capitalism and have trained themselves in ways conducive to getting ahead in any society based on private ownership and markets. Others have learned behavior and values that are dysfunctional for success in a private ownership economy; one might argue that their behavior is well adapted to surviving on the margins of such a society but not to succeeding in its mainstream ... From the ethical point of view, the goal of socialism is to annihilate the opportunities that are unequal as a consequence of unequal access to or ownership of the alienable means of production. Equal ownership rights in the means of production would go only part way toward rectifying those inequalities, because the skills and preferences of people are themselves a consequence of past unequal opportunities.[11]

This observation brings us to the second response to the alienation objection.

The educational response

The second response starts to come into view once we entertain the following thought: Why take the existing link between social class and asset management capacity as a given? Could the state not do things to weaken this link? The proposal, in other words, is to connect citizen's stake initiatives with a concerted effort to break, or at least weaken, the link between class and asset management capacity. It is to design and complement such initiatives with a view to cultivating asset management capacity on the part of members of historically asset-poor groups.

Easily said, but how might this be done? I don't have a definitive answer to this question, but there are some possibilities that we may note. One indication of how citizen's stake-style policies might incorporate the concern to cultivate asset management capacity is provided by the recent experiments with so-called Individual Development Accounts (IDAs) in various parts of the United States.[12] IDA schemes originated in the non-profit sector but have now been given further support from states and federal government. A typical scheme works as follows. A community of eligible individuals, e.g., those with incomes below a specified threshold, is identified. Eligible individuals are offered the opportunity to set up individual accounts into which they will try to direct savings each month. Any saving they actually make is matched, e.g., the state may contribute $2 for every $1 the account-holder saves. Once a certain amount has been saved, individuals can withdraw their funds for approved investment purposes (such as courses of education, training, or putting a down-payment on a house). The generous subsidies obviously make these schemes attractive and make it likely that they will result in an immediate improvement in the asset position of their beneficiaries. But typically the schemes are designed on the premise that beneficiaries will make better use of the opportunities they provide if they receive some training in the mechanics and logistics of saving. Thus, in many schemes individuals are required to attend financial education classes as a condition of receiving matching funds or withdrawing funds from their account. These classes include "diverse topics such as household budgeting, personal financial management, establishing and repairing credit, goal setting, and principles of investing."[13] One cross-sectional survey of participants in the American Dream Demonstration IDA project found that 85 percent of participants completing the survey felt that the financial education classes helped them to save more, e.g., by identifying specific saving strategies suited to their circumstances. Another study found that the level of saving increased with hours of financial education, though only up to a point.[14]

We do not have sufficient evidence as yet to assess whether these schemes are effective in developing the long-term asset management capacity of otherwise asset-poor individuals. But if programmes of this kind are successful in this way, we should bear in mind that the effects may be felt not only by the immediate savers themselves but by others around them. Skills learned by a parent on an IDA programme might be conveyed to her children, so that they reach maturity with greater asset management capacity than they otherwise would have. In this way, such programmes might contribute to the breaking down of intergenerational cycles of asset poverty, and we might therefore consider them as a helpful complement to more universalistic citizen's stake schemes.

Another possibility, which has been mooted in the British debate over the Labour government's Child Trust Fund (CTF), is to integrate financial education directly into universalistic capital grant schemes themselves.[15] Under the CTF scheme, each British child will receive a personal account at birth into which the state will pay, depending on parental income, an initial sum of £250–500 (with further small sums being added to their accounts as they grow up). Topped up by family contributions, the money in the account will accummulate as the child grows up, giving her a modest capital stake on maturity that she will be free to use as she wishes. Now, could one not add an educational dimension to the CTF scheme? Lessons focusing on CTFs might be included as part of the curriculum. Children could perhaps track how their CTFs are growing. Teachers could ask children to explore how their accounts would have grown had the funds been invested in different ways, and could use this as a device for introducing children to different investment possibilities and to frame a discussion about their respective advantages and disadvantages. Teachers could organize discussions about what people might do with their accounts on maturity. Representatives of universities, vocational training schools, small business associations, trade unions, as well as financial institutions, could come into schools and offer advice on how stakes can be effectively used.

At the same time, it can plausibly be argued that it is only by promising every child a generous citizen's stake that educators will be able to engage children from different social backgrounds with this topic. Schools could, after all, take it upon themselves to organize investment education classes for children in the absence of any citizen's stake policy. For children from deprived social backgrounds, however, such classes would probably then have an air of unreality. Children are surely much more likely to be receptive to such classes if they know that there is something like a decent capital stake there, in their name, waiting for them on maturity, than if they expect to inherit nothing.

The paternalism response

I turn now to the third response to the alienation objection: Paternalism. The paternalist response is to place restrictions on how a citizen's stake may be used so as to prevent individuals endangering the material basis of their freedom.

From a liberal standpoint – and citizen's stake proponents such as Ackerman, Alstott, and Van Parijs are self-consciously arguing from a liberal standpoint – paternalism is intrinsically suspect (not the same, of course, as being necessarily wrong). On the liberal view, for individuals to lead lives that are good, it is necessary that they live in accordance with their own judgments about what the good life is.[16] If, however, they are to be free to live in authentic accordance with their own conceptions of the good life, then they must be left free to take what risks they deem worthwhile. The state ought not, as a general matter, to substitute its judgment for that of the individual. The state's task, in general, is to ensure sufficient equality in initial circumstances, and not to direct individuals as to how to make the best use of their endowments.

Having said that, few liberal thinkers are absolute in their opposition to paternalism. As the second quotation at the head of this chapter indicates, John Stuart Mill famously argued that individuals should not have the freedom to alienate their own freedom through some kind of slavery contract, and this can reasonably be seen as a form of paternalism.[17] Mill's comment draws attention to two fundamentally different ways in which we might manifest our concern for freedom. Stated in rough, shorthand terms, it is a difference between an end-state and a side-constraint view of what it means to manifest concern for freedom. In the first case, we treat freedom, and, thus, a degree of non-dependency, as an end-state. We do not necessarily seek to maximize the sum of end-state freedom, aggregated across all people; but we do at least seek to ensure that each person always has a certain minimum amount of end-state freedom, and this goal admits, indeed mandates, some paternalism aimed at preventing people from subverting this end-state through their own imprudent choices. In the second case, we treat freedom of choice as a side-constraint.[18] The state may not act in ways that violate this side-constraint, even to prevent people from doing things that would render them dependent and thereby deny them freedom in the future. Mill, in his comments on slavery, commits himself to a version of the first view. Mill's position finds a clear echo, moreover, in the view that many contemporary liberals take about the limits of freedom of association. Many liberals argue that the freedom to join a given association, such as a church, should be balanced by adequate freedom to exit this association. On this basis, it is argued that members of religious associations should not be allowed, as some churches have demanded of their members, to waive their social security contributions and consequent rights to state welfare benefits, for this would make the members in question so reliant on their church for future material support as to fatally compromise their freedom to exit the church in the future.[19] In this view we see, again, a degree of paternalism aimed at protecting the individual from relationships of dependency that would undermine her freedom and expose her to exploitative and abusive treatment.

Turning to the debate over the appropriate form of the citizen's stake, advocacy of a CI, as opposed to a CG, seems to rest much more easily with the first, Millian view of how we appropriately manifest our concern for freedom, than with the second, more Nozickian view. And, indeed, an appeal to a Millian paternalism plays an important role in Van Parijs' argument for implementing the citizen's stake as a CI rather than a CG.[20] As presented in his book *Real Freedom for All*, Van Parijs' case for a CI proceeds from the claim that each citizen has, in principle, a right to an equal share of certain external assets, notably "job assets."[21] In practice, we cannot literally give people equal amounts of these assets, but we can equivalently give them each a sum of money equal to the per capita value of these assets, financed from a tax on their value; or, if the policy of strict equalization would have large disincentive effects, we can and should give each person the highest sustainable sum of money we can from the taxation of these assets. Van Parijs argues that this sum should be paid as a periodic and non-mortgageable income grant. But there is nothing in the logic of the external assets argument which implies the grant should be non-mortgageable. What considerations justify this stipulation? The non-mortgageability of the income grant means that it cannot be converted into a lump-sum and then "blown." And, as Van Parijs acknowledges in *Real Freedom for All*,[22] the obvious rationale for preventing this would seem to be a paternalistic one: specifically, to restrict people's freedom to act in ways that would alienate the material basis of their freedom. In Van Parijs' words:

> a mildly paternalistic concern for people's real freedom throughout their lives, not just 'at the start', makes it sensible to hand out the [citizen's stake] in the form of a (non-mortgageable) regular [income] stream – just as a mildly paternalistic concern for their formal freedom makes it reasonable to prohibit the permanent alienation of self-ownership.[23]

However, another way in which we might structure the citizen's stake so as to reduce the likelihood that people will alienate the material basis of their freedom is, of course, to restrict the range of purposes for which citizens will be able to use an initial lump-sum grant. We can make it less likely that they will blow their grant, and thus endanger their future freedom, by insisting that the grant be used only for specific, developmental, asset-building purposes. The kind of freedom-preserving paternalism that I have said supports a CI over a simple one-off, lump-sum grant does not, in fact, point unequivocally toward CI as opposed to this third type of citizen's stake, which we might call a *development grant*.

A number of proposals for this type of citizen's stake have been made in recent years. One example is the scheme recently proposed in

Britain by David Nissan and Julian Le Grand.[24] They propose that all citizens be endowed on maturity with a grant of some £10,000, which would go into an individual Accumulation of Capital and Education ("ACE") account, financed from a revamped inheritance tax. Each ACE account "would be handled by a set of trustees, whose purpose would be to approve the spending plans of individuals before releasing any capital."[25] Nissan and Le Grand mention education, training, business start-up costs, and housing down-payments as possible approved uses for the grant. This proposal has much in common with Robert Haveman's earlier proposal for a "universal personal capital account for youths."[26] Development grants have also been proposed in recent books by Roberto Unger and Cornel West[27] and by Ted Halstead and Michael Lind.[28] Halstead and Lind propose giving every newborn citizen of the United States a grant of $6,000 "as a down payment on a productive life." As with the CTF proposed by the British government, the sum would be invested and would grow as the child matures. On reaching adulthood, the use of these special trust funds would be restricted to various types of personal investments, such as: "Paying for the costs of higher education or vocational training, putting a down payment on a first home, covering serious health emergencies, or starting a legitimate business."[29]

Is paternalism justified?

Let us now briefly recap. We have seen, first, that the alienation objection to the idea of a citizen's stake (in the form of a CG) is a genuine objection, one which cannot be defused by invoking a distinction between choice-based and brute luck disadvantage, especially in the circumstances of societies like our own in which an individual's capacity to manage assets effectively is so influenced by class background. Second, there would seem to be two ways of reducing the problem to which the objection points: education and paternalism. The first approach will lead us to concentrate on developing strong "preventive" social policies to complement a citizen's stake. The second approach will incline us to restructure the citizen's stake itself, moving away from the CG model towards a CI or, perhaps, toward what I have termed a development grant. Two further questions must now be considered:

(1) Would adoption of the first, educational approach render unimportant the second, paternalist approach?

(2) To the extent that the paternalist approach retains relevance, do
we have good reason to prefer a CI to a development grant or vice
versa?

As regards the first question, there is no doubt that the absence of
the educational measures associated with the first approach makes the
paternalist measures associated with the second approach much more
urgent. However, even if educational measures of the relevant kind
are in place, I am not sure that the case for a supplementary paternalism evaporates. As Gerald Dworkin points out in an influential article
on paternalism, just about everyone is capable of moments of irrationality or weakness of will in which they commit themselves to
courses of action that risk tragic and irreversible consequences. Even
the solid, sensible middle-class citizen, as it were, can make a fatal
decision not to wear a seat-belt in the car, or a safety-helmet when
inspecting a building site.[30] In this article, Dworkin suggests that
solid, sensible citizens will be aware of this potentially tragic fallibil-
ity on their part, and, wishing to protect themselves against it, may
well desire various kinds of paternalistic intervention as a kind of
insurance policy against their less rational, weaker selves. This leads
to the following thought: A given paternalistic intervention is justifiable if it commands what one might call, with apologies to Rousseau,
a *prudential general will*. That is, a given paternalistic intervention is
justifiable if it is a restriction that all citizens would agree to, when in
a state of sober reflection on what really conduces to their own individual good, as a way of insuring themselves against individual
weaknesses of rationality and/or will that might have significantly
bad and irreversible consequences for their own welfare or freedom.[31]
The intervention is then something which supports people in the
pursuit of their goals, rather than an alien imposition on them.[32]

Viewed in this light, the case for a supplementary paternalism in the
design of citizen's stake policies does not seem unreasonable. Some
paternalistic restrictions can surely be defended as restrictions that
citizens would impose on themselves as an insurance policy against
the stakeblowing potential of periods of irrationality and/or weakness
of will. Van Parijs, we should note, explicitly invokes the prudential
general will idea in defending the "mildly paternalistic" CI option
over the alternative of a CG. He writes that the justification for pre-
ferring a CI "... consists in assuming a universal desire on people's
part, when 'in their right minds,' to protect their real freedom at older
ages against weakness of their will at younger ages and to do so pretty
homogeneously throughout their lifetimes."[33] Ackerman and Alstott

are not as far removed from this position, moreover, as they might at first sight appear. As noted above, their proposal is not, in fact, for a CG pure and simple, but for a hybrid form of citizen's stake that combines a CG on maturity with an age-related CI (a "citizen's pension" for which people are eligible at age 65). They insist that citizens not be allowed to capitalize their citizen's pension entitlements when young.[34] People in their youth cannot be expected to have a full appreciation of the interests of their aged selves, so far into the future, and so, they argue, we are justified in ring-fencing the citizen's pension from the ambitions of youth. This specific paternalistically motivated qualification of the CG proposal in its simplest form is perfectly plausible, but, by itself, it leaves individuals with a very large chunk of their lives in which to suffer the freedom-scuppering consequences of youthful irrationality and/or weakness of will. Given this fact, I find it no less plausible to think that additional paternalistically motivated departures from the pure and simple CG proposal would command a prudential general will.

The case for a hybrid stake incorporating a development grant

Turning now to our second question, if we were to move in a more paternalistic direction, which direction should it be? Should we move in the direction of a CI, in which citizens receive their stake as a non-mortgageable income stream, or in the direction of a development grant, in which citizens receive their stake as capital but subject to restrictions on how they may use their capital? I am not sure that either option, taken by itself, could command a prudential general will. On the one hand, I find it implausible that citizens – that is, the sober, sensible citizens whom we imagine as formulating this prudential general will – would really want to give up the option of starting their working life with an account that they can use for important investment purposes, as, presumably, they would if they were to choose to take their citizen's stake wholly in the form of a non-mortgageable CI. On the other hand, I find it no less implausible that such citizens would want to tie all of their stake up in a grant that can be accessed only for major investment purposes. Someone who is soberly, sensibly looking ahead, as we imagine these citizens to be, will anticipate not only investment needs that should be catered for, but also possible emergency needs that ought to be catered for. By emergency needs, I mean needs that have to do with the management of periods of crisis and transition in one's life – for example, after the break-up of a marriage or following the loss of a job or the death of a loved one. These are situations in which we may be particularly vulnerable, emotionally and often also economically, and so at particular risk of dependency. To help cope with these needs, and to minimize the economic pressures generated by such situations, citizens may wish to keep a portion of their stake as cash that they can access unconditionally, i.e., as something more like a CI or a CG than a development grant.

These points suggest that we should give more thought to possible hybrid forms of citizen's stake. One possibility, which speaks to the investment and emergency needs that sober, prudential citizens like those depicted above will anticipate, is to establish a universal citizen's account which combines a generous development grant with what I have elsewhere termed a time-limited citizen's income. A time-limited CI is an income grant that one can choose to draw on without satisfying a work-test (or means-test) but which can only be enjoyed for a fixed number of years (one, two, three?) over the whole course of one's working life. For example, individuals might have a right to draw up to a maximum of £20,000 in CI over the course of a working life, with, perhaps, a maximum of £8,000 drawable in any given year. A time-limited CI of this kind – obviously the figures I cite are purely illustrative – could then be combined with a capital grant of, say, £30,000 initial value, which citizens would be free to use for specified investment purposes such as higher education, vocational training, setting up a new business, and so on. The development grant speaks to anticipated investment needs; the time-limited CI to anticipated emergency needs. Prudently managed, a time-limited CI could provide individuals with crucial financial independence in periods of difficulty which might otherwise expose them to dependency. I would not claim, of course, to have demonstrated here the unique desirability of this hybrid type of citizen's stake. But, having once admitted paternalistic considerations into the analysis (at least along the lines proposed in Dworkin's influential article), I think it has some clear strengths that make it preferable to either the pure CI or pure CG models.[35]

Having said that, one must acknowledge that the proposal to implement the stake in part as a development grant, rather than as a CG or wholly as a CI, is subject to some forceful objections. For one thing, the development grant is likely to be more costly to administer than a CI or a CG; it costs resources to monitor that the stake is being used for the approved investment purposes.[36] Because of this some might object that it would be irrational of citizens to prefer this type of stake to a simple CG or CI. Why pour some of your precious stake into bureaucrats' salaries when you could take it as extra cash in hand?

There are, I think, two replies to this objection. First, while the administrative costs are real, and imply that citizens will have to pay a price for taking their stake as a development grant, we must not forget that according to the argument made above citizens also stand to gain some benefit from taking the stake in this form: The benefit of of being able to access directly a large portion of their stake for investment purposes while also being protected from the possibility of stakeblowing. If citizens value this benefit enough, then they may be quite willing to pay the price implicit in taking the stake as a development grant. It is not necessarily irrational to invest a portion of the stake in the sort of monitoring arrangements associated with the development grant if one values the combination of investment freedom and insurance against stakeblowing that this provides: the accessible cash value of the stake is lower, but there may be an offsetting welfare gain. Second, we should consider how the restrictions associated with the development grant will affect behavior and economic outcomes, and, thereby, the sustainable level of the stake itself. Imagine, for example, that the effect of taking the stake as a development grant, rather than as a pure CG, is to raise the level of investment in human capital, and that this, in turn, lowers the equilibrium rate of unemployment, or raises the rate of growth of the economy. As a result, it may be possible to sustain the stake at a higher overall level so that, even after allowing for higher administrative costs, the accessible cash value of the stake to the citizen is as great under the development grant option as under a pure CG. Of course, it is hard to judge the strength of these replies without hard data on the relevant administrative costs, on citizens' considered, self-regarding valuations of the benefits of the development grant, and on the aggregate economic impact of development grants relative to other forms of citizen's stake. But I think these replies suffice to show that the administrative costs objection to taking the stake (at least in part) as a development grant is not necessarily decisive.[37]

A second forceful objection to the development grant proposal focuses on "stakelosers" as opposed to stakeblowers. Whereas stakeblowers use their stakes in imprudent ways, stakelosers use their stakes in *ex ante* sensible ways, but just have bad luck in their investment decisions, e.g., use their stake to purchase training in skills that become outmoded in a way that could not reasonably have been anticipated. Taking the stake as a development grant will insure you against stakeblowing, but not against stakelosing. By contrast, taking the state as a CI will also insure you against the freedom-scuppering consequences of stakelosing. Doesn't this suggest that the sober, sensible citizens we have thus far imagined, concerned to protect their long-term interests, should lean more toward the CI option that the development grant? In reply, one can say that while there is, in this respect, a greater degree of risk attached to the development grant option, there is also something intrinsically attractive about taking the stake as a capital grant, immediately available for major invest-ment purposes, and citizens will naturally wish to strike a balance between this consideration and the risks attendant upon taking the stake as some form of capital grant. The possibility of stakelosing reinforces the point that prudent citizens will probably not want to take all of their stake as a development grant rather than a CI, but this does not mean that they would or, as prudent people, should elect to take all of their stake as a CI to the exclusion of a development grant.

CONCLUSION

I have argued that we should give attention to hybrid forms of citizen's stake which combine capital grant and CI components. And I have argued that in thinking about hybrids, we should give attention to development grants as well as pure capital grants of the kind proposed by Ackerman and Alstott. One possibility I have suggested is to combine a development grant with a modest, time-limited CI. Even with a citizen's stake of this kind, however, it will be far from impossible for people to blow their stakes and so alienate the material basis of their freedom. People could squander their time-limited CI so that no entitlement remains when they most need it. People could draw their development grants for ill-chosen educational purposes, or to finance ill-considered business ventures. They might use the grant to help buy a house, then sell the house, and lose the proceeds on a foolish gamble. This is one reason why I envisage a stake of this kind functioning alongside more conventional welfare state policies, and not as a full replacement for them.[38] And it is also why, in closing, I think it important to stress once more the importance of the educa-tional response to the alienation objection, the response which calls for an effort to cultivate the asset management capacity of citizens.

To some on the left, this will doubtless seem a nauseating prospect, an aspiration to turn every child into a good little bourgeois. If, however, we are aiming, in the name of freedom, at what John Rawls calls a property-owning democracy,[39] then we must indeed aspire to a society in which citizens have the characteristic skills and virtues of property-owners (or at least those skills and virtues of property-owners that are necessary for the long-term reproduction of personal freedom). In the long run, it may be that the relevant skills and virtues will percolate through a "stakeholder society" without the need for a conscious state policy aimed at cultivating these skills and virtues. But in the circumstances of our societies today, there is arguably a need for a strong proactive policy in this area to combat the existing link between the capacity for asset management and social class. To this extent, while redesigning distribution is essential to the goal of a free society, it may well not be enough.

NOTES

1 Stephen Spender (1951), p. 119.

2 I say "largely" because the proposal set out in their 1999 book, when described in full, is not in fact a proposal for a CG rather than a CI, but for a hybrid form of citizen's stake which combines a generous CG on maturity with an age-related CI (a "citizen's pension" of $670 paid to all from the age of 65). See Bruce Ackerman and Anne Alstott (1999), especially pp. 129–154 on the CI element of their proposal.

3 See, in particular, Ackerman and Alstott (1999); Philippe Van Parijs (1995); Van Parijs (1992), especially pp. 81–98; and Tony Fitzpatrick (1999).

4 Here I follow Jeremy Waldron, "Homelessness and the Issue of Freedom," in Waldron, *Liberal Rights* (1993), pp. 309–338. See also G.A. Cohen (1997), pp. 29–47, specifically pp. 41–43.

5 Philip Pettit (1997), pp. 85–87. See also Quentin Skinner (1998).

6 Pettit also argues, in contrast to Skinner, that interference as such does not diminish the freedom of the person subject to this interference if it tracks the interests of this person. Thus, for Pettit, not only is the absence of interference not *sufficient* for personal freedom, but it is also not *necessary* for freedom. I do not follow Pettit in making this second claim. Nor do I follow either Pettit or Skinner in asserting that the conception of freedom as involving non-dependency is somehow outside the "liberal" tradition of thinking about freedom.

7 For relevant analysis of the concept of exploitation, see Robert E. Goodin (1987), pp. 166–200.

8 See G.A. Cohen, "On the Currency of Egalitarian Justice," *Ethics* 99, 1989, pp. 912–944, and Ronald Dworkin, "What is Equality? Part 2: Equality of Resources," *Philosophy and Public Affairs* 10, 1981, pp. 283–345. I do not mean to imply that either Cohen or Dworkin would necessarily sympathise with the "So what?" response to the alienation objection.

9 This concern for vulnerability and resulting exploitation and domination is, I think, one of the considerations that Elizabeth Anderson advances for rejecting what she calls "luck egalitarianism." See Elizabeth Anderson,

"What is the Point of Equality?," *Ethics* 109, 1999, pp. 287–337.

10 See John Roemer, *Free to Lose: An Introduction to Marxist Economic Philosophy* (London, Radius/Century Hutchinson, 1988), pp. 152–153.

11 Roemer, *Free to Lose*, pp. 152–153.

12 A particularly helpful survey is provided by Ray Boshara, ed., *Building Assets: A Report on the Asset-Development and IDA Field* (Washington, D.C., Corporation for Enterprise Development, 2001). See also Larry W. Beeferman, *Asset Development Policy: The New Opportunity* (Waltham: MA, Heller School for Social Policy and Management, Brandeis University, 2001), especially pp. 27–28, 85–87.

13 See Colleen Dailey, "IDA Practice," in Boshara, ed., *Building Assets*, pp. 51–64, specifically p. 53.

14 See Sondra G. Beverley and Michael Sherraden, "How People Save and the Role of IDAs," in Boshara, ed., *Building Assets*, pp. 65–80, specifically p. 75.

15 See *Saving and Assets for All* (London, HM Treasury, 2001).

16 This view has been most explicitly and systematically defended by Ronald Dworkin. See Ronald Dworkin, "Foundations of Liberal Equality," in Stephen Drawall, ed., *Equal Freedom: Selected Tanner Lectures on Human Values* (Ann Arbor, University of Michigan Press, 1995), pp. 190–306, especially pp. 262–273.

17 See John Stuart Mill, *On Liberty* (Harmondsworth, Penguin, 1985 [1859]), p. 173.

18 I take the notion of a side-constraint, of course, from Robert Nozick. See Nozick, *Anarchy, State, and Utopia* (Oxford, Blackwell, 1974), pp. 28–30.

19 For relevant discussion, see Brian Barry, *Culture and Equality* (Oxford, Polity, 2000), pp. 155–193, especially pp. 163–164.

20 In view of Erik Olin Wright's class-power argument for CI over CG, I am not sure that only an appeal to Millian paternalism will settle the issue in favour of CI. This is, however, the appeal that Van Parijs makes in his book, *Real Freedom for All*. See Erik Olin Wright, "Basic Income, Stakeholder Grants, and Class Analysis," chapter 4 in this book.

21 See Van Parijs, *Real Freedom for All*, especially pp. 89–130.

22 Ibid., pp. 45–48.

23 Ibid.

24 See David Nissan and Julian Le Grand, *A Capital Idea: Start-up Grants for Young People* (London, Fabian Society, 2000).

25 Nissan and Le Grand, *Capital Idea*, pp. 12–13.

26 See Robert Haveman, *Starting Even: An Equal Opportunity Program to Combat the Nation's New Poverty* (New York, Simon and Schuster, 1988), pp. 168–171.

27 See Roberto Mangabeira Unger and Cornel West, *The Future of American Progressivism: An Initiative for Political and Economic Reform*

(Boston, Beacon Press, 1998), p. 62. Unger and West write: "American democracy should work toward the generalization of a principle of social inheritance. Everyone should be able to count on a minimum of resources. These resources are the tools of self-reliance, not an alternative to self-reliance. People should have a social-endowment account so that society can do for everyone a little bit of what family inheritance does for a few. At major moments in their lives – when they go to college, make a down payment on a house, or open a business – they should be able to draw on this account." I interpret Unger and West to mean that the account should be geared specifically to these investment purposes, though, strictly speaking, what they say here does not rule out use of the account for other purposes.

28 See Ted Halstead and Michael Lind, *The Radical Center: The Future of American Politics* (New York, Doubleday, 2001), p. 101.

29 Halstead and Lind, *The Radical Center*, p. 101. They estimate that their proposed scheme would cost $24 billion annually.

30 For an excellent discussion of these problems, see Michael Lewis, "Perhaps There Can be Too Much Freedom," paper prepared for the Real Utopias conference, "Rethinking Redistribution: Designs for a More Egalitarian Capitalism," A. E. Havens Center for the Study of Social Structure and Social Change, University of Wisconsin-Madison, May 2–5, 2002.

31 See Gerald Dworkin, "Paternalism," in Richard Wasserstrom, ed., *Morality and the Law* (Belmont: CA, Wadsworth, 1971), pp. 107–126, especially pp. 120–123.

32 The idea of a prudential general will probably has to be qualified to some extent. In any given case, it is possible that a minority has values such that they would reject a proposed paternalistic intervention even in the state of sober, considered judgement we here imagine – for example, a religious group might regard the wearing of seat belts in cars as contrary to God's will. Can paternalistic measures still be justified in view of the possible burden to such minorities? Adopting a Rawlsian approach to the question, we might ask whether parties in an original position, behind a veil of ignorance, would consent to a degree of paternalism as a way of protecting their long-term interests given this risk of burden. I think that a reasonable balancing of interests by parties in the original position would suggest something like a principle of supermajoritarian paternalism: measures are justified if a sufficiently large majority regard the measures as restrictions they would consent to in a state of considered judgement. The parties might also consider supplementary principles, such as one aimed at compensating minorities for their burdens based on how costly it is for members of the minority groups to pursue their goals as a result paternalistic measures. I do not think the parties would choose a complete rejection of paternalism, for that would be to give effectively no weight to their very real interest in being

able to enact laws to protect themselves against their fallible selves. For Rawls's own discussion of the issue, see John Rawls, *A Theory of Justice: Revised Edition* (Cambridge: MA, Harvard University Press, 1999 [1971]), pp. 218–220.

33 Van Parijs, *Real Freedom for All*, p. 47.

34 See Ackerman and Alstott, *The Stakeholder Society*, pp. 133–142.

35 I should add that I think a hybrid citizen's stake with a similar struture can also be defended on non-paternalistic grounds, as a way of balancing justice-related concerns for freedom and reciprocity. I have developed this argument in another paper, "Freedom, Reciprocity, and the Citizen's Stake," in Keith Dowding, Jurgen De Wispelaere, and Stuart White, eds., *The Ethics of Stakeholding* (Basingstoke, Palgrave, pp. 79–93.

36 In discussion at the conference for which this paper was originally written, Julian Le Grand indicated that monitoring the use of development grants for the purpose of establishing a new business was particularly tricky, and that this problem had discouraged the British government from structuring the Child Trust Fund on the model of a development grant.

37 A further point to bear in mind concerns the degree to which there are administrative economies in stakeholder schemes: that is to say, the extent to which the cost of administering a single dollar of a development grant varies with the level of the grant. If there are economies of scale in the sense that the unit administrative cost falls as the average grant level rises, then the relative desirability of taking some of the stake as a development grant may increase as the generosity of the grant increases. Citizens may quite reasonably feel that it not worth paying, say, twenty-five cents to administer each dollar of a very modest development grant, but that it is worth paying, say, five cents to administer each dollar of a large development grant.

38 See Will Paxton, "Assets: a third pillar of welfare," in Sue Regan, ed., *Assets and Progressive Welfare* (London, Institute for Public Policy Research, 2001), pp. 17–33.

39 See John Rawls, *A Theory of Justice: Revised Edition*, pp. xiv–xvi, and *Justice as Fairness: A Restatement* (Cambridge: MA, Harvard University Press, 2001), pp. 135–140.

REFERENCES

Ackerman, Bruce and Anne Alstott. 1999. *The Stakeholder Society*. New Haven, CT: Yale University Press.

Anderson, Elizabeth. 1999. "What is the Point of Equality?," *Ethics* 109, pp. 287–337.

Barry, Brian. 2000. *Culture and Equality*. Oxford: Polity.

Beeferman, Larry W. 2001. *Asset Development Policy: The New Opportunity*. Waltham, MA: Heller School for Social Policy and Management, Brandeis University.

Boshara, Ray, ed. 2001. *Building Assets: A Report on the Asset-Development and IDA Field*. Washington, D.C., Corporation for Enterprise Development.

Beverley, Sondra G. and Michael Sherraden. "How People Save and the Role of IDAs," in Boshara, ed., *Building Assets*, pp. 65–80.

Cohen, G.A. 1997. "Back to Socialist Basics," Appendix: "On Money and Liberty," in Jane Franklin, ed., *Equality*. London, Institute for Public Policy Research, pp. 29–47.

— 1989. "On the Currency of Egalitarian Justice," *Ethics* 99, pp. 912–944.

Dailey, Colleen. "IDA Practice," in Boshara, ed., *Building Assets*, pp. 51–64.

Dworkin, Gerald. 1971. 'Paternalism', in Richard Wasserstrom, ed., *Morality and the Law*. Belmont, CA: Wadsworth.

Dworkin, Ronald. 1981. "What is Equality? Part 2: Equality of Resources," *Philosophy and Public Affairs* 10, pp. 283–345.

— 1995. "Foundations of Liberal Equality," in Stephen Drawall, ed., *Equal Freedom: Selected Tanner Lectures on Human Values* (Ann Arbor, University of Michigan Press, pp. 190–306.

Fitzpatrick, Tony. *Freedom and Security: An Introduction to the Basic Income Debate* (London, Macmillan, 1999).

Goodin, Robert E. "Exploiting a Person and Exploiting a Situation," in Andrew Reeves. ed. 1987. *Modern Theories of Exploitation*. London: Sage, pp. 166–200.

Halstead, Ted and Michael Lind. 2001. *The Radical Center: The Future of American Politics*. New York: Doubleday.

Haveman, Robert. 1988. *Starting Even: An Equal Opportunity Program to Combat the Nation's New Poverty*. New York: Simon and Schuster.

Lewis, Michael. 2002. "Perhaps There Can be Too Much Freedom," paper prepared for the Real Utopias conference, "Rethinking Redistribution: Designs for a More Egalitarian Capitalism," A. E. Havens Center for the Study of Social Structure and Social Change, University of Wisconsin-Madison, 2–5 May.

Mill, John Stuart. 1985 [1859]. *On Liberty*. Harmondsworth: Penguin.

Nissan, David and Julian Le Grand. 2000. *A Capital Idea: Start-up Grants for Young People*. London: Fabian Society.

Nozick, Robert. 1974. *Anarchy, State, and Utopia*. Oxford: Blackwell.

Paxton, Will. 2001. "Assets: a third pillar of welfare," in Sue Regan, ed., *Assets and Progressive Welfare* (London, Institute for Public Policy Research, pp. 17–33.

Pettit, Philip. 1997. *Republicanism: A Theory of Freedom and Government*. Oxford: Oxford University Press.

Rawls, John. 1999 [1971]. *A Theory of Justice: Revised Edition*. Cambridge, MA: Harvard University Press.

— 2001, *Justice as Fairness: A Restatement* (Cambridge, MA: Harvard University Press.

Roemer, John. 1988. *Free to Lose: An Introduction to Marxist Economic Philosophy*. London: Radius/Century Hutchinson.

Saving and Assets for All. 2001. London: HM Treasury.

Skinner, Quentin. 1998. *Liberty Before Liberalism*. Cambridge: Cambridge University Press.

Spender, Stephen. 1994 [1951]. *World Within World*. New York: St. Martin's Press.

Unger, Roberto Mangabeira and Cornel West. 1998. *The Future of American Progressivism: An Initiative for Political and Economic Reform*. Boston: Beacon Press, 1998.

Van Parijs, Philippe. 1995. *Real Freedom for All: What (if Anything) Can Justify Capitalism?* Oxford: Oxford University Press.

Van Parijs, Philippe, ed. 1992. *Arguing for Basic Income*. London: Verso, 1992.

Waldron, Jeremy. 1993. "Homelessness and the Issue of Freedom," in Waldron, *Liberal Rights*. Cambridge: Cambridge University Press.

White, Stuart. "Freedom, Reciprocity, and the Citizen's Stake," in Keith Dowding, Jurgen De Wispelaere, and Stuart White, eds. 2003. *The Ethics of Stakeholding*. Basingstoke: Palgrave, pp. 79–93.

4

Basic Income, Stakeholder Grants, and Class Analysis

Erik Olin Wright

At the core of the class analysis of capitalist society in both the Marxian and Weberian traditions is a simple idea: Workers are separated from the means of production and, by virtue of that, from their means of subsistence. As a result, they must enter the labor market and seek employment in order to acquire the means of life. This double separation – from the means of production and the means of subsistence – is the material basis for the basic power imbalance between capital and labor in capitalism: Workers must sell their labor power in order to live and thus, ultimately, are forced to accept terms of exchange and working conditions which they would not if they had viable options.[1]

This characterization of the power imbalance in the core class relations of capitalism is generally associated with Marxist class analysis, but the same basic idea is present in Weber as well. Weber writes that for workers in a capitalist economy:

> ... the inclination to work [depends on] the probability that unsatisfactory performance will have an adverse effect on earnings ... [This] presupposes [that] the expropriation of the workers from the means of production by owners is protected by force. (Weber 1922 [1978]: 151) ... willingness to work on the part of factory labor has been primarily determined by a combination of the transfer of responsibility for maintenance to the workers personally and the corresponding powerful indirect compulsion to work, as symbolized in the English workhouse system, and it has permanently remained oriented to the compulsory guarantee of the property system. (Weber 1922 [1978]: 153)

In the Marxist tradition, two of the central indictments of capitalism stem from this class relation: first, workers are *exploited* because
they must work harder and longer for capitalists than is needed simply
to provide for their own standard of living; and second, they are
alienated because they enter into employment relations within which
they are deprived of power over both their laboring activities and the
fruits of that activity. Both of these properties of the class relations of
capitalism are rooted in the core power imbalance that accompanies
private ownership of the means of production in capitalism. These
indictments of capitalism are not, in the first instance, claims about
injustices in capitalism. They are claims about how a particular form
of class relations imposes harms on people. The thesis is that the lives
of most people would be better if the exploitation and alienation generated by private ownership of the means of production were reduced
or eliminated.[2]

The traditional Marxist remedy for this power imbalance was
socialism. Socialism reunited workers with the means of production
– and thus with their means of subsistence – in the form of collective
ownership of the means of production organized through the state.
This, it was thought, would end capitalist exploitation, since workers
would democratically control the surplus generated by production,
and it would end alienation, since workers would control the conditions of production.[3]

Critics of the power imbalances of capitalist class relations are now
much less sanguine about the possibility of comprehensive socialism
as a solution to the harms generated by capitalist relations.[4] While the
historic experience of the Soviet Union is not decisive proof of the
impossibility of comprehensive economic planning, it now seems to
most critics of capitalism that markets cannot be dispensed with, and
thus alternatives to "actually existing capitalism" need to be compatible with well-functioning market institutions.

In this theoretical and normative context, both Stakeholder Grants
and Unconditional Basic Income (UBI) can be thought of as strategies
of potentially transforming class relations within capitalism in ways
that partially counteract the power imbalances of those relations.[5]
Both of these proposals accept the basic economic framework of capitalist society – private ownership of the means of production, robust
markets, investment driven by profit maximization, and so on. Both
of these proposals see the efficiency properties of markets as sufficiently important that any redistributive project must operate within
constraints imposed by well-functioning markets. But both proposals
also believe that quite substantial redistribution is possible within

these constraints. What I will argue is that while both of these proposals, if sufficiently generous, would impact the power imbalances of capitalist class relations, basic income does so in a way which is likely to have more profound consequences for the character of class relations in capitalist society. This is not a claim that with respect to the arguments of liberal-egalitarian theories of justice, basic income better satisfies principles of justice than do stakeholder grants, nor is it a claim that on pragmatic grounds basic income is either more efficient or more politically feasible than stakeholder grants. These are important issues, but I will not address them. What I will try to show is that with respect to the goal of redressing the power imbalance between labor and capital, basic income is likely to have more profound effects than stakeholder grants.

Stakeholder grants give each citizen, upon reaching the age of adulthood, a lump-sum grant of assets that they can use for any purpose they choose. Ackerman and Alstott propose that this stake be $80,000. From the point of view of its impact on class relations, the critical issue is whether the stake is sufficiently large to enable the recipient to realistically begin a small business (perhaps by leveraging additional funds from credit institutions).[6] If the stake makes this possible, then it effectively makes it possible for workers to acquire their own "means of production," thus potentially breaking their dependency on selling their labor power in order to acquire their means of subsistence. Unconditional Basic Income gives each person a monthly stipend sufficiently high to live at what might be considered the no-frills respectable economic level. It thus challenges the power imbalance within class relations of capitalist economies by directly reuniting people with the means of subsistence, rather than with the means of production needed to generate their means of subsistence.

In one sense, of course, basic income and stakeholder grants are convertible one into the other: If a person put the $80,000 stake into a low-risk account of some sort that yielded 6 percent return a year, then in about 20 years it would yield an income of over $1,000/month. Similarly, if a person received a basic income and simply saved it in a low-risk account while continuing to work in the ordinary labor market then eventually it would become a stake. The difference, then, between the two programs is that in a basic income system you are guaranteed a flow of resources, but must take initiative and wait to acquire a stake, whereas in a stakeholder grant system you are guaranteed a stake, but must take initiative and wait to acquire an income.

In the discussion that follows I will bracket the question of the economic feasibility of either a system of stakeholder grant or basic income. In both cases this obviously depends upon the level of generosity of the program. I will assume that the sustainable level of stakeholder grants is sufficiently high to make self-employment a feasible option for virtually everyone and that the monthly stipend of a basic income is sufficiently high to provide for a culturally acceptable, modest standard of living. The question, then, is which of these would, in the long run, have the deepest ramifications for class relations in capitalism.

STAKEHOLDER GRANTS

Being one's own boss is certainly a core aspiration of many workers in the United States. In my 1980 comparative class analysis survey, 58 percent of employees in the United States (66 percent of male employees and 47 percent of female employees) say that they would like to be self-employed someday (Wright: 1997: 116).[7] Stakeholder grants would certainly increase the proportion of employees who would attempt this, and probably the proportion who would succeed as well. So, generous stakeholder grants are likely to have some real impact on capitalist class structures: A higher proportion of the population will be able to "be their own boss" in a capitalism with stakeholder grants than in one without.

Nevertheless, there are three main reasons why one would expect the overall impact of stakeholder grants on the power imbalances of capitalist class relations to be relatively modest. First, a certain proportion of recipients of stakeholder grants will simply use the grants for short-run enhanced consumption. From the point of view of the equal opportunity rationale of stakeholder grants this is perhaps unfortunate, but it is not a fundamental problem. The premise of the stakeholder grant program is that people should have the opportunity to take responsibility for their own futures and that giving people a stake significantly equalizes this opportunity. If some people are imprudent, this does not undermine the "starting-gate equality" objectives of stakeholder grants. Still, it does reduce the impact of stakes on class structure.

Second, a very high proportion of small businesses fail, typically within a year. There is little reason to assume that there will be a higher success rate in businesses started by young adults with stakeholder grants than currently exists among people who start small businesses out of their savings, and perhaps reasons to expect a higher failure rate (because of inexperience). In any case, most people who attempt to create small businesses with their stakes will fail. This does

not mean, of course, that the equal-opportunity rationale of stakeholder grants is vacuous – the opportunity to fail is an inherent
feature of the opportunity to compete in a market economy. But it
does limit the breadth of the impact of stakeholder grants on relations
of class power.

Third, even for those small business which succeed, many will exist
within various kinds of social relations that subordinate them to
capital through credit markets or contractual relations such as fran-
chises, suppliers, subcontractors and so on. This does not imply that
the situation of a self-employed person in a small business embedded
in such relations is no different from that of an ordinary worker: Self-
employment still gives most people some measure of real autonomy.
Still, for many people, being self-employed only modestly equalizes
the power relations to capital within which they gain a living.

BASIC INCOME

A generous, unconditional basic income which would allow employees a meaningful exit option from the employment relation directly
transforms the character of power within the class relations of capitalist society. First, in a capitalism with basic income people are free
to engage in non-commodified forms of socially productive activity,
that is, productive activity which is not oriented towards the market.
There is a wide range of activities which many people want to do but
which are badly organized by either capitalist markets or public
institutions. Prominent among these is care-giving labor – the care
of children, of the elderly, and, in many situations, of the ill. Non-
commodified forms of engagement in the arts, in politics and in
various kinds of community service would also be facilitated by UBI.
Frequently people with serious interests in these kinds of activities
would be willing to do them at relatively modest earnings if they were
provided through markets – witness the very low standards of living
accepted (if reluctantly) by actors, musicians, political activists, and
community organizers. The problem for many people is not so much
the low earnings, but the inability to find employment in these kinds
of activities. Unconditional Basic Income makes it possible for people
to choose to do this kind of activity without having to enter into an
employment relation. In this way it contributes to a shift in the
balance of power within class relations.

Second, for those people who still enter into ordinary capitalist
employment relations, UBI would contribute to a greater symmetry of
power between labor and capital even in the absence of collective

organization on the part of workers. This would be particularly salient for workers in low-skilled, low wage jobs. Often workers in such jobs suffer both from low wages and from miserable working conditions. The realistic exit options of low wage workers under a UBI system would increase their bargaining power with employers. Of course, this might mean that many such low-skill jobs would disappear, but since many low-skilled people will still want discretionary income above the no-frills UBI level, there will still be potential workers willing to take such jobs. The difference is that the balance of power within which the attributes of such jobs are determined would be shifted towards workers.

Third, an Unconditional Basic Income could also contribute in various ways to increasing the collective strength of workers, not just their individual leverage within employment relations. One of the factors which defines the context for the formation of working-class collective organization is the extent to which unions help employers solve various kinds of problems. As has been noted in discussions of union density, there seem to be two equilibria in these terms: capitalism appears to operate best under either high union density or low union density (Calmfors and Driffill, 1988; Wright, 2000). One of the contexts in which high union density is advantageous for employers is when there are chronically tight labor markets. In such situations, employers face the problem of escalating wages as firms bid up wages to poach employed workers from other firms. From the point of view of individual workers such wage escalation might seem like a good thing in the short run, but if this bidding process means that wages rise more rapidly than productivity, then in the longer run this is unsustainable and leads to a general destabilization of capitalist labor markets. In these contexts, then, a strong labor movement can enforce wage-restraint on employers and workers in exchange for greater economic security and a more stable economic setting for productivity-enhancing technical change.

Unconditional Basic Income generates some of the same pressures as tight labor markets and thus may lead employers to be more receptive to the high union density equilibrium. Where workers individually have easier exit options, employers may have greater incentives to agree to new forms of collective cooperation with organizations of workers. Such collective cooperation is an element in what is sometimes called "high road" capitalism, a model of capitalism in which labor and capital engage in much closer collaboration over the design and regulation of work, production and innovation than is characteristic of conventional capitalist organization in which employers have more or less unilateral control over basic production decisions. Such closer collaboration, if it is stably institutionalized, constitutes a relative equalization of power within capitalist class relations. Insofar as UBI makes such a high cooperation equilibrium more feasible, therefore, it contributes to a shift in the balance of class power towards workers.

CONCLUSION

Taking these considerations together, if it is economically sustainable, Unconditional Basic Income seems likely to underwrite a set of social and institutional changes which more profoundly reshape the power relations of capitalism than will a program of stakeholder grants. The argument for basic income, in these terms, is more like a public goods argument than a simple individual social justice argument, since changes in power relations affect the overall dynamics and conditions everyone experiences in a society – not simply those immediately party to the power relation. Let me explain.

The ideal of "Equality of opportunity," as it is conceived in much liberal egalitarian discussion of justice, involves trying to distinguish between those conditions of life for which people can reasonably be held responsible and those for which they cannot. Social justice requires trying to minimize those inequalities outside of individual control, and redistribution is one way of accomplishing this. Both UBI and stakeholder grants can be defended as significant steps in the direction of remedying unjust failures of such equality of opportunity. On these grounds, in fact, some people might prefer a generous stakeholder grant system to UBI insofar as it might be thought as better embodying the responsibility ideal of equal opportunity. In some ways UBI looks like a paternalistic program, in which, to avoid the risk of individuals squandering redistributed resources, the state doles out a stipend to people rather than giving them a single, large lump-sum payment. In a UBI program people can still squander their BI, but they can only do so one month at a time. If avoiding paternalism is a high priority within a conception of equality of opportunity, and if equality of opportunity is the central justification for redistribution, then stakeholder grants might be preferred over UBI.

The defense of UBI offered here is not, however, primarily about social justice as such. It is about creating the conditions under which a stable move towards more equal power within class relations can be achieved. The issue of equality of power has strong public goods features. Consider another context in which we worry about equality of power: The right to vote. We don't allow people to sell their right to vote to anyone, even though many people would want to do so if given the opportunity and there would surely be a market for such sales if they were permitted. It could be argued that this too is paternalism: The state prevents people from engaging in a voluntary transaction in order to prevent them from doing things which, in the long run, would cause harm. The justification for this prohibition is not simply that it would ultimately be harmful to the particular persons who sell their right to vote, in the same sense that taking an addictive drug might be harmful. Rather the argument is that selling votes would undermine democracy and be harmful even to those who did not sell their votes: It would be harmful because of the concentrations of power that a free market in votes would create, and this ultimately undermines the ideal of political equality of citizens. Legal prohibitions on the selling of votes therefore is defended above all because of a judgment about the *collective* consequences of alternative distributions of power within our political institutions.

Power within class relations have some of these same public goods qualities. And in these terms, a relatively generous universal basic income – if it were sustainable – is likely to contribute to an equalization of such class power more than a generous lump-sum grant to young adults. The monthly flow of income that is an essential part of UBI, therefore, is not simply a form of paternalism designed to prevent individuals from squandering their resources, but a way of insuring the stability of the social process by which power relations are shifted.

NOTES

1   The claim that this relation is properly described as embodying a "power imbalance" may be contentious to some economists, since many economists see the labor exchange as a purely voluntary contract within which power is absent. Capitalists do not really have power over workers, the arguments go, because workers are always free to quit if they do not like what they are told to do. The counter-argument is that the capitalist ownership of the means of production is backed by force in the form of state-enforced property rights, and this gives them effective power over workers given the basic scarcity of capital and the necessity for workers to seek employment from some employer. For contemporary discussions of the power dimension of the relation between labor and capital that are addressed to the skepticism of neoclassical economists, see Bowles and Gintis (1990) and Bartlett (1989).

2   It may also be the case, of course, that issues of justice and fairness are closely linked to these indictments of capitalist class relations. The language

of "exploitation" certainly has a connotation of injustice even if, on closer inspection, it is not a simple matter to link a class analytic concept of exploitation to philosophically rigorous understandings of justice.

3 Socialism was also seen as a remedy for a third traditional Marxist indictment of capitalism: The "anarchy of the market" in capitalism generates various forms of waste, inefficiency and negative externalities. Socialism, as a system of democratic economic planning, was thought to be a solution to these macro-economic problems as well as the micro-economic issues of exploitation and alienation in the lives of workers.

4 By "comprehensive socialism" I mean an economy within which private ownership of the means of production has been largely abolished and markets have been replaced with democratic planning as the basis for economic regulation and coordination. One can, of course, be a skeptic of comprehensive socialism and remain a socialist critic of capitalism. The problem then becomes thinking through the ways in which socialist elements can be infused into capitalist relations in ways which neutralize the power imbalances of capitalism. Whether the limits on such a process mean that the amalgam in an optimal institutional equilibrium would be more socialistic or capitalistic is not something, I believe, which can be known in advance of institutional experiments.

5 In one of the earliest systematic defenses of basic income, Philippe Van Parijs and Robert van der Veen (1985) characterized unconditional basic income as "A Capitalist Road to Communism" which would by-pass socialism as a way of neutralizing the undesirable consequences of capitalist class relations for individual autonomy and freedom.

6 In Ackerman and Alstott's proposal, the central rationale for stakeholder grants is to remedy as much as possible a problem of inequality of opportunity generated by the fact that some young adults receive substantial inter-generational transfers of wealth and others – the large majority – do not. While using the assets from a stakeholder grant to underwrite self-employment is one of the uses to which the grants can be put, people are free to use the opportunity afforded by the grant in any way they see fit.

7 The proportions of male and female *workers* – rather than all employees – who would like to be self-employed in the United States are virtually the same as for all employees: 66 percent of male workers and 46 percent of female workers in the US report that they would like to be self-employed. The proportions of employees in other countries who want to be self-employed are generally much lower than in the US: 49 percent in Canada, 40 percent in Sweden, 31 percent in Japan, and 20 percent in Norway.

REFERENCES

Bartlett, Randall. 1989. *Economics and Power*. Cambridge: Cambridge University Press.

Bowles, Samuel and Herbert Gintis. 1990. "Contested Exchange: new micro-foundations for the Political Economy of Capitalism," *Politics & Society*, 18:2: 165–222.

Calmfors, L. and J. Driffill. 1988. "Bargaining Structure, Corporatism and Macro-economic Performance," *Economic Policy*, 6: April, 13–61.

Weber, Max. 1922 [1978]. *Economy and Society*, edited by Gunther Roth. University of California Press.

Wright, Erik Olin. 1997. *Class Counts: Comparative Studies in Class Analysis*. Cambridge: Cambridge University Press.

— 2000. "Working-Class Power, Capitalist-Class Interests and Class Compromise," *American Journal of Sociology*, Volume 105, Number 4, January, 957–1002.

5

Democratizing Citizenship:
Some advantages of a basic income
Carole Pateman

The chapters by Philippe Van Parijs on basic income and Bruce Ackerman and Anne Alstott on a stake (or capital grant) contain very valuable insights into both these ideas. They also provide arguments about feasibility and the best way to present stakeholding or a basic income to gain public support. I am going to focus on the reasons for advocating a basic income and how a theoretical argument for it should be framed. By a "basic income" I am referring to the payment of a regular sum by a government to each individual (citizen) over an adult life-time, with no conditions attached. A "stake" means a one-time unconditional capital grant from a government to all individuals (citizens) at, say, age 21.[1]

My view is that in the current political climate in the United States and Britain a stake is likely to prove more acceptable to public opinion than a basic income. Indeed, the Blair government in Britain has introduced the Child Trust Fund. The government is providing £250 for a capital account for each child born after 1 September 2002, to be invested until the child is 18 (parents can add a limited sum yearly). A basic income stands more chance of being introduced in Europe where, as Van Parijs illustrates in his chapter, income support policies have already moved in a direction where a basic income, albeit probably of a partial character, could be seen as a logical "next step."

Stakeholding, I agree, would be an advance over current arrangements in the United States and in Britain. But which is to be preferred: a capital grant or a basic income?

The answer to that question depends upon the reasons why each of these ideas is being advocated. All ideas and policies are invariably put forward for a variety of different reasons and involve different hopes about what might be achieved. The reasons that eventually become most prominent in public debate then help shape practical outcomes. All human activities have unintended and unforeseen consequences, so we cannot be certain of the results of introducing either a basic income or stakeholding, not least since a great deal hinges on the level of the income or capital grant. But because the direction of change depends, among other things, on the reasons why the change is advocated and what it is expected to achieve, the manner in which the theoretical case is made for a basic income or a stake is crucial.

I became interested in the idea of a basic income some years ago for two main reasons. First, because of the part that basic income could play in furthering democratization, i.e. the creation of a more democratic society in which individual freedom and citizenship are of equal worth for everyone. The second, and closely related, reason is because of its potential in advancing women's freedom. My argument is that in light of these reasons, a basic income is preferable to a stake. A basic income is a crucial part of any strategy for democratic social change because, unlike a capital grant, it could help break the long-standing link between income and employment, and end the mutual reinforcement of the institutions of marriage, employment and citizenship. In the early twentieth century, Bertram Pickard declared that a state bonus (a forerunner of a basic income) "must be deemed the monetary equivalent of the right to land, of the right to life and liberty" (1919: 21). My conception of the democratic significance of a basic income is in the spirit of Pickard's statement.

I will begin with some general arguments about why, if democratization is the goal, a basic income should be preferred to stakeholding, and then discuss the institution of employment and some questions about free-riding and the household.

A BASIC INCOME AND SELF-GOVERNMENT

My argument for a basic income shares the view of Van Parijs and Ackerman and Alstott that both a basic income and a stake expand individual freedom. However, our reasons for holding this view and our conceptions of individual freedom are very different. Basic income in Van Parijs' *Real Freedom for All* and stakeholding in Ackerman and Alstott's *The Stakeholder Society* are justified in terms of freedom as individual opportunity. Despite the many other differences between the form and content of their arguments, they agree about the conception of freedom to be promoted. I am concerned with another conception of freedom; individual freedom as self-government or autonomy, which I see as a political form and as central to democracy. In *Real Freedom for All* Van Parijs explicitly rejects any necessary connection between individual freedom and democracy; if there is a connection it is merely contingent (1995: 8–19, 15–17).[2]

Individual freedom as autonomy or self-government has been neglected in the academic debates about stakeholding, but it is central to democracy. Modern (universal) democracy rests on the premise that individuals are born, or are naturally, free and are equal to each other. That is to say, they are self-governing or autonomous. If their self-government is to be maintained they must become citizens with rights and interact within institutions that further autonomy. In this conception, freedom includes not only individual economic (private) opportunities, and the opportunity to participate in collective self-government, but also individual autonomy. The latter tends to be overlooked, in part because "democracy" has become identified with collective (national) self-government, especially through "free and fair elections." Other forms of government that deny or limit individuals' freedom fall out of the picture, such as government in marriage or the workplace. In so far as self-government in these areas has received attention in political theory it has been directed to the workplace rather than to marriage, despite three centuries of feminist analysis that has highlighted the denial or limitation of wives' self-government and the political significance of the institution of marriage.

Individual self-government depends not only on the opportunities available but also on the form of authority structure within which individuals interact with one another in their daily lives. Self-government requires that individuals not only go about their lives within democratic authority structures that enhance their autonomy, but also that they have the standing, and are able (have the opportunities and means) to enjoy and safeguard their freedom. A basic income – set at the appropriate level – is preferable to a stake because it helps create the circumstances for democracy and individual self-government.

Little attention has been paid in recent academic debates to the democratic significance of a stake or a basic income. Participants have tended to focus on such questions as social justice, relief of poverty, equality of opportunity or promotion of flexible labor markets rather than democracy. I do not want to downplay the importance of these questions, or suggest that they are irrelevant to democracy, but they involve different concerns and arguments than explicit attention to democratization. Academic discussion today is too often conducted in a series of separate compartments, each with its own frame of reference. In political theory, for instance, discussion of social justice has usually been undertaken by one set of theorists and democratic theory by others, with the two discussions seldom intersecting. The terms of the debate about stakeholding have tended to be confined within the framework provided by republicanism, libertarianism, utilitarianism, and liberalism. And, rather oddly in ostensibly "political" theory (though in keeping with the times), political argument is being displaced by neo-classical economic concepts and theories.

The narrowness of the debate is exacerbated by the striking absence of the arguments and insights provided by feminist scholars. Some feminists are opposed to a basic income, but their arguments are absent too. Many years of scholarship about marriage, employment and citizenship are virtually ignored in debates about basic income and stakeholding, and women's freedom (self-government) and its implications for a democratic social transformation has hardly been mentioned.

Now that the nostrums of neo-classical economics enshrined in national and international policy-making have begun to look a little tattered, the way is being opened for some new ideas. The idea of a basic income is not, strictly speaking, new; advocates usually trace it back to Tom Paine, and I have mentioned one of its earlier incarnations as a state bonus. But it is now being more widely discussed, and current circumstances (as I shall show below) offer a much more favorable environment than in years past. A basic income offers not just an alternative to highly bureaucratized public provision, and to the eligibility doctrines that have been resurrected in recent years, but an opportunity to move out of the very well-worn ruts of current discussions of welfare policy. As Brian Barry has stated, "basic income is not just another idea for rejigging the existing system." Rather, it has the potential to lead to "a different way of relating individual and society" (1997: 161). Or, at least, it has that potential if it is argued for in terms of democratization and women's freedom.

A DEMOCRATIC RIGHT

One reason for the democratic potential of a basic income is that it would provide an important opportunity, namely, *the freedom not to be employed*. Participants in the debates about a basic income tend to skirt round this distinctive implication, but, as I shall argue, it is central to its democratizing possibilities – provided that the income is set at an appropriate level. Neither the idea of a basic income not that of a capital grant say anything about the level at which they should be set. The level proposed will depend on the reasons for supporting such proposals. My assumption is that, for a basic income to be relevant for democratization, it should be adequate to provide what I call a modest but decent standard of life. This is a level sufficient to allow individuals to have some control over the course of their lives, and to participate to the extent that they wish in the cultural, economic, social and political life of their polity.

It might be objected that the level of basic income has more to do with practical feasibility than why the proposal should be supported. The objection always raised to basic income or stakeholding is that both schemes would cost far too much, but political imagination is required here.[3] Besides, before turning to problems of implementation and cost we need to know *why* a basic income or stakeholding scheme should be introduced at all, and what level of income or grant is entailed, given those reasons.

If interest in a basic income is, say, as a means to relieve poverty – a goal that I certainly share – then the level of income will differ from the level required when a basic income is advocated as part of a wider strategy for democratization. Van Parijs (above, page 23) remarks that the fight for a basic income "is no game for purists." But if we are going to be "tinkerers and opportunists"in attempts to get a basic income squarely on the political agenda, we need to be clear about what we are being opportunistic about, including wider goals and the level of the income. What is it that we shall be sacrificing if, as no doubt will be the case, compromises are necessary in practice? Perhaps my notion of a level of basic income sufficient for a modest but decent standard of life makes me a "purist," but this is necessary to appreciate the differences between arguing for basic income as an element in a democratic social transformation, or advocating it as a means of improving existing systems of income support. The latter is no doubt more politically feasible, but a great deal of democratic value in the idea of a basic income is lost if immediate political feasibility dominates the academic discussion.

The idea of a basic income has much less political and theoretical interest if the payment is assumed to be below subsistence level and seen merely as a way to alleviate poverty. Thus I would take issue with Van Parijs (15) when he states that "the central case" for a basic income is as a "specific way of handling the joint challenge of poverty and unemployment." To be sure, a basic income is a way of handling this challenge, but this is not, I would argue, the central reason to be interested in the idea. On the face of it, Ackerman and Alstott's case for stakeholding seems much closer to my own argument. They focus not on poverty or unemployment but on citizenship: "Stakeholding is not a poverty program. It is a citizenship program" (1999: 197). A capital grant, they write, creates a "proud culture of free citizenship" (14). But the citizenship in question is economic citizenship; a stake is an "economic birthright."[4] In *The Stakeholder Society*, they state that "just as one person-one vote expresses political citizenship, an equal stake expresses economic citizenship" (1999: 33). The comparison between a basic income and universal suffrage is instructive, but I part company with Ackerman and Alstott in their bifurcation of citizenship.

When I first began to think about basic income I was alerted to the comparison between the suffrage and a basic income by a little-noticed passage in T. H. Marshall's famous *Citizenship and Social Class*: "To have to bargain for a living wage in a society which accepts the living wage as a social right is as absurd as to have to haggle for a vote in a society which accepts the vote as a political right" (1963: 116). There are, however, two problems with Marshall's argument that are pertinent here. First, as is well known, he separated citizenship into three different components, civil, political and social rights. But whether the division is into three parts, or follows Ackerman and Alstott's two-part economic and political citizenship, the result is the same; attention gets diverted into endless wrangles about which category is primary and which can properly be seen as "rights" (do social rights count?). Second, Marshall linked standard of life to employment, by which he meant male employment, a matter I shall discuss shortly.

Van Parijs also refers to universal suffrage. In making his comment about purism and tinkering, he compares the fight for a basic income to the fight for universal suffrage and neither, he states, is an "all-or-nothing affair." This is a curious comment. Countries with restricted suffrage – even restricted to the male half of the population – are often called "democracies," but that reveals less about the suffrage than about a more general wariness of the full implications of democratization. The suffrage is either universal, i.e. encompassing all adults, or it is not. Partial enfranchisement means that there are qualifying conditions that only some of the adult population can meet (typically, owning property, being male, having a white skin, or belonging to a certain ethnic group). Where such eligibility conditions exist a vote is a privilege, not a right. Universal suffrage is democratic precisely because the vote ceases to be the privilege of a part of the population and becomes a right of all adults. To be universal, the qualifying criteria for suffrage have to be reduced to a bare minimum that everyone can meet with time, such as an age requirement and length of residence for naturalization, or that all can meet barring accidents of nature, such as being of sound mind.

My argument is that a basic income should be seen, like the suffrage, as a democratic right or a political birthright. By a "democratic" right I have in mind a fundamental right in Henry Shue's sense of a "basic right." Basic rights "specify the line beneath which no one is to be allowed to sink." Rights are basic "if enjoyment of them is essential to the enjoyment of all other rights" (1996: 18, 19). Subsistence is one of Shue's basic rights, which he defines as "what is needed for a decent chance at a reasonably healthy and active life of more or less normal length, barring tragic interventions" (1996: 23). Building on this line of argument, a basic income, at a level sufficient for a modest but decent standard of life, can be seen as a fundamental or democratic right. Such an income is necessary to enable all citizens to participate as fully as they wish in all aspects of the life of their society.

A basic income as a fundamental right can more reasonably be compared to the suffrage than can a stake. Citizenship and the suffrage are for life, and a basic income is a right that also exists over a citizen's life-time, whereas a capital grant is a one-off payment at the beginning of adulthood. A stake provides young people with a valuable start, but what of the rest of their life as citizens? A basic income provides the life-long security that helps safeguard other rights. Universal suffrage is the emblem of equal citizenship, and underpins an orderly change of government through free and fair elections, so enhancing citizens' security. A basic income is the emblem of full citizenship, and provides the security required to maintain that political standing. Another way of making this point is that a basic income as a democratic right is necessary for individual freedom as self-government, which is a political freedom.

One of the major disagreements between Ackerman and Alstott and Van Parijs in their essays is over the latter's prohibition on the capitalization of (future) basic income into a single payment. Van Parijs minimizes the difference between basic income and a capital grant, and remarks that the difference between the two "would be essentially annulled if the recipients could freely borrow against their future basic income stream" (1). I shall leave aside the issue of whether the future income stream can be used as collateral for, e.g., a mortgage on a house, and concentrate on prohibition against conversion of a basic income into a single lump-sum. The question is whether this constitutes a significant limitation on individual freedom.

Ackerman and Alstott argue that it does: a basic income stands in
the way of individual freedom. Young people are hindered in achieving their goals if they cannot choose to capitalize their basic income
as a capital grant. Ackerman and Alstott, therefore, see a basic
income as "a fancy name for a restraint on alienation" (8). The
restriction on conversion, they argue, makes basic income into the
equivalent of a "spendthrift trust," the beneficiary of which has to
apply to a trustee, who administers the trust according to a set of conditions, in order to be able to use the money. They see basic income
as a "universal spendthift trust" (9). To treat adults as potential
spendthrifts "demeans their standing as autonomous citizens" (9). In
contrast a stake would "promote the real freedom of young adults on
the threshold of life" (20)

It might; but the most obvious problem is that a lump-sum capital
grant could very easily and quickly be squandered or lost. Many
responsible individuals could lose their capital even if they avoided
Las Vegas or drugs. Small businesses have a high failure rate despite
the best efforts of their owners, and stock markets crash. Of course,
Ackerman and Alstott are aware of the problem of stakeblowing and
they supplement the individual stake with an old-age pension that is
provided, unconditionally, as right of citizenship. But stakeholding
plus a retirement pension is insufficient for democratic citizenship.
Too long a period of citizens' lives is open to the vagaries of chance
and the market.

For individuals to be able to decide in which form to receive their
income means that entrepreneurial activities would no doubt be
encouraged as well as trips to Las Vegas. Ackerman and Alstott see
the risk of individuals losing their lump sum as part of individual
freedom. As they write in *The Stakeholder Society*, they are "interested in opportunities, not outcomes," and they present a basic
income as a cushion for failure, whereas a stake "is a launching pad
for success" (1999: 24, 215). But the launch might well end in a crash.
Equality of opportunity is a democratic principle, but the freedom
involved in young people being able to convert a basic income to a
capital stake hardly looms large from the perspective of democratization and individual freedom as self-government.

Ackerman and Alstott also criticize a basic income on the grounds
that it "encourages a short-term consumerist perspective" (10). The
only sense in which, as far as I can see, a basic income might do this
is if it were introduced at a level below that required for a modest but

decent standard of life. A payment below subsistence level might be seen, at least by those well above the poverty level, as merely an extra bit of discretionary income available for immediate spending. But even this would be mitigated if the tax system came into play for those at higher income levels. There seems no good reason why a basic income implemented at the level I am suggesting would encourage consumerism. Indeed, one could make the opposite case; by breaking the link between income and the labor market it would allow individuals, if they so wished, to abstain from the race to accumulate ever more material goods and help combat the identification of freedom with consumerism.

EMPLOYMENT

A basic income would have two important consequences for democratization. First, it would allow individuals more easily to refuse to enter or to leave relationships that violate individual self-government, or that involve unsafe, unhealthy or demeaning conditions. It would, as Van Parijs states, endow "the weakest with bargaining power" (10), but the bargaining power is a by-product of the full standing as citizens that a basic income helps create. Basic income is not (as Marshall saw) about bargaining but self-government, rights and democratic citizenship. A basic income would also support citizens' participation in collective self-government by opening up opportunities for citizens to develop their political capacities and skills. A guaranteed standard of life would mean that participation in social and political life would not require heroic efforts on the part of any citizens.

The second consequence, and a crucial difference between basic income and stakeholding, is that a basic income would give citizens the freedom not to be employed. Both a basic income, if set at the appropriate level, and a capital grant would provide enlarged opportunities for individuals, but the opportunities provided by a basic income would be far wider than those offered by a stake, since the new opportunities would not be confined to the competitive market. A basic income, like a stake, would make it possible for anyone (at any point in their life, not merely while they are young) to go back to school, to retrain for a new occupation, or to open a business. But a basic income providing a modest but decent standard of living would do much more.

In the *Constitution of Liberty*, Friedrich von Hayek – like G.D.H. Cole from a very different point on the political spectrum – argued that employment fostered an outlook among employees that was an impediment to freedom. The employed, he wrote, are "in many respects alien and often inimical to much that constitutes the driving force of a free society" (1960: 119). His solution was that there should be as many gentlemen of private means as possible to counteract the deleterious effects of employment. Such gentlemen have large basic incomes, albeit not provided by a government. At a very much lower level of resources, a basic income democratizes the freedom open to a gentleman of private means to spend time in scholarly pursuits, good works, writing poetry, cultivating friendships, hunting, or being a drone or a wastrel. A basic income would allow individuals at any time to do voluntary or political work, for example, to learn to surf, to write or paint, to devote themselves to family life, or enjoy a quiet period of self-reassessment or contemplation.

By opening up this range of opportunities and uncoupling income and standard of life from employment, a basic income has the potential both to encourage critical reassessment of the mutually reinforcing structures of marriage, employment and citizenship, and to open the possibility that these institutions could be re-made in a new, more democratic form. A capital grant given to young people with the aim of assisting individual economic success lacks the same potential. In *The Stakeholder Society*, Ackerman and Alstott argue that a stake encourages individuals, in a way that a basic income cannot, to reflect upon what they want to do with their lives and appraise their situation. "Civic reflection" and attention to "the fate of the nation" become possible when economic anxieties are lifted (1999: 185). A "purer form of patriotism" will arise out of the "simple gratitude to the nation" that citizens will feel as they think about their capital grant and the debt that they owe to their country for the economic citizenship that comes with stakeholding (1999: 186; see also 43–44).

Patriotism and gratitude, however, have only a tenuous connection to individual freedom. Provision of a one-time capital grant will no doubt encourage individuals to consider what courses of action are open to them, and might even foster reflection on the debt they owe to their country. But it seems implausible that it would help promote reflection on the political implications of the structural connections between marriage, employment and citizenship. Both the wide variety of opportunities made possible when employment becomes truly voluntary, and the fact that women's freedom would be greatly enhanced, mean that, unlike a stake, a basic income has the potential to open the door to institutional change – providing that democratization is at the forefront of discussion and that feminist arguments are taken seriously.

The freedom not to be employed runs counter to the direction of much recent public policy and political rhetoric (especially in Anglo-American countries, though the policies are international), and this makes stakeholding more palatable than basic income in the current political climate. The effect of such policies and rhetoric is to draw even tighter the long-standing link between employment and citizenship, at the very time when a reassessment has been made possible by changing circumstances. The institution of employment is a barrier to democratic freedom and citizenship in two ways. First, economic enterprises have an undemocratic structure, a point that I shall not pursue here.[5] Second, as feminist scholars have demonstrated, the relationship between the institutions of marriage, employment and citizenship has meant that the standing of wives as citizens has always been, and remains, problematic.

The Anglo-American social insurance system was constructed on the assumption that wives were not only their husbands' economic dependents but lesser citizens whose entitlement to benefits depended on their private status, not on their citizenship. Male "breadwinners," who made a contribution from their earnings to "insure" that they received benefits in the event of unemployment or sickness, and in their old age, were the primary citizens. Their employment was treated as *the* contribution that a citizen could make to the well-being of the community. Ackerman and Alstott acknowledge this in their criticism of "workplace justice" (6–7), and their recognition that unconditional retirement pensions would be particularly important for the many older women whose benefits still largely derive from their husbands' employment record (1999: 145–46). That is to say, only paid employment has been seen as "work," as involving the tasks that are the mark of a productive citizen and contributor to the polity. Other contributions, notably all the work required to reproduce and maintain a healthy population, and look after infants, the elderly, the sick and infirm – the caring tasks, most of which are not paid for and are undertaken by women – have been seen as irrelevant to citizenship.

FREE-RIDING AND THE HOUSEHOLD

The debates about basic income also center on the figure of a man in – or avoiding – paid employment. This is very clear in one of the major criticisms of, and apprehensions about, the idea of a basic income; that is, that it would encourage free-riding and idleness. Free-riders breach the principle of reciprocity by obtaining the fruits of the efforts of others and contributing nothing themselves in return; a basic income, it is charged, would "inspire a segment of the able population ... to abjure work for a life of idle fun"(Anderson, 2000: 16). But who is being seen as so prone to idleness and fun? The assumption guiding the discussion of basic income is that the problem is about men and employment.[6] A much greater problem about male free-riding to which a basic income is directly relevant, but about the household not employment, is therefore ignored.

Van Parijs appears to be an exception to the prevailing view of free-riding. Unlike most other participants in discussions of basic income he has noticed that free-riding exists "on a massive scale" in household interactions (1995: 143). But who are the free-riders in the household? Barry notes that full-time housewives can be seen as free-riders (1996: 245). But they can only be seen in that way if "work" is taken to mean paid employment.[7] As feminist scholars have emphasized for a very long time, housewives are working (unpaid) by undertaking the necessary caring work. Given the major contribution they already make for no monetary return at all, wives (women) are hardly likely to be the target of the objection that a basic income would lead to idleness and fun.

The majority of wives are now in some form of paid employment, but their labor force participation is usually different from that of men. This reflects the legacy of a wage system that enshrined the belief that husbands (men) not wives (women) are the "breadwinners."[8] Many more women than men work part-time and women earn less than men. The private and public sexual division of labor, that is to say, continues to be structured so that men monopolize full-time, higher paying and more prestigious paid employment, and wives do a disproportionate share of unpaid work in the home. Given the structure of institutions and social beliefs, this appears as a "rational" arrangement. The mutual reinforcement of marriage and employment explains why husbands can take advantage of the unpaid work of wives and avoid doing their fair share of the caring work. That is why there is massive free-riding in the household – by husbands.

Neither free-riding by husbands, nor its scale, is usually acknowledged in discussions of basic income and stakeholding. This is because marriage and the household rarely enter the argument. The narrow parameters of discussion, and the influence of the assumptions of neoclassical economics, preclude attention to institutional structures and their interrelationships. Van Parijs is an exception in recognizing that

a problem of free-riding exists in households, but his neo-classical theoretical apparatus leaves him unable to acknowledge that the problem
is one of men (husbands) and the work of caring for household
members. His argument is that free-riding arises merely because of differences in individual tastes or preferences. Free-riding, Van Parijs
states, occurs when benefits enjoyed by both partners in a household
are produced by only one of them, the partner who happens to care
most about the particular benefit. His example is that the partner who
most strongly values tidiness will make sure that the home is tidy.

"Tidiness" is part of the more general work of housekeeping, and
there is abundant empirical evidence that shows that the female
partner is most likely to do the housework, including tidying up. The
empirical data do not show this pattern just by chance – female
partners do not by some quirk happen to prefer tidiness more strongly
than their male partners. The institution of marriage, and social
beliefs about what it means to be a "wife" or "husband," have
vanished in Van Parijs's analysis and there are merely two individuals,
indistinguishable except for their different tastes for tidy surround-
ings. His theoretical approach in *Real Freedom for All* precludes
analysis of the structure of relations between the sexes, and a crucial
area of debate is, therefore, removed from discussion of basic income.

Indeed, some advocates of a basic income argue that it would make
it easier for women to do "their" work in the home. Van Parijs
remarks (2000: 7) that some women would probably use their basic
income to "lighten the 'double shift' at certain periods of their lives."
But, he continues, "who can sincerely believe that working subject to
the dictates of a boss for forty hours a week is a path to liberation?"
One can have grave doubts on the latter score – but also ask, first,
whether working for a husband at home is the right path either, and,
second, ask why *men* might not use their basic income to take on their
fair share of the caring work.

Now is the time to ask the second question. The conditions under
which the institution of employment and the Anglo-American social
insurance system was constructed have now crumbled. "Old
economy" male breadwinner jobs are being swept away in global
economic restructuring and "downsizing." New jobs have been
created but many are low paid, lacking benefits and temporary, and
economic insecurity is widespread. Views about femininity, masculin-
ity and marriage are changing too, but since we are still in the midst
of all these changes it is hard to know what the eventual outcome will
be. Still, times of rapid change provide opportunities to investigate
new ideas and look critically at old arrangements – including the

moral hazard of institutions that give incentives to men to avoid their fair share of the unpaid work of caring for others. It has now become possible to rethink the connections between income and paid employment, between marriage, employment and citizenship, between the private and public division of labor, between caring work and other work, and reconsider the meaning of "work." But such rethinking requires a different approach from that taken by many participants in the debate about stakeholding and basic income. This is crucial if proper account is to be taken of women's freedom, which has received rather short shrift in discussions of a basic income.

As early as 1792, Mary Wollstonecraft argued in *A Vindication of the Rights of Woman* that rights, citizenship and full standing for women required economic independence, whether a woman was married or single. As Ackerman and Alstott emphasize, a capital grant would be a step in this direction, but a basic income would for the first time provide all women with life-long economic independence. Thus feminists might be expected strongly to support the introduction of a basic income.[9]

Yet this is not the case. Some feminists are critical of the idea because they fear a basic income would reinforce the existing sexual division of labor and women's lesser citizenship. They argue that the provision of an income without having to engage in paid employment would, in light of women's position in the labor market combined with lingering beliefs about the respective places and tasks of women and men, give women an even greater incentive to undertake more unpaid caring work in the household, and, conversely, men would have another incentive to free-ride. A basic income, that is, would reinforce existing limitations on women's freedom.[10]

This objection illustrates the importance of the reasons advanced for supporting a basic income. The probability of feminist fears being borne out is higher, for example, when the argument is made that to avoid weakening the "incentive to work" a basic income should be below subsistence level. This "incentive" is promoted with men and paid employment in mind. A basic income at this level provides no incentive for wives to "work" (i.e. enter paid employment); rather it would encourage them to do more unpaid caring work. Again, to support basic income on the grounds that it would improve the living standards of the poorest sectors of the population does not promote consideration of the structural connections between marriage, employment and citizenship, and the private and public sexual division of labor. Without the debates about basic income being informed by feminist arguments and a concern for democratization (and genuine democratization necessarily includes women's freedom and standing as citizens), the discussion will revolve around ways of tinkering with the existing system, rather than encouraging thinking about how it might be made more democratic.

Putting democratization at the center requires attention to institutional structures, especially the institutions of marriage and employment. For instance, Ackerman and Alstott remark in *The Stakeholder Society* that the "case for stakeholding does not ultimately rest on its effects on employment, marriage, or crime. It rests on each American's claim to respect as a free and equal citizen" (1999: 209). However (leaving crime aside), the respect accorded to women and men as free and equal citizens has a great deal to do the institutions of marriage and employment. It is not possible to understand women's lesser citizenship, as Ackerman and Alstott show in their discussion of social security, without understanding the relationship between their position as wives and men's position as workers.

Similarly, Van Parijs argues that while "a defensible long term vision" of an unconditional basic income at the highest sustainable level is vital, nevertheless more limited and politically feasible proposals are also essential. He states that a household-based guaranteed minimum income "would definitely be a major change in the right direction" (16–17) – but the right direction according to which reasons? Household-based schemes disregard not only all the problems about the sexual division of labor, and the fact that women earn less than men, but also income distribution *within* households. Can it be confidently assumed that income would be distributed equally between husband and wife? A basic income is important for feminism and democratization precisely because it is paid not to households but to *individuals as citizens*.

A focus on individuals does not imply resort to the atomistic individualism of neo-classical economics. The problem of women's self-government and full standing as citizens is visible only when individuals are conceptualized within the context of social relations and institutions. A household-based basic income allows the problem of marriage, employment and citizenship to be avoided since wives (women) disappear into the category of the "family" or "household." To treat a basic income as a payment to households, rather than individuals, ignores the question of who performs the work of caring for household members. That is, it is tacitly assumed that reciprocity exists and that free-riding is only a problem about men avoiding employment.

This assumption is nicely illustrated by the picture of a male surfer on the cover of *Real Freedom for All*. In academic discussions, the surfer is used to represent non-contributors. But in the popular political imagination and the media other symbols of free-riding are present, such as the African-American "welfare queen," or, more recently, the "illegal immigrant" or the "asylum seeker."[11] The figure of the surfer not only obscures the problem for democratization of popular attitudes embodied in these other symbols, but also obliterates the systematic avoidance of one form of contribution – the vital caring work – by men who are *in employment*.

Nor do the numerous suggestions for conditions to be placed on payment of a basic income as a solution to free-riding – Atkinson's (1996) "participation income" is a well-known example[12] – get to grips with free-riding by men in the household. While the notion of a "contribution" may be broadened to include, e.g., the work of caring for others, as in Atkinson's proposal, this is insufficient to focus attention on the structural problem of the connections between marriage, employment and free-riding by husbands. While payment of a basic income to a husband for his "contribution" through employment and to his wife for her "contribution" in the home is to recognize that she does indeed make a socially valuable contribution, this does little to calm the fears of some feminists that a basic income will merely reinforce women's lesser standing and the idleness of husbands in the household.

An adequate discussion of free-riding and reciprocity in debates about basic income is hampered by, on the one hand, the prevalence of an economistic or contractual sense of "reciprocity." In this interpretation of the term the recipient must make a contribution directly in return for every benefit received, a view that magnifies the problem of free-riding. On the other hand, by ignoring the household, participants in the debate tacitly presuppose that "reciprocity" in another sense, i.e., mutual aid, characterizes domestic interactions.[13] To refocus the debate about basic income around its significance for democratization would mean replacing the preoccupation with one kind of free-riding with an examination of how to reinforce reciprocity in the sense of mutual aid across the social order. And that, in turn, would require widening the terms of debate, engaging with the large body of feminist analysis, moving away from the assumptions of neo-classical economics and developing a political argument.

*

In conclusion, I want to make two further points. First, schemes for a conditional basic income raise another problem. In effect, these proposals declare irrelevant the comparison of basic income with universal suffrage as a democratic right. The criteria for eligibility for a conditional income may be very generously interpreted, but there are always likely to be individuals who fail, or refuse, to meet the conditions. What, then, is their status? Are they, like individuals who lack the franchise, to become second-class citizens? So long as a basic income is conditional, a privilege not a right, the problem of second-class and lesser citizenship cannot be avoided. The use that citizens make of their freedom is open to no guarantees. Democratic self-government entails that they decide for themselves how and when they will contribute, or whether they will contribute at all. If the cost of improving democratic freedom for all citizens is the existence of some drones, then, I submit, it is a cost worth paying.

Second, let me emphasize that a basic income is not a panacea. In itself, a basic income would not, for instance, provide an adequate stock of affordable housing, sufficient good quality education, adequate health-care, an end to racism, or violence-free neighborhoods. Yet if a genuinely democratic society in which the freedom of women is as important as that of men remains an aspiration, it is hard to see that there is a substitute for an unconditional basic income.

NOTES

1 I am focusing on adults and citizens here; a more complete account would also discuss non-citizen residents and children.

2 Van Parijs' argument is libertarian, or, more exactly, a "real libertarian" argument that departs in some significant respects from typical libertarianism. I comment further on Van Parijs in Pateman (2003).

3 Others are much more qualified than I to discuss this aspect, but how public monies are allocated – guns or butter – is as much a political as an economic question. Ackerman and Alstott (1999) provide a detailed discussion of how a capital grant could be financed through a wealth tax. However, neither wealth taxes nor income taxes are popular at present, so I would suggest consideration of an alternative, hypothecated, form of taxation, such as a Tobin tax on speculative financial trading, or a tax on polluting and other environmentally destructive activities. Even better, I would advocate fewer guns and much more butter.

4 Claus Offe (2000) also argues in terms of universal economic citizenship in his proposal for sabbatical accounts, which he presents as a gradualist and experimental approach to basic income.

5 See Pateman (1970 and 2002).

6 The consequence for employment rates of a basic income is hard to determine in the abstract. On the one hand, it would act as a disincentive for

individuals to be employed, since, *ex hypothesis*, they could live on the income. On the other hand, precisely because the income is paid whether or not individuals are employed, they could enjoy a better standard of life by taking a low paid job than by living on a basic income alone. It would thus act as an incentive to employment, and improve the flexibility of the labor market.

7   McKay and VanEvery (2000: 281) remark that critics of the free-rider objection argue in "masculinist terms which ignore the implicit relegation of family carers to this category."

8   For a discussion of support for this legacy in the Netherlands, see Plantenga, Schippers and Siegers, 1999.

9   For some examples of discussion of the importance of a basic income for women, see Walter (1989), Parker (1993), McKay and Vanevery (2000), McKay (2002), and on stakeholding Alstott (2000).

10   Like Robeyns (2001) I have frequently encountered this objection when I have talked about a basic income. It is less often seen in academic discussions.

11   My thanks to Harvey Goldman for his comments about the surfer at a talk I gave at UC San Diego in 2001.

12   For a conditional stake see Goodin (2003).

13   To apply "reciprocity" in the first sense to the household would have dire consequences, not least for infants. Political theorists in an earlier era saw reciprocity in my second sense as the primary law of nature. That is, they recognized that a social order *is* a system of generalized mutual aid and mutual forbearance. If reciprocity in this sense of the term breaks down, social order begins to disintegrate.

REFERENCES

Ackerman, Bruce, and Alstott, Anne L. 1999. *The Stakeholder Society*. New Haven, CT: Yale University Press.

Alstott, Anne L. 2000. "Good for Women." Symposium: "Delivering a Basic Income," *Boston Review*, Oct.–Nov.

Anderson, Elizabeth. 2000. "Optional Freedoms," in Symposium: "Delivering a Basic Income," *Boston Review*, Oct.–Nov.

Atkinson, Anthony. 1996. "The Case for a Participation Income," *Political Quarterly*, 67: 67–70.

Barry, Brian. 1996. "Real Freedom and Basic Income," *The Journal of Political Philosophy*, 4: 242–276.

— 1997 "The Attractions of Basic Income," in *Equality*, ed. Jane Franklin. London: Institute for Public Policy Research.

Goodin, Robert. 2003. "Sneaking Up on Stakeholding," in *The Ethics of Stakeholding*, Keith Dowding, J. De Wispelaere and S. White, eds. Basingstoke: Palgrave.

Hayek, Friedrich von. 1960. *The Constitution of Liberty*. Chicago: University of Chicago Press.

Jordan, Bill. 1998. *The New Politics of Welfare*. London: Sage Publications.

Marshall, T. H. 1963. "Citizenship and Social Class," in *Sociology at the Crossroads and Other Essays*. London: Heineman.

McKay, Ailsa, 2002. "Arguing for a Citizen's Basic Income: A Feminist Perspective," paper presented at the annual meeting of the American Political Science Association, Boston.

McKay, Ailsa and VanEvery, Jo. 2000. "Gender, Family, and Income Maintenance: A Feminist Case for Citizens Basic Income." *Social Politics: International Studies in Gender, State, and Society* 7, 2: 266–84.

Offe, Claus. 2000. "The German Welfare State: Principles, Performance and Prospectives after Unification," *Thesis Eleven*, 63: 11–37.

Parker, Hermione. 1993. *Citizen's Income and Women*. BIRG Discussion Paper 2. London: Citizen's Income.

Pateman, Carole. 1970. *Participation and Democratic Theory*. Cambridge: Cambridge University Press.

— 2002. "Self-Ownership and Property in the Person: Democratization and a Tale of Two Concepts." *Journal of Political Philosophy* 10.1: 20–53.

— 2003. "Freedom and Democratization: Why Basic Income is to be Preferred to Basic Capital," in *The Ethics of Stakeholding*, Keith Dowding, Jurgen De Wispelaere, and Stuart White, eds. Basingstoke: Palgrave.

Pickard, Bertram. 1919. *A Reasonable Revolution: Being a Discussion of the State Bonus Scheme—A Proposal for a National Minimum Income*. London: Allen and Unwin.

Plantenga, Janneke, Schippers, J., and Siegers, J. 1999. "Towards an Equal Division of Paid and Unpaid Work: The Case of The Netherlands," *Journal of European Social Policy*, 9. 2: 99–110.

Robeyns, Ingrid. 2001. "Will a Basic Income Do Justice to Women?" *Analyse and Kritik: Zeitschrift fur Sozialtheorie* 1. 88–105.

Shue, Henry. 1996. *Basic Rights: Subsistence, Affluence, and U.S. Foreign Policy*. 2nd edn. Princeton: Princeton University Press.

Van Parijs, Philippe. 1995. *Real Freedom for All: What (If Anything) Can Justify Capitalism?* New York: Oxford University Press.

— 2000. "A Basic Income for All," *Boston Review*, October/November, 4–8.

Walter, Tony. 1989. *Basic Income: Freedom from Poverty, Freedom to Work*. London: Marion Boyers.

Widerquist, Karl. 1999. "Reciprocity and the Guaranteed Income," *Politics and Society*, 27, 3: 387–402

Wollstonecraft, Mary, 1993 [1792] "A Vindication of the Rights of Woman," in *Political Writings*, ed. Janet Todd, Toronto: University of Toronto Press.

6

Implementing Stakeholder Grants: the British case

Julian Le Grand

Britain is the first country actually to begin the process of implementing the idea of stakeholder grants. The government of Tony Blair has introduced what it calls a Child Trust Fund. This is a universal grant, topped up by a means-tested addition, given to every baby at birth, invested in a fund and available for use when the child reaches 18. It raises a number of issues, both theoretical and practical, that are of more general interest and form the focus of this short chapter.

THE PRECURSORS

As Ackerman and Alstott have noted, the pioneer in this area was Tom Paine, who suggested that every 21-year-old man and woman should receive an endowment of £15, financed from an inheritance tax. "The subtraction will be made at the time that best admits it, which is, at the moment that property is passing by the death of one person to the possession of another ... The monopoly of natural inheritance to which there never was a right, begins to cease."[1]

In more modern times in the UK a similar idea was put forward by the economist Cedric Sandford in the early 1970s and discussed by A. B. Atkinson in his pioneering work on wealth inequality.[2] Both explored the idea of a capital grant, although not one necessarily connected with the inheritance tax and not necessarily provided at the age of majority: Atkinson, for instance, discusses the possibility of including a capital element in the state pension.

Unaware of these predecessors, over ten years ago I published a proposal for a grant to everyone on reaching the age of majority financed out of a reformed inheritance tax, terming the idea a "poll grant."[3] More recently, influenced by developments in the US, especially the work of Michael Sherradon and Bruce Ackerman with Anne Alstott, similar ideas have acquired momentum in British policy circles.[4] In 1999, a capital grant at the age of majority was discussed in several contributions to the *New Statesman* magazine.[5] In 2000 Gavin Kelly and Rachel Lissauer of the influential centre-left think-tank the Institute of Public Policy Research (IPPR) reviewed schemes designed to promote asset ownership and proposed a "baby bond": A grant of £1,000 made at birth.[6] And in the same year, the Fabian Society produced a pamphlet by myself and David Nissan advocating a capital grant of £10,000 to every 18-year-old.[7]

This momentum has carried through to government. Just before the election of June 2001, in a star-studded event at No. 10 Downing Street, Prime Minister Blair, the Chancellor of the Exchequer, Gordon Brown, and the Secretaries of State for Education and Social Security, David Blunkett and Alistair Darling, launched proposals for a "child trust fund." This has now been implemented.

THE POLICY

The government has set up a Child Trust Fund for each child born on or after 1 September 2002. The government starts the fund off with a £250 voucher, and will make a further contribution when the child is seven (the exact amount has yet to be decided). Children born to parents below a threshold income will receive a furhter £250. Parents can pay into the fund, which will be invested in a wide range of vehicles including equities. Neither parents nor children will have access to the Fund until the child reaches 18; there will then be no restrictions as to use. Financial education would be provided to both parents and children.

Issues

The government's proposals, together with the other contributions to the US and British debates, raise a number of issues, especially with respect to the Child Trust Fund, that need resolution before the idea can become practical policy. They include timing, finance, universality and possible restrictions on use. Some comments on each follow.

Timing

Should the grant be given at birth in the form of a "baby bond," as the government and the IPPR have proposed, or at the age of majority, as Paine, Ackerman and Alstott and I have argued? There are arguments on both sides. In favour of a grant at birth, since the money is to be invested for eighteen years, less can be given up-front. This would make the grant allocation easier politically, because it apparently saves the government money (in reality, of course there is no saving, since the government is simply losing the income that it could have earned by investing the grant itself). Another advantage is that the fund can be seen to accumulate by both parent and child, thus serving a useful financial educational purpose. On the negative side, this very visibility may make the fund unpopular with parents, especially poor ones, who will see money accumulating that they might feel they could have put to good use, but which they are unable to touch. Also, depending on how each of the funds is invested, children may end up with different amounts on reaching the age of majority – an outcome that could be regarded as unfair.

This last point raises questions as to the appropriate investment strategy for a "baby bond," and the related issue as to who would manage the investment. Should the funds be invested in savings accounts, equities or government bonds? Should government or private sector financial institutions manage the fund? What should be the role of the parents in managing the investment – or indeed of the children?

In the British case, the government preferred the private sector to manage the funds. The private sector, although interested for long-term reasons, was worried about the small size of the amounts involved and the difficulty of covering their fixed costs. This was resolved by confining fund management to a few finance institutions, from whose offerings parents would choose.

Finance

Where would the money to finance the stakeholding grant come from? The British government does not specify this in its proposals. Ackerman and Alstott finance their much more generous scheme from an annual wealth tax. Kelly and Lissauer finance their baby bond through reducing tax reliefs for pensions.

I have argued that the best way to finance this potentially popular spending proposal is by linking it to reforms to a hitherto unpopular and inefficient tax – inheritance tax.[8] Hypothecating, or earmarking, inheritance tax revenues to capital grants could provide the means for rehabilitating a much despised tax. It also has an obvious popular appeal: The wealth of one generation is visibly spread around so as to fertilise the growth of the next.

Inheritance tax is a misnomer in the UK. What we have is a tax on estates that bears no relation to the amount any individual inherits, either from the estate in question, or over a lifetime. And the tax is largely voluntary. The Inland Revenue estimated that in 1995 total marketable personal wealth stood at £2,013bn. This measure excludes wealth that cannot be realized, such as accrued pension rights. In contrast, the yield from inheritance tax is pitiful, just £1.7bn in 1997–98. Wealth passes almost untaxed between generations through lifetime gifts, through exempt items such as agricultural land and forestry, and through devices such as discretionary trusts which can defer tax liabilities for decades.

It is against this scale of wealth transfer that suggestions such as capital grants should be measured. There are approximately 650,000 18-year-olds in Britain, so it would cost £6.5 billion to give them each £10,000. The current yield of £1.7bn would pay for about £2,500 per recipient.

Yields, and hence the grant, could be increased in subsequent years by reforms that have long been on economists' agendas, but that have lacked political support. These include shifting the basis for the tax from the donor to the recipient, and extending it to include lifetime inheritances and gifts. This would encourage the wealthy to pass on their wealth to those who have not already been substantial beneficiaries, as by so doing they could reduce the taxman's take. The system would require that everybody had a lifetime gift and inheritance allowance, say of £50,000, which could be received free of tax. Thereafter tax could be levied at progressive rates to maintain incentives for wealth to be spread around. A review of exempt items and Trust law should also be undertaken to broaden the base of the tax.

In theory receipts could collapse with such a tax if bequests were directed only to those who had not used up their inheritance tax allowance. However, if that occurred a fairer distribution of inherited wealth would have been achieved, and there would be less need of an additional system of grants. More likely, however, is that wider bequests would happen mainly at the margins, as people would continue to want to help their own children first. As they did so they would be taxed to pay for grants for those less fortunate.

It would not be necessary to impose penal rates of inheritance tax to finance a substantial reallocation of capital. Indeed an ideal system would have rates that most regarded as reasonable, to minimize incentives for avoidance or evasion.

What might such rates be? The inadequacies of the existing inheritance tax mean we have very limited information indeed about the extent of wealth bequeathed or given on a year by year basis. But a crude estimate by Le Grand and Nissan suggested that a reformed inheritance tax would need to be levied at an average rate of around 15 percent to finance £10,000 per young adult. If higher education subsidies were reduced *pari passu* (as they should be if equity is to be maintained), the savings from this could also be used to finance the grant and the inheritance tax rate could be lowered yet further. Since the participation rate of the relevant age group in higher education is now running at around one third, this means that the inheritance tax rate could be lowered to 10 percent. Alternatively, the rate could be kept at 15 percent and the savings in higher education spending could be used elsewhere within the education budget or for other public services. In short, there is every opportunity here to levy a modest tax on gifts and bequests, and still make sure every young person has the capital needed to get off to a good start.

The insignificant contribution of inheritance tax to financing public spending, and the sense of the state as inherently wasteful, have meant that avoiding such tax has never attracted much moral opprobrium. The ease of avoidance of inheritance tax reflects the lack of public support for it. But if the proceeds of the tax were visibly distributed through stakeholding grants, perhaps that perception could change.

Universality

Should the grant be universal or means-tested? The British government's proposals involve both a universal and a means-tested element, where the relevant "means" are parental income.

The case for a universal grant is part of the more general case for universal benefits over ones targeted on the poor. Universal benefits contribute to the sense of national community, whereas targeted ones can be socially divisive. Also targeted benefits require a cumbersome apparatus for determining eligibility: One that is expensive to administer and can be demeaning to the recipient. In contrast universal benefits require only the information necessary to determine that the individuals concerned fall into the relevant category: In this case, simply their age.

But there is an additional, more fundamental reason for a universal grant. Everyone born into a developed country benefits from a share in a common inheritance: A set of capital assets, including buildings and other physical infrastructure, transport links, capital equipment and agricultural land. The vast majority of these are the results of the labors and efforts of previous generations, the members of which have struggled together to produce what is in effect a gift of wealth to the next. It is largely because of this inheritance that the current inhabitants of any developed country are as wealthy as they are; without that enormous accumulation of capital over the centuries, no amount of efforts by the current generation could generate the levels of current production that maintain our standards of living.

This idea, that the wealth of one generation is a common asset to the next, is important for it cuts across the argument that individuals who have created wealth should be free to give it all to their children. Ownership gives personal command of resources, but it is not easy to justify this persisting beyond the grave, especially when, as we have seen, the life chances for many are reduced by lack of access to start-up capital. How can one argue that people have as great a right to inherited wealth as to, for instance, the income or profits that result from their own efforts? It would seem fairer if the right to our national patrimony was more equally distributed – as would happen if our proposal for a universal capital grant were implemented.

A standard argument used against any universal benefit is what we might call the "Prince William" objection: should the benefit be paid to the better off who are unlikely really to need it, such as Prince William, as well as to the really needy? The answer is, in general, yes: for this is a price that has to be paid if the other advantages of universality are to be obtained and the problems of means-tested targeting avoided. Moreover, if the grant is financed through inheritance tax then, as parents pay the tax, a significant portion of their wealth will now be going to pay for the start-up costs for thousands of other children, as well as their own. In the prince's case, an exception may be made as long as his family, uniquely, are exempt from inheritance tax.

It is also worth noting that the children of the better off already receive a form of grant through subsidies to higher education. Although with the recent introduction of tuition fees and student loans these subsidies are being reduced, they remain considerable. Most students come from middle-class backgrounds. Hence the proposal can be viewed as simply a means of extending an already existing subsidy to the better off to those less fortunate. It also has the implication that higher education subsidies can be further reduced without making anyone worse off, since one potential use for the grant could be to pay for tuition and living expenses while acquiring further education.

Restrictions on use and eligibility

Political support for the scheme would depend not only on its method of finance but also on what happens at the other end: what the recipients of the grant did with the money. The intention of these schemes is to encourage investment and hence the accumulation of capital (financial, physical or human). Hence it would be desirable for grants to be spent on investment opportunities. There would be no surer way to lose popular and political support for a system of capital grants than a few well-publicized cases of young people blowing their grants on cocaine or wild holidays.

The size of the grant may in itself be of importance here. While it may be tempting to launch such a scheme with a small grant to introduce the idea, as the British government is doing, there is a danger then that it is seen to be insignificant by the recipient, who might then feel quite justified in blowing it for a bit of fun. The sum needs to be seen as significant, providing a one-off opportunity that justifies careful consideration. Instinct says that a grant of a thousand or two may fall between stools, being insufficient for most worthwhile investments. Hence my and David Nissan's suggestion of a £10,000 grant.

It would be possible to make a respectable case for this level of grant to be given unconditionally on the grounds that ultimately adults do have to take responsibility for their own lives, and that young adults have to learn to do so. As it is, there would be plenty of social pressure on 18-year-olds not to blow their grants; to add to that pressure by confining the grants to only certain kinds of spending might be seen as unacceptable state paternalism.

Indeed, this is the argument put forward by Ackerman and Alstott, who do not put any restrictions on how their grant is to be used. However, they do restrict the recipients to those with a high school diploma and without a criminal record. Interestingly, the possibility of these kinds of restrictions has not been raised in the British case. This is perhaps because it is felt that they would exclude precisely those who would most benefit from the scheme.

Currently the British Government is proposing no restrictions on the use of its child trust fund. This is largely because of the impossibility of policing the restrictions. So it is important for those who advocate restricting use to spell out how the restriction process might work. Nissan and I have suggested that the grants could be paid into a special account held in the individual recipient's name either in a local commercial bank or in a local branch of a network of publicly owned savings institutions set up by the government specifically for this purpose. The account would have a special name: since its purpose is for the (A)ccumulation of (C)apital and (E)ducation, this suggests the simple acronym ACE. ACE accounts would be handled by a set of trustees, whose purpose would be to approve the spending plans of individuals before releasing any capital; hence individuals would only be able to draw money from the account to spend on approved purposes, as defined by the trustees.

Having quality ACE trustees would clearly be important to this aspect of the scheme. For they would not only have to vet the spending plans, but also ensure that the money was spent in the way proposed. They could be specially employed by the local institution to vet the spending plans of all the grants being given out by that branch; alternatively they could be drawn from panels of local business people and other community leaders, on a voluntary basis, perhaps through the Business in Community scheme.

What sort of investment purposes should they approve? One obvious possibility is higher and further education: a way of accumulating human capital and hence of increasing an individual's value to the labor market. The grant could be used to contribute to the fees and maintenance costs for a university education, or to the costs of more vocational forms of training. To ensure compliance, it could be paid through the educational institution concerned, in much the same way as the present student grant and loan scheme.

Another use for the grant might be for the down payment on a house or flat purchase. Unpublished research by Gavin Smart suggests that for many poor people, the down payment is the biggest obstacle to homeownership; once the down payment is made, people have a commitment to their homes and usually manage to keep up the mortgage payments regardless of any income or employment problems they encounter. Again to ensure compliance the payment could be made directly to the vendor.

The grant could also form part of the start-up costs of a small business. The development of a business plan and its approval by the trustees would be essential – which makes it the more desirable to include local business people among the trustees.

What should happen if no worthwhile uses are proposed for an individual's ACE account? One option would be for the grant to be put towards a personal or stakeholder pension. The pension schemes could be drawn from an approved list, and payment made directly from the ACE account to the scheme.

Such arrangements could not prevent all abuse, and it would be pointless to pretend otherwise. Assets bought through trustee-approved distributions must at some future date be saleable, and use of the proceeds could not easily be monitored. It is not unheard-of for the offspring of the wealthy to fritter away their fortunes; and it will always be in the nature of some of the recipients of our capital grant to do so. What counts is for everyone to get his or her opportunity. Thereafter, as in many other aspects of life, it should be up to them.

Conclusion

Stakeholding grants are an idea whose time has come – at least in Britain. It is to be hoped that some at least of the British discussions will be of use to other countries that may be considering going down this road.

NOTES

1 Quoted in Ackerman and Alstott (1999), p. 182.
2 Sandford (1971), pp. 250–254; Atkinson (1972) pp. 233–236.
3 Le Grand (1989), p. 210.
4 Sherradon (1991), Ackerman and Alstott (1991).
5 These included an article by the ex-US Secretary of Labor Robert Reich (14 June), an editorial endorsing the idea (13 September) and articles by the present author and David Nissan (26 July, 4 October).
6 Kelly and Lissauer (2000).
7 Nissan and Le Grand (2000).
8 Le Grand (1989); Nissan and Le Grand (2000).

REFERENCES

Ackerman, Bruce and Alstott, Anne. 1999. *The Stakeholder Society*. New Haven, CT: Yale University Press.
— 2001b. *Delivering Savings and Assets, The Modernisation of Britain's Tax and Benefit System*, Consultation Paper No. 9 (London: HM Treasury).

Kelly, Gavin and Lissauer, Rachel. 2000. *Ownership for All*. London: Institute for Public Policy Research.

Le Grand, Julian. 1989. 'Markets, welfare and equality.' Ch. 8 in Julian Le Grand and Saul Estrin, eds. *Market Socialism*. Oxford: Oxford University Press.

Nissan, David and Le Grand, Julian. 2000. *A Capital Idea: Start-up grants for young people*. London: Fabian Society.

Sandford, Cedric. 1971. *Taxing Personal Wealth*. London: Allen and Unwin.

Sherradon, Michael. 1991. *Assets and the Poor*. Armonk, NY: M.E. Sharpe, Inc.

7

A Swedish-Style Welfare State or Basic Income: Which should have priority?

Barbara R. Bergmann

The Stakeholding and Basic Income proposals (Ackerman and Alstott, 2001; Van Parijs, 2001) both involve taxing large amounts from some citizens to finance large cash payments to all citizens. I take the major aim of both to be to make living standards more equal than they otherwise would be, to reduce individuals' dependence on the labor market, and to provide more choices, greater opportunities, and more security, particularly to those who happen to be born to low-income parents. While these are desirable ends, I am going to argue that, for people holding progressive views, a Swedish-style welfare state, with state provision of a long list of expensive services, plus targeted cash payments to those in special circumstances, has higher priority. As an analysis of the Swedish budget will show, we cannot do both at current levels of per capita income. A generous welfare state is currently incompatible with large universal cash payments because of the problems that accumulate as the rate of taxation is pushed to very high levels. The time to consider introducing Universal Basic Income in each country is after the establishment of a well-funded welfare state. It could then be phased in slowly, as productivity rises and the labor needed to produce a given level of Gross Domestic Product (GDP) falls.

The funds that Universal Basic Income or Stakeholder grants would require currently have alternative uses that are of higher priority. In particular, there is a class of "merit goods" – goods and services that it is in the public interest that every citizen have access to – that are best provided universally by government. Cash payments that are targeted toward people in particularly needy circumstances might also have higher priority than Basic Income or Stakeholder grants. These include children's allowances and unemployment insurance, and above-subsistence-level pensions to the elderly and to the disabled. There is a practical limit to the portion of the GDP that can be taken by taxes. If the list of merit goods and targeted cash payments that progressives would have good reason to endorse is long and expensive, then at current levels of GDP little or no taxing capacity may be left over to finance the large cash payments required by the Basic Income or Stakeholder schemes. Which goods deserve to be placed in the class of merit goods, what targeted cash payments are of high priority, how much it would cost to provide these things, and what the limits of taxation should be taken to be are, of course, issues that need explicit discussion.

If the list of merit goods is taken to be short and the cost (plus the cost of other government functions and cash payments to those in special circumstances such as old age or disability) are well inside the taxation limit, then their provision need not interfere with the financing of a sizeable Basic Income or Stakeholder scheme. But if, as I shall argue, the list of such goods is taken to include those currently provided to citizens of the most advanced welfare states, such as Sweden, then there will be little or no room for sizeable universal cash grants at current per capita income levels.

Apart from the problem of finance, there are other disadvantages to the near-term all-at-once adoption of these schemes. The disincentives to work they entail would make the taxation problem even more acute. Under present conditions, they probably entail retrograde effects on gender equality. They would reduce the power of parents vis-à-vis their teenage children.

The Stakeholder proposal has severe disadvantages beyond those which both cash grant schemes share. The most obvious is the possibility that a not insubstantial portion of the citizenry would put large sums of money to uses that most people, quite reasonably, would not want to subsidize out of public funds raised from taxpayers: Gambling, drugs, alcohol, fancy cars and clothing or jewelry. The Stakeholder proposal would be likely to cause dissaving, and a reduction in the capital stock below what it otherwise might be.

In the United States, it makes political sense for progressives to put their limited energy toward advancing welfare state provisions before attempting to sell Basic Income. Even with the ascendancy of the right wing in the US, it is possible to add government-provided services to the budget, as the debate about drug benefits for the elderly suggests. It is likely to be more feasible politically to add to the list of government-funded goods and services than to institute and maintain a program of large cash payments to all citizens, since waste and reduced work effort are the probable result of such payments. Both in terms of politics and in terms of human needs, putting the achievement of Basic Income ahead of the achievement of the welfare state is putting the cart before the horse.

MERIT GOODS

We label a good or service a "merit good" when (a) we decide that everyone who is in a position to utilize it should have access to it and (b) when, in the absence of government provision, there are people who would not or could not acquire it on their own. The decision that all should have access to a good may be based on expected benefits to society, or on humanitarian considerations, or some combination of both. The worry that at least part of the population will not buy a sufficient quantity and quality of a high-priority good out of their own income will most often arise in the case of a good that is expensive relative to households' income, which may totally preclude some from buying it, or might force them to make inordinate sacrifices of even higher-priority goods if they are to buy it. The worry may also arise from a paternalistic judgment that households will not choose the right thing.

Obviously, different individuals will have different lists of merit goods. The extreme libertarians of the Cato Institute would have an empty list. But most people would have at least some things on their list. Here are mine.

Schooling

The most obvious case of a merit good, and one that is in effect recognized as such by liberals and most conservatives alike, is elementary and secondary schooling. Even those conservatives in the United States who would like to see many or most children educated in privately run schools do not question that the public purse should pay for at least a major part of the cost of that education. Schooling is a merit good because (a) it is perceived as something no child should be denied, for the child's own sake, for the economy's sake and as the foundation of the kind of social and political life we desire, and (b) because we have good reason to fear that some parents would fail to provide it in the quality and quantity deemed necessary.

Nobody would contemplate reducing or eliminating the government's funding for schooling and distributing the funds to the citizenry as a cash grant that could be used for anything the recipient chose.¹ Thus, including an item on your list of merit goods entails your deciding that it has higher priority for the funds it requires than a cash grant that would cost the same amount.

Schooling also illustrates an important issue relating to quality. Low-quality and high-quality schooling are really two different services, and it is high-quality schooling that is clearly the merit good we should aim for. That quality is not currently provided in many countries. In the United States, higher salaries for teachers, which would allow for a far more rigorous process of teacher selection and training, would be a necessary condition for more adequate quality, as would reduced class size, better provision for dealing with disruptive students, and more funds for schools with a high concentration of students needing special services. Such quality-enhancing reforms might well require a doubling of current education budgets.

Health care

A second obvious candidate for merit good status is health care, including access to dental care and pharmaceuticals. Most developed countries do provide this on a universal basis, and therefore treat it as a merit good. However, as in the case of schooling, there is a quality issue that needs to be attended to. In Great Britain, people with painful and disabling conditions must wait years for medical treatment, and older people are excluded from certain treatments. Britain's current Prime Minister, who in his first four years of office did not find his way clear to allocate enough money to put the health service on a decent footing, has proposed establishing a Stakeholder scheme, awarding considerable sums of money to healthy people in their early twenties. This would be a truly feckless policy. The situation in the United States is even worse, with 40 million people with no health insurance. To be campaigning for a program of large cash payments in a country where this is the case would be a striking inversion of priorities.² Another quality issue that needs addressing is nursing home care for the disabled elderly.

If better schooling and high-quality, timely health services were the only goods judged to be "merit goods," then we might well have room for greatly expanded cash grants. However, there are arguably others with higher priority than cash grants.

Childcare

A family with two pre-school children in the US needs to spend $12,000–20,000 a year to buy care in a childcare center. School-age children with working parents need after-school care, and recreation programs during the summer. Many parents buy relatively cheap "informal" care of probably inferior quality and safety, but even that takes a big share of the income of low-wage parents. A program offering free, universal care would cost upwards of $120 billion a year; a program with co-payments from higher-income parents might cost $60 billion. If the very low salaries currently provided to childcare workers were to be improved, an additional 20 percent would be added to the cost.

While a generous Basic Income allowance might be used to pay for childcare, families with pre-school children who used it that way would be living at a considerably lower standard than other families. Government provision of child care as a service allows families with pre-schoolers to live at the same standard as those of the same income who do not need to buy care. Moreover, the Basic Income grant would do nothing to upgrade childcare quality. Most parents would spend much of it on other things. The provision of childcare would significantly raise the standard of living of low-wage families with children, as the money they currently spend on care could be used to buy other things.

Free or partially subsidized college expenses

Nobody with the ability to take advantage of higher education, including graduate education, should be precluded from doing so by financial considerations, as many are now.

Mental health care

The large number of homeless people testifies to the need for more residential facilities for people with mental problems. Previously provided facilities were of low quality, and that contributed to the indifference of the public toward closing them. The community-based mental health facilities that were promised in their place never materialized. We should be providing treatment on demand, much of it residential, for drug, alcohol, and gambling addiction. For those not needing care in therapeutic facilities, generously subsidized access to pharmaceutical and talking therapies should be provided. Parents with children with developmental deficits and people taking care of parents with Alzheimer's need special help.

Decent housing

The United States currently has a program helping low-income people with their housing costs. It works on the principle that families should not have to spend more than 30 percent of their income for housing. But the program is not an entitlement, so limited appropriations allow only a small percentage of families eligible for this kind of aid to receive subsidies. In an adequate welfare state, the program would be fully funded.

Public transportation

Public transportation requires at least partial subsidization. Greater provision would slow global warming, reduce sprawl, preserve green spaces, save energy, revitalize city centers.

Social work services

Far more generous funding of child protection services would be desirable, as well as services that work with troubled youth, released offenders, and people with trouble managing their family lives or finances.

Basic income would not ensure the private purchase of merit goods

One thing to notice about the menu of merit goods I have outlined is that the Basic Income and Stakeholder schemes would not by themselves ensure the provision of any of these things to all citizens. Unless a well-developed welfare state were established first, those people who currently lack these kinds of merit goods, as many do today in the United States, would remain without them despite their Basic Income grants. While under such schemes lower-income citizens who took jobs would be more affluent than they are now, and many would (as they do now) fail to buy health insurance, suffer with poor quality public schools, send their children to low-quality care, fail to get the mental health treatment they need, live in slummy dwelling units, and so on.

Most of these goods and services are very expensive, relative to income, and the boost that Basic Income would give to the income of low-earners would not suffice to ensure that everybody would choose to include them in their household budget, or indeed could do so. The situation would be even worse for those who chose to refrain from paid work. In the case of many of these merit goods, such as high-quality education and health insurance, the failure of a family to include them may be without obvious immediate negative consequences to the family, so the temptation to exclude them will be high.

Under a welfare state, with the provision of all of the merit goods I have listed, plus cash grants to citizens with special needs, even those with jobs with a relatively low wage would have access to the basic goods and services needed for a decent standard of living. If instead we provide only the Basic Income and few or no merit goods beyond education, then many will still lack important ingredients of decency.

THE PROBLEM IN FINANCING BASIC INCOME

If one agrees that it is a high priority to provide a substantial and expensive list of good quality merit goods to all citizens, then Basic Income or Stakeholder's payments, if adopted, must be in addition to the provision of merit goods, not instead of such provision. Is this possible under current conditions? One way to consider this question is to look at Sweden's welfare state, which provides most if not all of the merit goods listed above. We can then ask whether it would be feasible for Sweden to tack a Basic Income scheme on to its existing budget. Relevant magnitudes are shown in Table 7.1.

Table 7.1. *Distribution of Swedish Gross Domestic Product, 2000 (percent share).*

Consumption expenditure by households:	51%
financed by income from wages andother personal after-tax income	32
*financed by government cash benefits to households**	19
Consumption expenditures, public sector*	26
Non-consumption portion of GDP (investment, net inventory change, net exports, other):	23
*financed by public sector**	15
financed by private sector	8
TOTAL GDP	100%
total public sector (sum of * items)	60%

Source: Calculations based on data from the Swedish Ministry of Finance.

Government revenue in Sweden totals 60 percent of GDP, as compared with about 30 percent in the United States. Of this, Swedish government cash payments to households with special characteristics (old-age pensions, payments to the disabled, unemployment insurance, child allowances, paid parental leave, etc.) take up 19 percent. Another 26 percent of GDP goes for the purchase or production of goods and services provided by government to citizens. These include the kinds of merit goods I listed in the previous section, as well as services like garbage collection, defense, policing, inspection, administration, etc. The remaining 15 percent of GDP in the government's budget is used to finance items considered to be fixed capital investments, such as roads and other permanent structures.

Consumption expenditures by households amount to about 51 percent of Swedish GDP, of which, as we have seen, 19 percent of GDP is financed from government cash payments. The remaining 32 percent of GDP that households spend for consumption is financed by the wage and property income that is left to households after they pay their taxes.

Adding a Basic Income to the Swedish budget would require large cash payments to the sizeable body of people not currently receiving any such payments from government, namely the citizens who are not unemployed, not retired, without young children, not disabled, etc. Sending a check equal to a poverty line income to every adult between the ages of 20 and 65 would take about 15 percent of the GDP of a country with a per capita income such as that of Sweden or the United States.[3] Some of those currently receiving cash payments from government would receive more than they now do under a Basic Income scheme. It is unlikely that any would receive less.

Assuming that no diminution is desired in public sector consumption expenditures, the funds to finance the additional cash payments to households would have to come from an increase in government revenue. The precise amount required would depend on the characteristics of the scheme that was adopted, including the extent to which the current cash payments to households in special circumstances were discontinued or diminished. However, the amount of the increase could not be small, and the reward in terms of after-tax income that came to those participating in production would be considerably lowered.

A Basic Income in a country with a welfare state as developed as Sweden's would have to be financed by a shift of funds from the first category in Table 7.1 to the second.

For example, if an extra 15 percent of GDP were added to cash payments by government to households, those extra funds would have to be taxed away from households' wage and property income now devoted to buying consumer goods, now 32 percent of GDP, leaving households just 17 percent of GDP as their net reward for their participation in the production of the entire GDP.[4] That could hardly be tolerated.

So at present levels of per capita GDP, we must choose between the list of merit goods and cash payments for those in special circumstances (the welfare state) on the one hand, and the Basic Income scheme on the other. You cannot have both. Some compromise might be possible – a smaller Basic Income combined with a stripped-down list of merit goods. Those who advocate the Basic Income scheme should indicate which of the menu of merit goods they propose to do without.

If we choose to develop the welfare state first, then at a later date, as productivity growth occurs, it will be possible to use some of the additional resources to phase in universal cash payments. However, it is not necessarily true that in the near future such payments would be judged to be the best use of the additional resources generated by growth. Additional or better quality goods that might be provided by government, and greater payments to citizens in special situations might take priority. Sweden, for example, currently has plans to augment the welfare state they already have by increasing subsidies for child care from their present level.

However, we may reach a stage where people feel content with the already achieved list of government-provided goods and special needs cash grants. Then as the economy grows, the absolute level of spending on them could be maintained, but that would amount to progressively smaller percentages of GDP being spent that way. Some of the additional income could be distributed as a tax-financed uniform payment to all citizens. These payments could start small and grow over time.

PROS AND CONS OF THE WELFARE STATE

Those of us who favor giving merit goods priority over Basic Income have to face the fact that like any other human system, the welfare state is subject to problems and abuses. A government service that starts out as adequately financed may through time be allowed to deteriorate through a failure to continue to allocate sufficient resources, as the case of the British health service shows. The distribution of government expenditures may unduly reflect the clout of certain parts of the electorate (the elderly, for example), or be the result of energetic lobbying by small self-interested groups, rather than the result of a rational assessment of needs based on humanitarian considerations.[5]

Lack of competition may cause public authorities to produce a narrow range of unattractive goods and services, which poorly meet the needs and tastes of the population. In the United States, there is a tendency for government-provided goods to be unevenly distributed. Less resources go to public schools in low-income neighborhoods than to those in higher-income neighborhoods. The corps of civil servants that administers programs may grow to excessive size and become dictatorial, inefficient, dilatory, and corrupt, tendencies that were in full flower in the Soviet Union. All of these possibilities certainly exist. The experience of France, the Low Countries, and the Scandinavian countries suggest, however, that these tendencies can, at least in certain contexts, be overcome. It is certainly simpler to administer a Basic Income scheme than it is to see to the production of a whole raft of government-provided services, or for government to fund and supervise the provision of such services by private firms. But these countries have shown that high quality government provision is possible.

WORK INCENTIVE AND GENDER ISSUES

For many of its adherents, a major attraction of Basic Income is that the guarantee would allow those who wished to refrain from working at a paid job to do so. If a sizeable Basic Income benefit were to be introduced, and significant numbers were to decide to do without earned income, the supply of goods and services traded for money would suddenly fall. Yet the number of claimants on that supply would stay the same. There might be an increase in the amount of unpaid work, but the net effect on the average standard of living would most likely be negative. Per capita consumption and per capita income would fall. Presumably, only people working for wages would pay income and payroll taxes, and so a reduction in their numbers would reduce tax revenues, just as the need would be arising for increased tax revenue to finance the Basic Income grants.

The fewer people there are to pay taxes, the higher must tax rates be to achieve any particular amount of revenue. The higher the tax rate on earned income, the less the reward from working for pay. This looks like a vicious circle: Fewer working for pay, causing lower tax revenues, requiring an increase in tax rates, causing fewer to work for pay, and so on.

Van Parijs discusses at some length the possibility that Basic Income provision could be structured so as to make work for pay rewarding, by keeping the marginal tax rate low. However, even at a zero tax rate for the lower income ranges, the "income effect" of receiving a sizeable cash grant will reduce the incentive to take a paid job.

A second, even more serious effect, and one that would probably be fatal to continuance of the scheme, if not to its adoption, would be resentment of those publicly supported with no special circumstances like disability or old age to justify that support.[6] For better or worse, the activity of supporting oneself through paid work is now a requirement for respect in Western society, for rich and poor alike. Being a non-jobholding person supported by the paid work of other family members still brings respectability, but not full respect, as men's and women's roles in the economy become more alike. Being on the public dole without having some disability that justifies it brings no respect whatever.

One frequently mentioned aim by proponents of Basic Income would be to allow parents to stay home with young children. Under current cultural conditions, the vast majority of those who would do that would be women. As Ingrid Robeyns (2000) argues, a withdrawal from the labor force by many women would be likely to reverse at least some of the progress that women have made in status and wages in the last half of the twentieth century. Many if not most employers have come to see women as likely to be continuous labor force participants, not inevitably destined to leave the workforce, and therefore as people worth training, worth putting into jobs leading to promotion, worth considering for promotion. This kind of progress would be reversed if a higher proportion of women withdrew from the labor force when their first child was born. For this reason, the full-blown implementation of Basic Income schemes in the near future should not appeal to those for whom gender equality is an important goal. Perhaps in the future, economic, housekeeping, and parenting activities will have become less differentiated by gender. Then Basic Income would affect the behavior of both sexes more equally, and would have lost its anti-equality effect.

A final problem with Basic Income would be a loss of power over children by their parents. If children's payments were large enough to allow them to live apart from their parents (perhaps with other teens), parents might be under pressure to let teenagers live separately on "their own" money. The availability of Basic Income for life would make the prospect of taking up a career less attractive, and reduce some teens' educational efforts. For modern parents, getting children through the teenage years without major damage is difficult enough now. Basic Income might well make it a nightmare. This is not a problem that is likely to diminish through time.

CONCLUSION

At current levels of per-capita income and production, there is no room in the budget for both the Swedish welfare state and Basic Income. One must choose one or the other to do first. The fully developed welfare state deserves priority over Basic Income because it accomplishes what Basic Income does not: It guarantees that certain specific human needs will be met. Both the welfare state and Basic Income reduce inequality of condition. But the welfare state does so with greater efficiency, because it takes better account of inequalities due to differences in needs. If I need an expensive operation and you don't, giving both of us a Basic Income grant will not go far to make our situations more equal. Only the provision of health services has the chance of doing that.

People on the left, who have limited energy, should in the immediate future concentrate on achieving provision of a satisfactory menu of government-provided merit goods. When this has been accomplished, then will be the time to consider starting to phase in Basic Income. If through time the capital intensity of production and productivity rise, then as a result the demand for labor may shrink.[7] A progressively lower labor force may become desirable, and Basic Income grants may be the best way of distributing an increasing share of the national income. But in the near and medium-term future, in a country like the United States which is very far from providing a decent list of high priority merit goods, Basic Incomes' attractive features don't trump extending the guarantee of merit goods to all citizens.

NOTES

1 I am not, of course, suggesting that the proponents of cash grant schemes would favor doing this, or that doing it would be necessary if we were to want to fund a cash-grant scheme. I am merely trying to demonstrate that publicly funded schooling has higher priority than cash grants.

2 Nobody would consider it sensible to say that we could make sure everybody had health insurance by distributing even large cash payments.

3 I have used American magnitudes to estimate this. The poverty line income for an individual under 65 was $8,959 in the year 2000. There were

162.6 million people between 20 and 65, and GDP was $10,000 billion. The calculation is roughly applicable to countries like Sweden that have similar levels of per capita GDP to the United States.

4 I am ignoring here the amount of wage and property income that house-holds use for investment that is presumably included in the 8 percent of GDP the private sector uses to finance such expenditure.

5 "Tax expenditures," the tax breaks to particular groups, are also pertinent.

6 The resentment shown in the United States in the last few decades against those single mothers receiving cash welfare grants predicts the state of public opinion under a Basic Income scheme. Single mothers' welfare payments were considered to be justified, at least by some, on the grounds that they were doing valuable work by taking care of their own children. But that justification did not prevent vitriolic and eventually successful attacks on the system of cash welfare grants, attacks that were probably supported by a majority of American voters. Those without children who wanted to depend on public support would not even have that justification.

7 A rise in productivity through time is by no means guaranteed forever. A big rise in demand for the kinds of personal services that cannot be assisted by capital goods is possible, reducing the ratio of the value of output to labor.

REFERENCES

Ackerman, Bruce and Anne Alstott, "Why Stakeholding?," paper prepared for the conference on Rethinking Distribution, Madison, WI, July 2001.

Robeyns, Ingrid. 2000. "Will a Basic Income Do Justice to Women?," *Analyse und Kritik,* 22 (2). Summer.

Van Parijs, Philippe. 2001. "Basic Income: A Simple and Powerful Idea for the 21st Century."

8

The Effects of a Basic Income Guarantee on Poverty and Income Distribution[*]

Irwin Garfinkel, Chien-Chung Huang, and Wendy Naidich

INTRODUCTION

A universal demogrant, credit income tax (Garfinkel, 1983), or, to use the current term, a Basic Income Guarantee (Van Parijs, 1992, 2001) is a universal cash benefit paid to all citizens. Entitlement is based only on citizenship. The same benefit is paid to all regardless of income, wealth, or work history. Benefit amounts vary only with age.

Advocates of BIG stress different justifications, including promotion of freedom, increased economic efficiency, and reduction in poverty. For example, Widerquist and Lewis (1997) in good Rawlsian fashion assert that the ultimate goal of social policy is to reduce poverty to the greatest extent possible, and go on to argue that Guaranteed Income "is the most efficient and comprehensive method to attack poverty" (1). Research supports this claim. Programs aimed directly at poor people via income-testing have done little to alleviate poverty (Burtless, 1994). These programs create strong disincentives to work in the legitimate labor market, are stigmatizing, and promote divisions among population groups rather than solidarity (Garfinkel, 1982). Non-income-tested programs, on the other hand, have been highly effective in lifting people out of poverty as well as

* This research was supported by a grant from the Institute for Socioeconomic Studies, White Plains, New York, Leonard M. Greene President. The earlier version of this paper was included as an appendix in the book *The National Tax Rebates: A New America with Less Government*. Leonard M. Greene. 1998. Washington: Regency Publishing, Inc. Address for correspondence: Irwin Garfinkel, School of Social Work, Columbia University, 622 West 113 Street, New York, NY 10025. We thank Leonard Greene for his support and encouragement of universal tax credits.

in serving non-poor people. Entitlement to BIG is based on citizenship rather than income. As such, BIG does not involve a separate income test with an implicit marginal tax rate on income that is higher than marginal rates in the positive tax system. This is a special appeal of BIG. Under the present system, as our poorest citizens who are aided by our safety net programs begin to earn income, they must forfeit a large portion of their means-tested transfers as their income rises. The rate of this marginal tax is significantly higher than the highest rates in income tax rate – 50 percent to 60 percent is common, and, if the loss of Medicaid is at stake, over 100 percent – making it difficult for a family to work itself out of poverty, and discouraging low income persons from supplementing their income by working.

As detailed by Van Parijs (1992, 2001) Widerquist (2001a, 2001b), proposals for BIG range from very small (Friedman, 1966) to so big as to be unachievable (Schutz, 1996). In the 1960s a number of economists, including three future Nobel Prize winners, proposed variants of BIG, which in those days was referred to as the Negative Income Tax (NIT). Milton Friedman (1966) advocated a very small NIT – a refund of unused income tax deductions – as a substitute for all other social welfare programs. James Tobin advocated a far more generous NIT – a universal tax credit or demogrant – as a substitute for only a limited set of existing programs. James Meade's proposal for Great Britain was similar to Tobin's. A fourth economist, Robert Lampman (1971), who unlike the other three specialized in income transfer policy, advocated a modest NIT not as a substitute for, but rather as an addition to, the existing set of income transfer programs. The range of generosity in today's proposals for a BIG is equally impressive. At the same time, there is little empirical evidence on the effects of variations in generosity on costs and poverty reduction.

Whether it is described as a demogrant, a guaranteed income, or one of a number of other labels, most advocates believe that BIG should be judged by the degree to which it reduces poverty. Surprisingly, however, there are few empirical estimates of the extent to which various BIG proposals reduce poverty. This chapter is designed to fill that gap. In the next section of the chapter, we describe the benefit structure and financing of four different BIG Plans. In sections three and four respectively, we describe the data and methodology and report our estimates of poverty reduction and costs. In section five, we discuss a few considerations for the optimal size of a BIG. The chapter ends with a brief summary and conclusion.

THE BIG PLANS

Benefit structure

The BIG alternatives examined in this simulation are designed to place a high percentage of families above the poverty threshold, whether the family includes a productive (working) adult or not. For families in which there are members who can work, the BIG amounts will be given to help them escape from poverty through their endeavors to work.

We simulate four different BIG plans that we have named as follows: Standard Plan, Children Plus Plan, Single-Parent Plus Plan, and the Adult Plus Plan. The first plan, the Standard Plan, provides a baseline from which the other plans depart. In the Standard Plan, all children up to age 18 receive a BIG of $2,175 per year; all adults between the age of 18 and 65 receive a $4,000 per year BIG. The elderly receive $8,000 or their social security payment. In all plans Old Age, Survivors, and Disability Insurance (OASDI) beneficiaries are held harmless, meaning that OASDI recipients receive either their OASDI benefit or BIG, whichever is higher. The benefit structure of the four plans are summarized succinctly in Table 8.1.

The BIG, in all plans, is taxable. The net gain for people with higher incomes is smaller than for people who are poor. For example, if a person pays a federal income tax rate of 40 percent, the net gain of the BIG of $4,000 is only $2,400.

The Children Plus, Adult Plus, and Single Parent Plus plans, respectively, focus higher benefits on children, prime-age adults, and single parents. Note from Table 8.1 that the Children Plus Plan not only raises the benefits per child from $2,175 to $4,000, but also lowers the benefit per adult from $4,000 to $3,150. Similarly, the Single Parent Plus Plan not only raises the benefit to a single parent from $4,000 to $6,000, but also raises the benefit to all children from $2,175 to $3,000, and lowers the benefit for all other adults to $3,000.

Financing of the BIG plans

Three of the four BIG plans are paid for solely by offsets from Old Age, Survivors, and Disability Insurance (OASDI) and the elimination of 115 other existing federal programs. The Adult Plus Plan, the most generous of the plans, requires additional taxation of all citizens amounting to slightly over 5 percent of gross income for all citizens. Table 8.2 illustrates how the Standard Plan is financed. In 1994, there

Table 8.1. *The Basic Income Guarantee Plans.*

Plan name	Benefits	Financing
Standard Plan	Elderly (E) $8,000; Adult (A) $4,000; Children (C) $2,175 OASDI kept harmless.	Offsets from OASDI. Elimination of 115 programs. Elimination of personal exemptions. Taxation of BIG benefits.
Children Plus Plan	E $8,000; A $3,150; C $4,000 OASDI kept harmless.	Offsets from OASDI. Elimination of 115 programs. Elimination of personal exemptions. Taxation of BIG benefits.
Single-Parent Plus Plan	E $8,000 First A with children $6,000 Other A $3,000 C $2,700 OASDI kept harmless.	Offsets from OASDI. Elimination of 115 programs. Elimination of personal exemptions. Taxation of BIG benefits.
Adult Plus Plan	E $8,000; A $6,000; C $2,000 OASDI kept harmless.	Offsets from OASDI. Elimination of 115 programs. Elimination of personal exemptions. Taxation of BIG benefits. Imposition of a federal contribution equal to a proportional tax rate of 0.0548.

were approximately 70 million children, 160 million non-aged adults, and 30 million aged adults. Thus, the gross costs of the Standard Plan equal 70 million times $2,175, plus 160 million times $4,000, plus 30 million times $8,000, or $1,032 billion. Making the BIG taxable and eliminating exemptions raises $170 and $118 billion in tax, reducing the net cost of the BIG to $743 billion.

As described above, recipients of OASDI receive either their existing OASDI benefits, or the BIG, whichever is higher. As of 1994,

Table 8.2. *Financing the BIG Plan.*

PROGRAM	1994 Budget (Million)
I. Gross costs of BIG	1,030,888
II. Financing	1,031,418
1. Revenue from taxing BIG	169,851
2. Eliminating Personal Exemptions	118,227
3. Offsets in Social Security: The amounts of Old Age, Survivors, and Disability Insurance ($312.84 billion) minus harmlessness costs of standard plan ($37.15 billion).	275,694
4. Elimination of Federal Programs	467,646
A. Tax Exemption/Exclusions	256,400
B. Direct Income Support Programs	89,845
C. Special Needs/Social Services	48,057
D. Housing	36,406
E. Business/Economic Development	14,883
F. Student Loans	9,033
G. Farm Subsidies/Price Supports	8,616
H. Employment Programs	4,406

OASDI beneficiaries received $313 billion. Because they can receive either the BIG or their OASDI benefit, but not both, most of the cost of the BIG for these beneficiaries is offset by existing OASDI benefits. Indeed, as Table 8.2 shows, all but $37 billion of the current costs of OASDI, or $276 billion, offset the costs of the BIG.

The last section of Table 8.2 contains a list of the eliminated programs. The budget numbers included in this part of the table are taken from one of two government-published records that reflect actual expenses: the 1993 Green Book or the 1995 Catalog of Federal Domestic Assistance. As indicated in Table 8.2, the total expenditures for the excluded programs were $467 billion in 1994, including $256 billion of Tax Expenditures programs, $90 billion of Direct Income Support Programs, $48 billion of Special Needs and Social Service Programs, $36 billion of Housing Subsidies, $14 billion of Business and Economic Development, $9 billion of Student Loans, $9 billion of Farm Subsidies and Price Supports, and $4 billion of Employment

Programs. A more detailed list of programs included in these broad categories is provided in Appendix A. The Adult Plus Plan requires additional financing equivalent to a proportional tax on all income of 0.0548 percentage points.

DATA AND METHODOLOGY

Micro-simulation models provide useful tools for analyzing the effects of proposed changes in government programs especially when the changes involve interactions among more than one government program, and behavioral responses such as decisions to work. Therefore, we use a micro-simulation model to estimate the effectiveness, first, of existing anti-poverty measures and, then, of four proposed BIG plans, in reducing poverty, decreasing the poverty gap, and redistributing income. The approach takes data on a large number of families and mimics the way that current and then alternative government programs would apply to each individual described in the records (Citro and Hanushek, 1991).

The micro-simulation model that we use does not incorporate behavioral changes that might result from changes in the transfer structure. For example, low-income mothers dependent on TANF would be encouraged to work because unlike TANF, their BIG would not be reduced if they worked. The effect on low-income men could go the other way. That is, to the extent that most such men are not now receiving benefits, BIG will provide them with more income and thereby increase their ability to work less if they so choose. Low-income men currently receiving benefits, like low-income mothers, will work more because unlike their current benefits, BIG would not be reduced if they earned more. BIG may also increase marriage. But none of these effects are captured by our micro-simulation. The no behavioral change micro-simulation that we employ measures the first round effects before anyone changes their behaviors. Some related micro-simulation work which incorporates changes in work effort finds that the first round effects on poverty and costs are very good estimates of the final total effects after taking account of changes in work (Meyer and Kim, 1998).

Using specific employment, income, and demographic data on each of the 63,756 families in the March 1995 Current Population Survey (CPS) sample, the micro-simulation replaces the reported level for 1994 of cash, in-kind and other programs, and tax benefits (including personal exemptions) for each family in the sample with a BIG. In a simplistic example, if a family of three receives AFDC, Food Stamps, and a housing subsidy, the income from these benefits would be sub-tracted from their current total income and replaced, in the Standard Plan, with $4,000 for the adult and $2,175 for each child for a total of an $8,350 BIG to this family. Each family in the sample is treated indi-vidually, and the data is maintained as part of the total. This is a far more exacting way of examining the effects of policy on poverty than techniques based on aggregate information.

Since we first ran these simulations, there have been significant changes in the welfare laws, the way the welfare benefits are funded, and the extent to which people participate in the program. Changes in welfare benefits were accompanied by changes in child-care benefits and job training programs. Also, use of the EITC increased as more people went to work in the late-1990s and the Balanced Budget Act of 1997 improved its enforcement; and, the tax laws have changed. Despite these numerous shifts, we have chosen to stay with the original 1995 data. If we had used a later year in the 1990s, we would expect that the simulation results might show smaller losses at the bottom, however we do not think that the results would be dramati-cally different for a number of reasons. The programs that have changed are relatively small programs; changes in some programs are offset by changes in others (e.g., while TANF recipients have decreased, EITC recipients have increased); and, many recent tax changes are set for the future. Additionally, remaining with the 1995 data provides more conservative estimates of the benefits of the BIG simulations. Data from 2000, at the peak of the business cycle, would likely result in overestimating how well the BIG plans would do in more typical times.

We used a six-step procedure in each simulation, except for the Adult Plus Plan in which a seventh was added. The steps of the micro-simulation model are:

1. Select representative population database, 1995 March CPS
2. Reconcile the microdata from the CPS with administrative record data
3. Impute the value of the in-kind and other programs
4. Calculate the value of the current system (post-transfer and post-tax income plus in-kind and imputed benefits) from pre-transfer and pretax income
5. Eliminate the current system
6. Simulate the BIG Plans
7. For Adult Plus Plan: add in the financing of the system

Step 1: Select representative population database

This simulation is based on the 1995 March CPS. The CPS, conducted by the US Bureau of the Census, is a monthly cross-sectional survey of a large sample of the US population. In the 1995 survey, CPS interviewed 63,756 families, which included 149,642 people. This sample is drawn from the US population of 69 million families or 262 million people. The survey contains data on labor force status and income for people aged 15 and older. Data collected for the basic CPS include demographic characteristics such as age, gender, race, marital status and educational attainment; and, labor force participation data such as usual weekly earnings, number of hours worked, and type of work. Annually, in March, supplemental employment and income-related data are collected including use of public and private transfer programs and receipt of non-cash benefits, such as food stamps. Income-related data is based upon income from the previous year.

Step 2: Reconcile the microdata (CPS) with administrative record data

For the AFDC and Food Stamps programs, for example, discrepancies were noted in both the number of recipients and the aggregate costs between the data from the CPS and the administrative data recorded in the 1996 Green Book and the 1995 Catalogue of Federal Domestic Programs. We therefore reconciled the data using the eligibility criteria described in the 1996 Green Book. Discrepancies are due, we believe, to the under-reporting of the receipt of benefits. Under-reporting occurs when recipients do not report the benefit at all, or report an amount lower than the actual amount of the benefit received. It may be the result of the stigma attached to receiving income-tested benefits.

If the number of recipients reported in CPS data was less than the number reported in the 1996 Green Book, we examined the CPS data to determine how many people who were eligible to receive the benefit did not report receiving it. If the number of recipients reporting the benefit plus the number of eligible people not reporting was equal to or slightly higher than the number reported in the administrative data, we assumed conformity. CPS data count the number of recipients during the previous year; Green Book data are based on the average monthly recipients. We expected, therefore, that the imputed CPS data would be somewhat higher than Green Book data. See Appendix B, p. 169, for additional detail on other programs.

Step 3: Allocate the value of the in-kind and other programs to the CPS data

The value of most in-kind programs and some other programs is not included in the CPS data. We, therefore, estimated the value of the benefits from these programs. This value was then added to each family's post-transfer and post-tax income to get the income of post-transfer, post-tax, and in-kind and imputed benefits. There are two parts to the calculation of in-kind and other programs:

(1) Determine the amount of in-kind and other program benefits that each family is likely to receive based on the budgeted amount. The allocation is based on the incidence assumption of each program as indicated in Column 2 of Appendix A (p. 163). Six different allocation methods were assumed because of the different methods that the programs use to distribute funds. Where CPS is indicated in the incidence assumption column of an in-kind benefit, the allocation method is described in Appendix B.

(2) Discount the amount calculated in the first step by a percentage to reflect the actual value of the benefit received. This reflects a discount for administrative costs and the fact that the actual value of in-kind benefits and services is lower than the value of cash. The Food Stamps Program in 1993 was $26 billion, of which $3.2 billion were for administration costs. In addition, in-kind benefits or services are worth less to recipients than cash because their use is restricted. Therefore, the aggregated value of food stamps for these recipients is less than $22.8 billion. To determine what percentage would show up in the family income of recipients, we estimated the value of the in-kind and other programs at three levels: 100 percent, 75 percent, and 50 percent (see Table 8.3). The 100 percent and 50 percent assumptions allowed us to bracket the high and low projections respectively. We used the 75 percent assumption, the intermediate projection, for the microsimulations believing that this most accurately reflected the actual benefit.

Step 4: Calculate the value of the current system (post-transfer and post-tax income plus in-kind and imputed benefits) from pre-transfer and pre-tax income

The family income presented in the CPS data reflects all cash transfers, without incorporating tax liability. This is the post-transfer, pre-tax income. In this step, we first calculate the pre-transfer, pre-tax income by subtracting all the cash-transfer benefits. Then, each family's tax liability for federal income tax, earned income tax credit (EITC), and payroll tax is deducted from the post-transfer, pre-tax income. We then distribute the in-kind benefits and other program benefits into post-tax, post-transfer income. This gives us the current system, each family's post-transfer, post-tax income plus in-kind and imputed benefits at the 100 percent, 75 percent, and 50 percent levels.

Step 5: Eliminate the current system

In this step, we removed all the benefits of the current system from family income. We started by removing in-kind benefits and benefits from other programs from the current system income at the 75 percent assumption. Then, we took away the tax exemptions and exclusions. Since the cash-transfer benefits were included in the CPS data, we deducted the value of the benefit at the micro level directly, using CPS data.

Step 6: Simulate the BIG plans

In this step, we allotted the BIG benefits to each person. The criteria to determine the amount of BIG was based on age and family status, that is, whether you are an adult in a one- or a two-parent family. Recipients of OASDI are treated differentially depending on whether the BIG amounts exceed their OASDI benefits.

Step 7 (for the Adult Plus Plan): add in the financing of the system

In the Adult Plus Plan, the cost of the BIG exceeded the cost of the current system by $233 billion. In order to finance this system, an increase in income tax rates of 0.0548 is imposed.

We make a number of assumptions that merit further examination. For example, the values attributed to in-kind benefits may vary from the actual value of these benefits.

EFFECTS OF BIG ON POVERTY AND INCOME DISTRITUION

To place our results for poverty reduction in historical perspective, we begin this section with a brief review of the recent trend in US social welfare expenditures and poverty rates. Then we present our simulation estimates of the effects of various BIG proposals on poverty, and the vertical and horizontal distribution of income.

The US context

After a sharp drop between 1959 and 1969, when the economy boomed and social spending increased substantially, the US poverty rate reached a low point of 11.1 percent in 1973 and leveled off through the decade (Danziger, Sandifur, and Weinberg, 1994). Social spending continued to grow during the 1970s even as the economy slowed, so that the poverty rate was kept in check (Burtless, 1994). The rate began climbing again in the 1980s and into the 1990s (US Bureau of the Census, 1995) as real wages of low-income people continued to fall, real government social spending declined, especially in programs directed at the poor, and the number of female-headed single-parent families increased (Burtless, 1994).

In 1994, the year we use as the point of departure for our simulations, the poverty threshold for a family of four was $15,141[1] and the percentage of people living in poverty was as high as in the late 1960s. The poverty gap – the amount by which the income of a poor family falls below the poverty line – for the median poor family had increased from about $1,300 to over $5,000, in 1990 dollars (Danziger and Weinberg, 1994). And the distribution of wealth in the US had become increasingly concentrated among the wealthiest Americans (Danziger and Weinberg, 1994). In 1994, the poverty rate after accounting for cash transfers was 14.4 percent for adults, 21.2 percent for children and 11.7 percent for the elderly, with female-headed single-parent families and minority households struggling disproportionately.

As the economy strengthened in the mid-1990s, the poverty rate peaked and then began to decline. By 2000, the percentage of people living in poverty had declined to 11 percent from its high of 15 percent in 1994; and, the poverty rate for children had declined to 16.2 percent after being as high as 22 percent in the mid-1990s. The poverty threshold in 2000 was $17,603.

The effect of BIG on poverty

All four BIG plans reduce the aggregate poverty rate and the aggregate poverty gap. This is true no matter which assumption is made about the value of in-kind benefits to recipients. In a few cases, some subgroups are made worse off, if we assume that the worth of in-kind benefits to recipients is 100 percent of its cost to taxpayers. This assumption is clearly false. Recipients gain nothing from administrative costs. We confine the rest of the comparisons to the assumption that recipients value the benefits at only 75 percent of cost. We believe that to be the most scientifically accurate of the assumptions.

Table 8.3. *The effects of the current tax transfer system and BIG plans on poverty.*

	Poverty rate of persons	Poverty rate of children	Poverty rate of elderly	Poverty gap (billion)
Pre-transfer[1], Pre-tax[2]	0.2243	0.2572	0.5038	189.68
Post-transfer, Pre-tax	0.1437	0.2170	0.1159	79.75
Post-transfer, Post-tax	0.1441	0.2121	0.1166	78.06
Current system[3] (100%)	0.0859	0.1206	0.0588	34.05
Current system[4] (75%)	0.1001	0.1455	0.0682	42.15
Current system[5] (50%)	0.1168	0.1729	0.0817	52.27
BIG Plans				
Standard Plan[6]	0.0783	0.1347	0.0029	28.97
Child Plus Plan[7]	0.0605	0.0809	0.0000	23.66
Single Parent Plus Plan[8]	0.0681	0.1026	0.0013	25.25
Adult Plus Plan[9]	0.0581	0.1128	0.0030	17.42

Notes:

1. Pre-transfer: Before any Cash Transfer (including General Assistance) Programs.

2. Pre-tax: Before Federal Income Tax, Payroll Tax, and Earned Income Tax Credit.

3. Current system: Post-transfer, Post-tax, and in-kind and all other programs except tax expenditures. The assumption is that the actual value of benefits from in-kind and other programs is 100 percent of face value of the benefit.

4. Same as 3, but the assumption is 75 percent of the face value.

5. Same as 3, but the assumption is 50 percent of the face value.

6. Standard Plan: Elderly $8,000, Adult $4,000, and Child $2,175 per year. OASDI kept harmless, i.e., people receive the BIG or OASDI, whichever is higher.

7. Child Plus Plan: Elderly $8,000, Adult $3,150, and Child $4,000 per year. OASDI kept harmless.

8. Single Parent Plus Plan: Elderly $8,000, First Adult with children $6,000, other adult $3,000, and Child $2,700 per year. OASDI kept harmless.

9. Adult Plus: Elderly $8,000, Adult $6,000, and Child $2,000 per year. OASDI kept harmless. Since the plan's cost exceeded the eliminated amounts by $233 billion, the authors finance it through a proportional tax rate of 0.0548.

All plans provide the elderly with an $8,000 benefit; this immediately raises all recipients above the poverty line. Hence, aged poverty rates fall to 0.3 percent or less.

The Adult Plus Plan does the best job of reducing the overall poverty rate – from 10 percent to under 6 percent. These are very significant improvements. Similarly, the poverty gap would be cut by more than half – from $42 billion to $17 billion. It is not surprising that the Adult Plus Plan does the best job of combating poverty. It is the most expensive to finance.

The Child Plus Plan, which requires the same financing as the Standard Plan, does virtually as good a job as the Adult Plus Plan in reducing overall poverty rates and nearly as well in reducing the overall poverty gap. The Child Plus Plan also does a better job of reducing child poverty down to 8 percent as compared to 11 percent for the Adult Plus Plan. Furthermore, the child plus plan does more to reduce poverty than the single parent plus plan. If we enriched the financing of the Child Plus Plan by the same 5 percent of taxable income that was done for the Adult Plus Plan and targeted all the extra funds on children, child poverty could be nearly wiped out.

The Effect on the vertical distribution of income

The redistribution effect of the current system on income shares is significant in comparison to the pre-transfer, pretax system. This is particularly true in the lowest and highest quintiles. Before transfer and tax, the lowest 20 percent of earners received less than 1 percent of the income; the highest received 50 percent. The current system raises the lowest quintile to 5 percent and reduces the highest quintile to 43 percent.

As indicated in Table 8.4, all of the BIG plans favor the first three quintiles. However, the degree of additional redistribution is small compared to the redistribution already achieved by the current system – less than a 1 percentage point increase in the first quintile in almost all cases. (The Adult Plus Plan is slightly higher at 1.24 percent.) In comparison, the two highest quintiles do not benefit under the BIG plan. The fourth quintile receives a slightly higher share (never more than 0.2 percent.) The highest quintile receives a lower portion. Under the Adult Plus Plan, in which we impose a tax on the states which is assumed to be equivalent to a proportional income tax on individuals, the income share in the highest quintile decreases more than 2 percent.

Table 8.4. *The effects of the current tax transfer system and BIG plans on the vertical income distribution.*

	1st Quintile	2nd Quintile	3rd Quintile	4th Quintile	5th Quintile
Pre-transfer, pre-tax	0.0085	0.0716	0.1530	0.2632	0.5038
Current system[1]	0.0511	0.1060	0.1648	0.2514	0.4267
BIG plans					
Standard Plan	0.0544	0.1086	0.1709	0.2526	0.4135
Child Plus Plan	0.0541	0.1084	0.1709	0.2533	0.4133
Single Parent	0.0539	0.1077	0.1717	0.2533	0.4134
Plus Plan					
Adult Plus Plan	0.0590	0.1118	0.1743	0.2531	0.4018

Note:
1. Current System: Post-transfer, post-tax, and post-imputation of in-kind and all other programs except tax expenditures, using the assumption that actual value of in-kind and other program benefits is 75 percent of face value.

The effect on the horizontal distribution of income

Table 8.5 presents the results of BIG plans on horizontal distribution of income. Perhaps the most striking aspect of Table 8.5 is the large percentage of families in the first four income quintiles who experience either significant increases or decreases in their incomes. In the standard plan, for example, over 80 percent of families in the bottom quintile gain or lose 10 percent or more, and the figures for the next three quintiles are 71 percent, 61 percent, and 46 percent. Note that within the first three quintiles, while more families gain than lose, a large minority of families in these quintiles experience significant losses. The BIG plans redistribute a lot of money even within quintiles because they are much less discriminatory than the current mix of programs.

Table 8.5. *The effects of the current tax transfer system and BIG plans on the horizontal income distribution.*

	1st Quintile	2nd Quintile	3rd Quintile	4th Quintile	5th Quintile
CURRENT SYSTEM					
Percentage of Winners[1]	0.7495	0.5317	0.2913	0.1450	0.0477
Percentage of Losers[1]	0.0725	0.3073	0.5500	0.7541	0.8482
Winners Mean Increase	5,883	9,512	11,503	12,441	19,723
Losers Mean Decrease	1,597	3,009	5,093	8,945	22,695
BIG PLANS					
Standard Plan					
Percentage of Winners	0.4706	0.4743	0.4358	0.3702	0.0578
Percentage of Losers	0.3601	0.2472	0.1702	0.0927	0.0606
Winners' Mean Increase	2,557	3,269	5,395	6,227	7,683
Losers' Mean Decrease	3,164	4,627	7,245	10,875	15,745
Child Plus Plan					
Percentage of Winners	0.4716	0.3106	0.4078	0.3752	0.1005
Percentage of Losers	0.3399	0.2550	0.1757	0.0968	0.0628
Winners' Mean Increase	2,241	4,233	5,816	7,638	7,880
Losers' Mean Decrease	3,033	4,547	7,350	10,797	15,676
Single Parent Plus Plan					
Percentage of Winners	0.4757	0.3050	0.4005	0.3995	0.0789
Percentage of Losers	0.3376	0.2555	0.1771	0.0991	0.0633
Winners' Mean Increase	2,116	4,352	6,059	7,291	7,266
Losers' Mean Decrease	2,978	4,559	7,340	10,674	15,660
Adult Plus Plan					
Percentage of Winners	0.4647	0.6014	0.4688	0.4445	0.0881
Percentage of Losers	0.3872	0.2390	0.1518	0.0899	0.0803
Winners' Mean Increase	3,551	3,791	6,603	7,114	8,624
Losers' Mean Decrease	3,217	5,737	9,202	12,605	16,864

Note:
Winners or losers are those with 10 percent more or less income than with the previous income base. The income base of current system is pretransfer and pretax, while the base of BIG plan is the current system.

HOW BIG SHOULD BIG BE?

With one exception, the plans simulated in this proposal are modest sized BIGs. All are financed from the elimination of other domestic programs and tax expenditures. The Adult Plus Plan requires an additional 5.5 percentage points in income tax rates to finance, but achieves more poverty reduction. Non-aged adult benefits could be raised another $2000 to equal the aged benefit of $8000 at an additional cost of $320 billion, or 5.7 percentage points of additional income taxation. Why stop with modest programs? Why not have a much bigger BIG?

There are several answers. First, BIG is not the only desirable social welfare program. Universal Education and health care are two achievements of the welfare state that few BIG advocates would (or should) quarrel with. Each increases human capital and hence the productivity of citizens more than any cash benefit can hope to achieve. Though the US pioneered the provision of free public education and the rest of advanced industrialized nations did not catch up in secondary education until after World War II, a few countries have surpassed the US in very early childhood education. Sweden and France, for example, have nearly universal provision of child care. For the US to provide free universal child care would cost around $120 billion (Bergmann, 2002). Other BIG advocates may want to add a universal wealth transfer to their menu of desired reforms (Haveman, 1988; Ackerman and Alstott, 1999). Ackerman and Alstott estimate that an $80,000 stake for all adults reaching age 18 would cost about $268 billion annually. Finally, some of the programs eliminated in our simulations are undoubtedly worth keeping, because for each dollar spent they produce more than one dollar's worth of benefits. For example, at a cost of about $50 billion, we could redesign a less expensive Unemployment Insurance System and retain Head Start, WIC, Child Care, Student Loans, and Job-Training Programs. This $50 billion shortfall could be financed either by reductions in the BIG of under $200 per person or by increased taxes. Other readers may want to retain other programs. For this reason, we encourage each reader to review the list of programs in Appendix A.

Second, in addition to social welfare programs, government provides law and order, defense, and transportation and communication infrastructure. These public goods must be financed as well as BIG and other social welfare programs. If the aggregate tax rate becomes too high, incentives will be blunted and productivity and growth will suffer.

Third, as a general matter in public finance, it is a mistake to rely too heavily on any single instrument – be it a tax or a transfer. Every tax and transfer has adverse incentives. In general the adverse effects grow more than proportionally with the size of the tax or benefit. Thus while a little or modest BIG is in our judgment highly desirable, a very big BIG is not desirable. Financing a very big BIG would require high marginal tax rates on earnings and other sources of income which will discourage work in the legitimate labor market for the bulk of the population, much like our current welfare programs discourage legitimate work amongst our poorest citizens.

The reader will note the similarity of the arguments made in this section to those made by Bergmann in her paper. We agree that the left in the US should not advocate BIG as a substitute for other advances in the welfare state such as universal health care and child care. Where we disagree is on the utility of a small-to-modest BIG as a substitute for many existing programs, including partial substitution and restructuring of social insurance programs (see Garfinkel, 1983) and as a complement to universal systems of health, education, and child care, and social insurance.

SUMMARY AND CONCLUSION

The BIG plans we simulate decrease poverty more effectively than the current system. This highlights the fact that some of the benefits in the current system, such as tax expenditures favor the rich instead of the poor or the middle class. All the BIG plans redistribute income from the highest quintiles to the lower ones. BIG not only more equitably distributes income among the quintiles, but the distribution of benefits is more equitable within the quintiles, particularly for people in the first quintile.

The different BIG plans have different effects on poverty and income distribution. Among them, the Adult Plus Plan is the most redistributive of the plans. It decreases the poverty rate of persons most significantly, and favors the first three quintiles, instead of only the first quintile. The Adult Plus Plan, however, is not self-financing. The equivalent of a proportional tax on income of 0.0548 is required to finance the plan. Thus, losers' mean decreases in the Adult Plus Plan are the highest among the plans. In contrast the Children Plus and the Single-Parent Plus Plans are self-financing and more focused on children and the first quintile. The disadvantage of the Children Plus Plan is that it may be too pronatalist. Similarly, the Single Parent Plus Plan, by rewarding single parenthood, may encourage its growth.

If the Single Parent Plus Plan is achieved via a child support assurance system, however, it will do more good at less cost and will have smaller effects on single parenthood than simply increasing benefits for all single parents (Garfinkel, 1992). These refinements, however, should not obscure the basic lesson. A small to modest BIG is a good fundamental building block for the modern welfare state.

Because other welfare state programs and other government functions are also valuable and because a very large BIG would have undesirable incentive effects, a small to modest BIG is preferable to a big BIG.

NOTE

1   The poverty threshold is a measure "developed in the early 1960s as an indicator of the number and proportion of people with inadequate family incomes for needed consumption of food and other goods and services" (Citro and Michael, 1995). It is based on the assumption that an adequate family income is three times the cost of the minimum diet. The poverty threshold is adjusted for family size and, for some family types, it is adjusted based on the age of the head of the household. The current method of calculating the poverty threshold does not incorporate the value of in-kind benefits, certain expenses incurred by families such as child care, or regional differences in cost of living. The poverty threshold is also infrequently reassessed and does not take into account current economic conditions. Although using three times the minimum food budget as a standard, when the poverty rate was first developed, raised people out of poverty, under current conditions in which housing costs are the most significant part of family budgets, the food standard is questionable.

REFERENCES

Ackerman, B. and Alstott, A. 2001. "Why Stakeholding?," mimeo.
— 1999. *The Stakeholder Society.* New Haven, CT: Yale University Press.
Bergmann, Barbara. 2002. "A Swedish-Style Welfare State Or Basic Income: Which should have priority?," mimeo.
Burtless, G. 1994. Public spending on the poor: Historical trends and economic limits," in S. H. Danziger, G. D. Sandifur, D. H. Weinberg, eds, *Confronting poverty: Prescriptions for change.* Cambridge, MA: Harvard University Press, pp. 51–84.
Catalogue of Federal Domestic Assistance. 1995. Washington, D.C.: Office of Management and Budget and the General Services Administration.
Citro, C. F. and Hanushek, E. A. eds. 1991. *Improving information for social policy decisions: the uses of microsimulations modeling,* Vol. 1. Review

and Recommendations. Washington, D.C.: National Academy Press.

Citro, C. F. and Michael, R. T. eds. 1995. *Measuring Poverty: A new approach.* Washington, D.C.: National Academy Press.

Committee on Ways and Means US House of Representatives. 1993,1994, and 1996. Overview of Entitlement programs: Green book. Washington, D.C.: Government Printing Office.

Danziger, S. H., Sandifur, G. D., and Weinberg, D. H. 1994. Introduction. In S. H. Danziger, G. D. Sandifur, D. H. Weinberg, eds, *Confronting poverty: Prescriptions for change.* Cambridge, MA: Harvard University Press, (pp. 1–19).

Danziger, S. H. and Weinberg, D. H. 1994. The historical record: Trends in family income, inequality, and poverty. In S. H. Danziger, G. D. Sandifur, D. H. Weinberg eds, *Confronting poverty: Prescriptions for change.* Cambridge, MA: Harvard University Press, (pp. 18–50).

Friedman, Milton. 1966. "The case for the negative income tax: a view from the right," In *Issues of American Public Policy* (J.H. Bunzel ed.), Englewood Cliffs (NJ): Prentice-Hall, 1968, pp. 111–120.

Garfinkel, Irwin. 1996. "Economic Security for Children: From means testings and bifurcation to universality," In I. Garfinkel, S. McLanahan, and J.L. Hochschild eds, *Social polices for children.* Washington, DC: The Brookings Institution, pp. 33–82.

— 1992. *Assuring child support.* New York: Russell Sage Foundation.

— 1983. "The role of universal demogrant and child support in social security reform: An essay in honor of George F. Rohrlich," *International Journal of Social Economics*, Vol. 10, No. 6/7, 12–20.

— ed. 1982. *Income tested transfer programs: The case for and against.* New York: Academic Press.

— 1979. "Welfare reform: A new and old view," *The Journal of the Institute for Socioeconomic Studies*, Vol. IV, No. 4.

Greene, L.M. 1998. *The National Tax Rebate: A New America with Less Government.* Washington/DC: Regnery Publishing Inc.

Haveman, Robert H. 1988. *Starting Even. An Equal Opportunity Program to Combat the Nation's New Poverty.* New York and London: Simon and Schuster.

Lampman, Robert J. 1971. *Ends and Means of Reducing Income Poverty.* Chicago: Markham.

Long, Sharon. 1986. "Food stamp research: Results from the Income Survey Development Program and the promise of the survey on income and program participation," Washington, DC: US Dept. of Agriculture, Food and Nutrition Service, Office of Analysis and Evaluation.

Meyer, Daniel R. and Rebecca Yeun-Hee Kim. 1998. "Incorporating Labor Supply Responses into the Estimated Effects of an Assured Child Support

Benefit," *Journal of Family Issues*, 19:534–55.

Schutz, Robert R. 1996. *The $30,000 Solution: A guaranteed annual income for every American.* Santa Barbara: Fithian Press.

US Bureau of the Census. 1995. Current Population Reports, Series P23-189: Population Profile of the United States. Washington, D.C.: Government Printing Office.

Van Parijs, Philippe ed. 1992. *Arguing for Basic Income: Ethical Foundations for a Radical Reform.* New York: Verso.

— 2001. "Basic Income: A Simple and Powerful Idea for the 21st Century," mimeo.

Widerquist, Karl. 2001a. "Perspectives on the Guaranteed Income, part I," *Journal of Economic Issues*, 35 (3): 749–57.

— (2001b). "Perspectives on the Guaranteed Income, part II," *Journal of Economic Issues*, 35 (4): 1019–30.

Widerquist, Karl and Lewis, Michael A. 1997. "An Efficiency Argument for the Guaranteed Income," The Jerome Levy Economics Institute Working Paper No. 212.

APPENDIX A: Detailed List of Programs that Offset Costs or are Eliminated: Budget Costs and Assumptions about their Incidence.

PROGRAM	1994 Budget (million)	Incidence assumption
I. Offsets in Social Security	275,694	CPS[1]
The amounts of Old Age, Survivors, and Disability Insurance ($312.84 billion) minus harmlessness costs of standard plan ($37.15 billion).		
II. Elimination of Federal Programs		
A. *Tax Exemption/Exclusions*		
Exc. of Pension Contribution & Earning	55,300	Note[2]
Deductibility of Mortgage Interest	45,500	Note[3]
Exc. Employer Contri. for Med. Care & Insurance Premiums	36,700	Note[2]
Exc. of Soc. Sec. & RR Benefits	28,000	Note[4]
Deduct. of property tax on Owner-occupied Housing	13,700	Note[3]
Exc. of Medicare Benefit	13,100	Note[5]
Deferral on Sale of Principal Residence	14,300	Note[3]
EITC	12,200	Note[6]
Tax Expenditure related to Employment	7,200	Note[2]
Individual Retirement Plans	6,200	Note[2]
Tax Expend. Related to Elderly & Disabled	5,900	Note[7]
Exc. on Sale of Resid. of person 55 & over	4,700	Note[8]
Deductibility of Medical Expense	3,500	Note[2]
Keogh Plans	3,000	Note[2]
Exc. of Interest on Bonds for Owner-Occupied and Rental Housing	2,800	Note[3]
Depreciation of Rental Housing in Excess of Alternative System	1,500	Note[3]
Credit for Child Medical Insurance Prem.	1,300	Note[2]
Low-Income Housing Tax Credit	1,500	PP
Subtotal	**256,400**	

(Cont'd.)

PROGRAM	1994 Budget (million)	Incidence assumption
B. *Direct Income Support Programs*		
Unemployment Insurance	27,274	CPS
Public Assistance (AFDC and	26,612	CPS
General Assistance)[14]		
SSI[15]		24,460
CPS		
SSI Administration costs[15]	3,695	GI[9]
Public Assistance Administration costs[15]	3,282	GI
Unemploy. Insurance Administration costs[15]	2,485	GI
Low Inc. Energy Asst.	1,737	CPS
Weatherization Asst.	206	CPS
Indian Gen Asst.	84	PP
Soc. Sec. Res. & Dev.	10	GH[10]
Subtotal	**89,845**	
C. *Special Needs/Social Services*		
Food Stamps	24,434	CPS
Food Stamps Administration costs[15]	3,665	GI
School Lunches	4,350	CPS
Head Start	3,325	CPS
Title XX - Social Service	2,807	PCP[11]
WIC	2,480	CPS
Child & Adult Care Food Prog.	1,355	PCP & PEP[12]
Various Food Programs	104	PP
School Breakfasts	958	CPS
Child Care Block Grant	892	PCP
Spec. Programs for the Aging	725	PEP
Empowerment Zones	640	GI
Comm. Serv. Block Grant	396	GH
Corp. for Nat. & Community Service	348	GH
At Risk Child Care	275	PCP
Summer Food Program	243	CPS
Emer. Comm. Serv. for Homeless	198	PP[13]
Nutrition Programs for the Elderly	149	PEP
Food Donation	118	PP
State Admin. Expenses for Child Nutrition	86	CPS
Emer. Food Asst.	80	PP

PROGRAM	1994 Budget (million)	Incidence assumption
C. *Special Needs/Social Services*		
Indian Child & Native American Programs	74	PCP
Refugee Assistance	62	PP
Family Preservation	59	PCP
CSBG Discretionary, Food & Demo	56	PP
Comprehensive Child Dev. Center	46	GH
Food for Soup Kitchens	40	PP
Runaway & Homeless Youth	36	PCP
School Milk Program	19	CPS
Social Service Research & Demo	13	PCP
Transitional Living for Homeless Youth	12	PCP
Fam. Support Ctr/Gateway	7	PCP
WIC Farmers Marketing Nutrition Program	5	PCP
Subtotal	**48,057**	
D. *Housing*		
S.8 Vouchers	14,576	CPS
Off. of Policy & Research	7,506	GH
Low Income Hsng Asst. (S.8)	5,158	CPS
Comm. Dev. Block Grant	3,003	PP
HOME	1,275	CPS
CDBG/States	1,232	GH
Supportive Housing for the Elderly	1,162	PEP
Pres. of Affordable Hsng	398	PP
Supportive Housing/Disabled	395	PP
Elderly Home Equity Conversion Mortgage	347	PEP
Shelter Plus	266	PP
Public & Indian Housing	263	GH
Supportive Housing	150	PP
Operating Assistance for Troubled Projects	136	PP
Emergency Shelter Grants	115	PP
S.8 Pension Fund Demo	100	PP
HOPWA	100	PP
Hope 1, Hope 2, and Hope 3	92	PP
Small Cities	54	PP
Youthbuild	40	PP

(Cont'd.)

PROGRAM	1994 Budget (million)	Incidence assumption
D. Housing		
Congregate Housing for the elderly	22	PEP
Housing Counseling Asst.	10	GH
Historically Black Colleges and University	6	GH
Subtotal	**36,406**	
E. Business/Economic Development		
Small Business Admin	14,568	GI
Appalacian Programs	213	GI
Overseas Private Investment	75	GI
TVA Eco. Dev.	18	GI
Comm. Asst. Prog. (Flood Insurance)	4	GI
Indian Business Dev.	3	GI
CD Revolving Loan Program	2	GI
Subtotal	**14,883**	
F. Student Loans		
Pell Grants	6,424	GH
Vocational Ed. Grants	955	PCP
Fed. Work Study	620	PP
Fed. Sup. Ed. Opty Grants	585	PP
Upward Bound	162	PP
Student Support Services	140	PP
State Student Incentive Grants	72	GH
Voc. Ed./Consumer & Homemaking	33	GH
Indian Higher Ed. Grants	29	PP
Voc. Ed./State Councils	9	GH
Legal Training/Disadvantaged	2	GH
College Asst./Migrant	2	GH
Subtotal	**9,033**	
G. Farm Subsidies/Price Supports		
Conservation Reserve Prog.	1,735	CPS
Wheat Stabilization	1,692	CPS
Free Grain Stabilization	1,538	CPS

PROGRAM	1994 Budget (million)	Incidence assumption
G. Farm Subsidies/Price Supports		
Commodity Loans & Purchase	1,524	CPS
Cotton Stabilization	1,323	CPS
Rice Stabilization	559	CPS
Wool & Mohair	201	CPS
Emergency Conservation	29	CPS
Farmer Owned Reserve Prog.	12	CPS
Small Farmer Outreach Trng	3	CPS
Subtotal	**8,616**	
H. Employment Programs		
JTPA	3,505	CPS
JOBS	872	CPS
Apprentice Trng Adv. Serv.	17	CPS
Emp. & Trng R&D	12	CPS
Subtotal	**4,406**	
Total programs can be eliminated	**743,340**	
Total programs can be eliminated (except OA and SSI)	**522,449**	

Notes:

1. CPS (Current Population Survey): The expenditure is distributed by micro level data.

2. The tax expenditure is allocated by the ratios of third party health care benefits according to income levels, as expressed in Table B1 in Irwin Garfinkel (1996).

3. The tax expenditure is allocated by the ratios of mortgage and tax credit according to income levels, as expressed in Table B1 in Irwin Garfinkel (1996).

4. The tax expenditure is allocated by the proportion of the Social Security and Railroad Retirement benefits received within each household.

5. The tax expenditure is allocated by the criteria of receipt or not of Medicare.

6. The tax expenditure is allocated by the formula of EITC.

7. The tax expenditure is allocated to subjects who are elderly or disabled in proportion to their income.

8. The tax expenditure is allocated to subjects 55 years old or over using ratios of mortgage and tax credit according to income levels, as expressed in Table B1 in Irwin Garfinkel (1996).

9. GI (General Expenditure related to Income): One-half of the expenditure is distributed equally to each family and the other one-half expenditure is distributed by the income portion of the family.

10. GH (General Expenditure related to Household): The expenditure is distributed equally to each household.

11. PCP (Program related to Child and Poverty): One-half of the expenditure is distributed equally to each poor household (below poverty) with child, the other one-half expenditure is equally allotted to families with child between one and two times poverty line.

12. PEP (Program related to Elderly and Poverty): One-half of the expenditure is distributed equally to each poor household (below poverty) with the elderly, the other one-half expenditure is equally allotted to families with the elderly between one and two times poverty line.

13. PP (Program related to Poverty): The 40 percent of the expenditure distributed to the families below ½ poverty level, the 35 percent expenditure to the families over ½ but below poverty level, and the other 25 percent expenditure to the families over poverty but below 1.5 poverty level.

14. Public Assistance, including AFDC and General Assistance, counted as two programs.

15. Program benefits and administration costs counted as one program, including SSI, Food Stamp, Unemployment Insurance, and Public Assistance programs.

APPENDIX B: Differences in and Reconciliation of Administrative Reports and CPS Reports on Expenditures and Recipients.

Program(s)	Admin Expend (billion)*	CPS Expend (billion)	Admin Number Recipient (million)#	CPS Number Recipient (million)	Avg Benefit/ Household	Imputation Assumption of Recipients	Imputation Assumptions for Benefits
OASDI: Old Age, Survivors, and Disability Insurance	312.88 billion (b) 273.49 b					Use the administrative numbers since the CPS data is somewhat skewed because some of the recipients are in institutions and therefore are not available to survey. (1994 Green Book, pp. 890–1)	
SSI	24.46 b	17.74 b				Same as OASDI.	
AFDC	22.79 b	16.49 b	5.04 million (m)	3.91 m		All eligible single mothers with family income lower than the government-guaranteed income are assumed to participate.	After participant imputation, the aggregate number matches the administrative data. Participant imputation results in 1.51 m recipients adding 6.3 b to the CPS benefit.

Program(s)	Admin Expend (billion)*	CPS Expend (billion)	Admin Number Recipient (million)#	CPS Number Recipient (million)	Avg Benefit/ Household	Imputation Assumption of Recipients	Imputation Assumptions for Benefits
Food Stamps	24.43 b	17.70 b	10.24 households (hh)			In addition to recipients reported in CPS, assume that families with incomes < 30% of the poverty line have an 80 percent probability of participation; families with inc. between 30-60 percent of poverty line have 50% participation; families with income 60-100% of poverty line have a 20% participation rate; and, all families eligible but over the poverty line reported (Long, 1986).	After participant imputation, the aggregate number matches the administrative data.

Program(s)	Admin Expend (billion)*	CPS Expend (billion)	Admin Number Recipient (million)#	CPS Number Recipient (million)	Avg Benefit/Household	Imputation Assumption of Recipients	Imputation Assumptions for Benefits
Housing: S8, Low Income Hsng Asst, and HOME	$21.009 b			5.36 m hh	$3,919		Assume total program benefits of housing are equally distributed to each household participating in program.
Energy Assistance: Includes weatherization assistance	$1.943 b		5.2 m hh	3.91 m recipients 2.37 are poor.	$193	Assume that the under-reported participants are families below the poverty line. The difference between the data from two sources is 1.29 m. There are 17.16 possible poor households, 2.37 million of which are reported in the data. The probability of a household not reporting is 1.29/(17.16-2.37)=0.087.	Assume that the imputed recipients have the mean benefit of the participants in the CPS data ($193). Then use a fixed ratio to bring the aggregate benefit to match the expenditures. The ratio to bring the fixed benefit per household to match the budgeted amount is 1.94.

Program(s)	Admin Expend (billion)*	CPS Expend (billion)	Admin Number Recipient (million)#	CPS Number Recipient (million)	Avg Benefit/ Household	Imputation Assumption of Recipients	Imputation Assumptions for Benefits
Farmers' Benefits: 10 programs as per Table 1 Section VII	$8.616 b			2.38 m hh			All farmers in the CPS data receive part of this benefit. Distribution is based on the income of each family in proportion to the aggregate income of farm families.
WIC	$2.48 b			3.37 m hh	$735	1.78 m households have one infant, and 1.59 m households have two children under 4. Assume that families with children under 4 and income at 185% of the poverty level are eligible. 6.5m families would be eligible. 3.37/6.5=.518. Use this ratio to determine actual recipients.	Each participant household gets benefits equally.

Program(s)	CPS Expend (billion)*	Admin Expend (billion)	Admin Number Recipient (million)#	CPS Number Recipient (million)	Avg Benefit/ Household	Imputation Assumption of Recipients	Imputation Assumptions for Benefits
Head Start	$3.32 b		0.74 m hh		$4,493	Families with child age 3–5 and family income lower than federal poverty line are eligible; this gives high estimate of 2.73 m. Use random function to draw hh's to participate; probability of .271. Assume each household has only one child participating. (1994 Green Book, pp. 836)	Each participant gets benefits equally. 3.325 b/0.74 = 4493.
JTPA: Six programs as per Table 1 Section IV (omits UI Admin)	4.406 b		1.85 m hh		$2,381	According to the CPS data, 13.74 m households are eligible. Calculation of probability is 1.85/13.74=.134 to estimate number of actual households to receive benefit.	Each eligible household has only one adult participating in the program. Each participant household gets benefits equally.

Program(s)	Admin Expend (billion)*	Admin CPS Expend (billion)	CPS Number Recipient (million)#	Number Recipient (million)	Avg Benefit/ Household	Imputation Assumption of Recipients	Imputation Assumptions for Benefits
School Lunch and Breakfast includes also Summer Food, Child Nutrition Admin and School Milk	5.65 b	6.00 b				A fixed ratio was used to bring the aggregate benefits down to match expenditures: 5.65/6.00=.9423. CPS data reflects the market value of these programs as reported by recipients. Administrative data reflects the actual government expenditure.	

* From 1995 Catalog of Federal Domestic Assistance # From 1996 Green Book

9

CIG, COAG, and COG:
A comment on a debate

Guy Standing

THE VISION THING

If one is talking about "Real Utopia" one must have a reasonably clear answer to two "grand" questions, which one feels inclined to ask in convivial company discussing the issues against the backdrop of a gorgeous lake in Madison, Wisconsin.

Bearing in mind that all theories of distributive justice espouse the equality of something, the first grand question is: *What is it that should be equalized in the Good Society of the twenty-first century?* The essence of the answer is that for real freedom, everybody in society must have *equal basic security*. This must be *unconditional* and *individualized*, the latter being critical for gender-related (and other) issues. The word "real" is used to signify that there must be a combination of "negative liberty" – the negation of deprivation and unchosen controls – and "positive liberty" – the opportunity to make informed and worthwhile choices. Real freedom might be described as the opportunity and capacity to function rationally and purposefully and to develop one's capacities or capabilities.

The complementary grand question is: *Assuming a veil of ignorance (not knowing where they would be in the distribution of outcomes), what sort of society would we want to leave for our children?* The gist of the answer is that they should be able to live in a society celebrating a diversity of lifestyles, constrained only by the need to avoid doing harm to others, and living in circumstances in which a growing majority of people work on their enthusiasms, to pursue their own sense of *occupation* – combining their competencies, or "functionings," varying their work status, and possessing the

175

means to be responsible to their family, neighbors and community. They should be able to live in an environment of *co-operative individualism*, in which individual freedom of action and reflection is backed by collective agency. This notion of development may be called *occupational security* – the security in which to develop capabilities and a working life in which one can combine forms of activity, including the stillness of contemplation.

I contend that a CI (Citizenship Income) is a necessary but not sufficient policy to give effect to the answers to the two "grand" questions, whereas, although it has its attractive properties and a laudable underlying motivation, a Citizenship Grant *in the way envisaged by Bruce Ackerman and Anne Alstott* would not be.[1]

A key term is *security*. Adequate socio-economic security is the bedrock of real freedom. However, one must allow that both as individuals and as society one could have too much security *or* too little security. Freedom does require democratically chosen restraints or constraints, to check recklessness and selfish opportunism. But these must presumably pass some veil of ignorance test. Bearing the desirability of basic security in mind, the ILO's Socio-Economic Security Programme has set out to establish two Policy Decision Principles.

The first, following Rawls but making security the locus of strategy, may be called the *Security Difference Principle*:

> *A policy, or institutional change, is just only if it reduces (or does not increase) the insecurity of the least secure groups in society.*

In other words, freedom cannot be advanced if, say, structural adjustment policies or "shock therapy" deliberately worsen the insecurity of those at or near the bottom of society. And this principle would hold regardless of claims made on behalf of political democracy.

This decision rule, or the principle of constitutionality, provides for a floor, to protect and enhance freedom in moving towards universal basic security. If one accepts that real freedom is the opportunity to pursue a life of dignified and dignifying work, then one must recognize that this is about *distributional* outcomes – the woman outworker, the laborer and the peasant should have the same (or equivalent) basic security as the lawyer, the economist or the shareholder.

The first policy decision rule should be complemented by one dealing with the threat of various forms of paternalism and state control, which also threaten freedom. This may be called the *Paternalism Test Principle*:

A policy, or institutional change, is just only if it does not impose controls on some groups that are not imposed on the most free groups in society, or if it reduces controls limiting the autonomy to pursue occupations of those facing the most controls.

Thus, unless husbands are subject to the same controls as wives, the poor the same as the rich, the unemployed the same as the employed, then policy, institutional or relational controls should be opposed as invalid. And they would remain invalid even if a political majority could be engineered to vote for them. Reducing the freedom of a minority (or a majority in the case of women in many societies) cannot be accepted, even if the change enhanced the freedom of others.

The *Paternalism Test Principle* will become crucial in the first decade of the twenty-first century, because of the dangers of ostensibly benign state paternalism. In the bristling machismo of the late twentieth-century, universalistic social protection without behavioral conditions was widely condemned by loaded words such as "nanny state" and "dependency." The irony is that state paternalism, in the form of workfare, welfare-to-work (*sic*) and other directive selective schemes, more deserves the epithet of nanny state – although such euphemisms should be treated with more disdain than they have been.

If the *Paternalism Test* and *Security Difference Principles* were to be respected, we should favor policies and institutions that move people's work away from external controls, and *towards* greater autonomy, security and equality. This is *not* just about laws and regulations. It is about work structuring – shaping work to suit people, not merely shaping people for jobs, or to make them more "employable" (*sic*), or even to give them more "human capital" or "human capability."[2] Freedom cannot be equated with capabilities or entitlements, unless one defines these terms so broadly that they lack specificity.

We should wish to provide basic security for all, since that is essential to facilitate the individual *freedom to develop*. It is a freedom to develop ourselves through a creative, multi-sided existence, in which our work and our contemplative sides are balanced and balancing.

In this regard, notions of freedom are clouded by economistic jargon that many distinguished observers have treated rather uncritically. Consider "human capital." Too many people see this in an unambiguously positive light. Thus, Amartya Sen sees "human capability" as merely "broader" than "human capital." In claiming a linkage between the two, Sen notes that the latter leads to the *"substantive freedom of people to lead the lives they have reason to value and to enhance the real choices they have.*"[3] One should go further: The human capability perspective *conflicts with* the human capital approach, in that the latter starts from the presumption that education (or, more accurately, schooling) should be valued in terms of its contribution to capital accumulation and growth. Education for its own sake, for the development of our contemplative capacity, is at best downgraded and at worst relegated to irrelevance.

Education is about *time* for contemplation as well as about exposure to the learning of techniques for acquiring fame and fortune. A prior condition for healthy education is basic social and economic security.

THE SOCIO-ECONOMIC CONTEXT

All the great Utopias painted throughout modern history have had characteristics of gentleness, conviviality, fraternity and social solidarity. Any progressive strategy should be compatible with those features. With that thought in mind, what is the biggest challenge that we face in the affluent parts of the world?

Let us be blunt. In the industrialized world, we live in an *apolitical era*, in which there is pervasive class fragmentation and a generalized lack of identity. The I-word dominates the We-word. The young are cynical – and rational – about the politics on offer. In 2000, for the first time, more of those under the age of 30 who voted in the US Presidential election voted for the Republican candidate than for the Democrat – about 40 percent for the former, 20 percent for the latter, and 40 percent for "independent." In France, in the first round of the French presidential election held in April 2002, a majority of that age group stayed in bed, leaving the extreme rightist candidate Le Pen, an odious character, to beat all candidates of the left. In the following weeks, chauvinistic individuals and groups in the UK and the Netherlands, among other places, attracted levels of electoral support that sent shivers of concern through the body politic.

In this context of disembedded populism, it may not seem an auspicious time to propose any form of Real Utopia. Yet surely that would be a faulty reading of the nature of the challenge. The fear should be that the cautious voices of the Lukewarm Left (LL) tendency that prevailed in the 1990s will continue to prevail, pandering to the *weakness-of-will* tendencies, not trying to create the collective agencies and spaces in which a progressive We can evolve. If this continues, the Young (and the not-so-Young) will continue to be disengaged.[4] Unless the Left offers a *politics of paradise*, its long-term prospects will remain bleak. It is not good enough for the LL tendency to say that the young should vote for them because if they do not do so a Bush or Le Pen or Berlusconi will obtain "power."[5] It is better for the LL politicians to be taught sooner rather than later that pragmatic adjustment to the dominant economic orthodoxy can *never* be part of the onward march.

One hypothesis to explain the declining turnout in national and sub-national elections in most affluent countries is that people are encouraged to be individualistic by market norms, whereas voting derives from a sense of social community and social relationships.

The significance of the political disengagement is that the Real Utopia project must surely be one that builds on the energies and the anger of youth, who have always provided the backbone of progressive movements, and not on the *adaptations* that youth are obliged to make in order to adjust to current realities. It must surely appeal not to their *weakness of will*, but to their enthusiasms.

What *asset* does Youth lack most? And what are the *reasons* for this? Coincidentally, what makes Youth *angry*?

The asset youth lacks most is *time*, both currently and, more importantly, in prospect as they move from "school" to "work." In modern affluent societies, there is constant pressure to use every moment, with work demands competing with the need to make contact with peers, through the internet, through emails, through mobile phones or whatever. Men and women in their twenties and thirties – and often in their forties and fifties – have to face *multitasking*, and take their work home, and their home to work. The reasons for this frenzied loss of time is that the pressure to consume and to compete is intensified in electronically connected individualistic capitalism. To pause is to risk becoming obsolescent, passed by in the latest splurge of gadgeting, or displaced by those people with the capacity to perform a revised set of tasks.

It is a lifestyle that is psychologically threatening, leaving both the successful and the failures teetering on the edge of a sort of hysteria. The notion of *bowling alone* is operating alongside the notion of *burnout*.

While this intense pressure on time causes some resentment – often turned inwards, resulting in a sense of inadequacy, stress and periodic burnouts – the younger generations are also infuriated by a sense of injustice, which is also unlike the sense of injustice that predominated in past generations.

In a global society, that takes the shape of revulsion against the gap between the affluence in the rich countries and the grinding poverty in low-income developing countries, and between the absurdly wealthy elites of the world and those detached from the mainstream of all society living a lumpenized existence of precariousness. But it also takes the form of anger about ecological decline, a worry that the quality of the environment is deteriorating as corporate greed and technological prowess threaten the sustainability of our planet. The poor in general, the hassled workers rushing to work on bus and underground, the slum dwellers, the inner-city dwellers, and numerous other groups live in crowded spaces, and they see the affluent living in spaces where they are in control of their environment. Youth see the rain forests shrinking, the range of species shrinking, the coral reefs shrinking, but they also crowd into cramped city spaces, on over-loaded buses or trains, in small costly apartments, permanently in a rush. Time and space are crowded, and they neither own nor control their own time or space. This contributes to a pervasive sense of exis-tential insecurity.

A progressive politics and vision must tap the most critical source of deprivation and anger of its potential supporters, and thus be about a redistribution of those assets perceived as the most scarce and most valued, and most unequally distributed. In a feudal society pro-gressives tapped the anger of the landless; in an industrial society they tapped the anger of those lacking the physical means of production. In the twenty-first century, the key assets lacking for youth and the median "middle-class" worker are *time* and *security*.[6] Progressives should be tapping the anger of those most likely to lack time and security.

The underlying malaise is not accidental. Modern capitalism has an interest in *time compression* among those who consume its products and among those who work to its rhythms. It is almost a truism that more and more people are living under a pressurized mix of induce-ments and incentives to "spend time" – purchase, possess, and display, that is the law of the modern prophets.[7]

In such circumstances, a subversive politics should be about wresting *control* over time for the "dispossessed," and it should recog-nize that such control is the essence of real security. As in every radical moment in history, the progressive vision should be about redistribut-ing the key scarce asset from those who possess too much of it to those with too little or none at all. No progressive agenda ever mobilized the masses unless it offered a strategy to redistribute the key scarce asset.

This is where we reach a dilemma for those wishing to create a Real Utopia: The demographics are in conflict with the potential politics. While youth are concerned by a lack of time and are angered by a sense of ecological injustice, a sense of deprived space, the age group that is growing as a proportion of the total population is the elderly. In part because of the nature of social policy derived from industrial society, this age group does not lack time. The welfare state, even in its residual Anglo-Saxon form, was built on the presumed norm of the laboring man, the "breadwinner," who received income transfers to compensate for "temporary interruptions of earning power." Old age was expected to be a short interruption between labor and death. Although never justified, it was the closest to a norm in the middle decades of the twentieth century. It certainly no longer applies in the early years of the twenty-first century.

There is no intrinsic reason for the over 50-year-olds to have a disproportionate share of society's "free time." Yet once having been granted it through PAYG pension systems during the second half of the twentieth century, they are scarcely likely to give it away – and in this they will be supported by those coming their way.

The demographic dilemma is compounded by the awkward fact that there is a obvious reason for the elderly having little opportunistic interest in the main source of anger motivating youth under globalized capitalism. Youth fear ecological decay, global warming, closing spaces and all the specters that come with them. Where will "We" go in 30 years' time, when the waves have come up round that island of peace and tranquility, when those frenetic years are behind Us? The elderly will understand this existential insecurity, and some will be motivated by altruism to the point of protesting alongside their grand-children. But they do not have a direct interest in those distant times, for the very simple reason that they do not expect to be around.

So, here we have the dilemma. The angry generations, the potential energizers for any Real Utopian project, lack time, lack security and feel the ecological pain. The growing generations – the "wrinklies," "grey power" – have ample free time and have only an altruistic concern for the primary source of anger among their younger citizens, a lack of "quality time." This is scarcely a recipe for a strong model of social solidarity. A formula for a new social solidarity has to be found – or we can kiss goodbye to any hope of a Real Utopia, and come to accept a landscape of Warholian politics, of populist individ-uals or parties flitting before electorates for their proverbial 15 minutes of fame and electoral fortune, catching the passing mood with a flurry of buzzwords, playing on the fears of the crowd, swayed by the turbulence of global capitalism. The crass politics of globaliza-tion and pervasive insecurity are populism and personalization. The politics of paradise must defeat that.

Recapturing control over time is a fundamental part of that politics. While preparing this note, I heard that, apparently, in the 1968 US presidential election the average "soundbite" from the presidential candidates lasted 45 seconds, suggesting some substantive reasoning process, whereas in the 2000 presidential election the average "sound-bite" had been shortened to eight seconds. A reasonable interpretation of this and other symptoms of time pressure is that the populace is suffering from a National Attention Deficit Disorder syndrome – reproducing at societal level a pervasive modern illness among children and young adults that is now a recognizable learning disorder. Induced to flit idly between a flurry of time-filling activities, it is scarcely surprising that youth seem to lack an appreciation of history.[8] Dare one say that lacking a sense of past time is a guide to a lack of a sense of future time? Do not expect a Real Utopia from those who lack a sense of where they have come from and where they are going.

The challenge is clear. The contours of the solution are no less clear – decommercialization of the spirit, decompression of time. Every imagined Utopia has met those challenges. An agenda for Real Utopia should at least face them.

COAG, CIG, AND COG

With these evaluative points in mind, consider the so-called "stake-holding grant" or "capital grant" idea, which should be called a Coming-of-Age Grant (COAG). In this section, I want to bring out differences between it and the Citizenship Income (CIG), but in doing so also highlight why a more generalized *social dividend* approach should give a place both to a CIG *and* to some form of Capital Grant. The variant of the latter that seems desirable is closer to what might be called a *Community Capital Grant (COG)*.[9]

Before considering each proposal, note that the COAG and the CIG have a common heritage and set of objectives, which might be summarized as a desire to enhance real freedom and a desire to promote a more egalitarian form of capitalism.

A danger of the debate between advocates of the CIG and the COAG is that both can be depicted as contrasting panaceas, when neither side believes in that. A CIG advocate would argue that a CIG is a necessary but not sufficient component of a package of policies to create the Good Society, whereas she might contend that a COAG is neither necessary nor sufficient. A COAG advocate might argue that while neither would be sufficient, a COAG would be helpful in enhancing economic freedom, whereas a CIG would not be politically feasible.

In considering the merits of a COAG and a CIG, one must reflect on the nature of modern capitalism. We are in the midst of a great transformation, in which the economy has been disembedded from society, such that there are no adequate systems of regulation, redistribution or social protection to moderate the inequalities and insecurities being thrown up.[10] Globalization and the spread of flexible, informal labor markets are associated with capital and labor *fragmentation*, in which *controls* (unfreedom) over workers and citizens are becoming more complex and indirect, and in which income flows are also becoming more complex. In brief, a small minority are receiving income mainly from capital, with a minority share coming from the performance of highly-paid labor (inter alia). At the top is an elite, blessed by absurdly high incomes and windfall gains that are a spreading dark stain on global capitalism. It is common to read of some executive receiving $10 million in bonuses, or *much* more. The stain is spreading, not just because more executives are joining that way of remuneration but because these incomes convert into huge wealth that is passed from generation to generation, producing the concentration of financial wealth that is the starting point for the COAG proponents.

Alongside the wealthy elite, a diminishing *core* group of workers are receiving income from a variable mix of wages, state benefits, enterprise benefits and capital (shares). Below both groups in terms of income, a heterogeneous group has mushroomed, which for present purposes may be called *outsiders* (flexiworkers, unemployed, and a lumpenized detached group of homeless or socially ill people scraping by). The outsiders put the fear of insecurity up the stomachs of the insiders, who in turn retreat into implicit or explicit "concession bargaining" with their firms.

One can complicate this basic labor market model, and for many purposes should do so. But for our purposes it is sufficient to depict the fragmentation in this way, to think of the implications of a COAG, CIG and COG.

THE ARGUMENTS OVER CIG

A CIG would be a basic income grant paid monthly, to each individual regardless of work status, gender, marital status or age, although a smaller amount would probably be paid to those counted as "children." It would be an equal amount paid to every legal resident, subject to some practical rule of time lived in the country. It would replace most other benefits, although supplements would be provided to certain groups with special needs, such as those with disabilities.

As such, a CIG would not be as radical as either its critics or some of its proponents like to believe. To some extent, it would amount to a consolidation of the patchwork of existing transfers coupled with a reduction in the number of conditions and administrative layers that exist today.

The standard objections to a basic income are that it would be too expensive, it would reduce labor supply, would offend some notion of "social reciprocity," would weaken governments' resolve to lower unemployment, and would weaken the use of a minimum wage. These objections are dealt with at length elsewhere.[11] Here we will deal just with the main ones in the process of concentrating on the advantages of moving in the direction of delinking basic income security from any labor obligation.

First, a CIG would be a means of integrating the tax-and-benefit system and consolidating much of the existing patchwork of out-of-work, in-work and out-of-labor-market income transfers and paternalistically provided social and personal services. In doing so, the gross cost would be the cost of shifting to a universal income support scheme, which would be the cost of including those currently not included. The net cost would be less because there should be a saving on administrative costs of policing the wide range of different conditions and tests for existing benefits, and a saving that would be hard to estimate in that by removing or reducing poverty traps, unemployment traps, and savings traps they would encourage more income-earning activity and more legal work activity. This is because any individual would start paying tax on any income earned above the basic income, and would not face a very high marginal tax rate going from non-employment to employment, or crossing a threshold of income. As for the alleged cost of "churning," paying out to everybody and taxing it back from most people, this objection is disappearing because of the integration of tax and benefits systems made possible by electronic processes.

The cost of existing systems is underestimated. The systems across Europe are riddled with poverty traps, unemployment traps, savings traps and behavior traps that are arbitrary, inefficient and inequitable. This is partly because of the spread of selective, means-tested and behavior-conditioned schemes. It is also partly because of the growing flexibility of working patterns and lifestyles.

Whatever the truth about long-term trends away from "permanent" (*sic*) regular full-time employment, it is both true and in principle desirable that more people at all ages move in and out of the labor force, take temporary jobs, combine several income-earning activities, and in the process do not conform to the simple three-stage model of life and work made the norm of industrial society, going straight from school or college into 30 or 40 years of employment and then sharply shuffling off the stage into retirement. Means-tested benefits are scarcely appropriate for such a society, and nor are those arbitrary behavioral tests that technocratic "Third Way" policymakers and their special advisers love so much.[12]

This leads to a key advantage of moving to a CIG. One of the main criticisms of basic income is that it would be a "handout," which would offend a sense of social reciprocity and lead to a fall in labor supply, to idleness, to shirking, and to a lack of discipline in jobs. This is a criticism from across the political spectrum. There are two ways of meeting it, one defensive and one normative. In assessing its validity either way, bear in mind that most advocates of a basic income envisage a modest amount sufficient just to cover basic subsistence needs, equivalent to the minimum income of social assistance schemes applied in many European countries.[13]

The defensive or pragmatic response to the criticism is to suggest that any adverse effect would be small or insignificant. The criticism presumes a pessimistic interpretation of the human species. We work for many reasons, and numerous surveys indicate that most people want to work and would do so even if they had enough income from other sources on which to subsist. Very few people are satisfied with basic subsistence, and aspire to much more. This is rather well known.

In any case, there are essentially two types of person who could be expected to reduce their labor supply, those with a high opportunity cost of doing income-earning activity (i.e., those wanting to pursue education or training, those wishing to care for relatives, those in poor health, etc.) and those doing low-productivity and/or onerous forms of labor. In both cases, we should want to induce labor-market and policy changes that would be welfare-enhancing. In the case of those with more socially or personally valuable non-labor activity, surely cutting back on a labor activity would be desirable. In the case of the person who withdrew from or cut back on the amount of time spent doing a low-productivity, onerous job, there would be a tendency for wages to go up, inducing others to fill the gap, or a tendency for labor-saving technological change to be introduced, or for people to realize that they did not want or need those jobs performed.

The normative response is based on an interpretation of the emerging mainstream character of twenty-first century capitalism.

We live in an era when globalization and market capitalism are eroding the social fabric so painstakingly erected during the twentieth century – and so assiduously presented to the rest of the world as the model to follow. One should not be atavistic about the erosion, since the era of welfare state capitalism had many flaws and limitations. But nor should we be lulled into thinking that the ill-defined "European social model" has essentially survived and is resilient enough to be sustainable with minor refinements.

While we should neither exaggerate nor belittle the changes taking place, it is reasonably clear that under the aegis of global market forces there is a widespread loss of identity – of class, community and occupation. Belonging to a fixed group is becoming harder. And yet there is a paradox – *individualization with homogenization*, or in plain language a tendency for people to be on their own, seemingly an individual, while all rushing to adopt a similar lifestyle, buying the same goods, watching the same films and TV shows, and so on. We live under incessant pressure to consume, and to labor to earn enough, which is never enough. Accordingly, at least in the middle-years of life more and more people are driven into an intense frenzy of labor-related activity. The story is too well known to need elaboration here. Electronic control systems, represented by personal computers with email plus internet imperatives, and by mobile phones, are only one side of this intensification, in which the borders of workplace and home, and of leisure and work, are blurred. We are losing control of time. This is not a "middle-class" phenomenon only, because the poor everywhere have rarely had any control to lose.

Providing a basic income as a citizenship right would provide a sense of basic security, and in doing so would help in the necessary process of gaining control over the sense of time. It would allow for more rational deliberation, more freedom in which to make choices about how to allocate time.

A related way of arguing for a basic income is by reflecting on the social struggles in the past century as capitalism has evolved. Broadly speaking, the progressive struggle in the early days of the twentieth century was to secure control over the means of production and to decommodify labor. This led to the twin policy of nationalization of production and the welfare state. The latter was, in effect, a way of decommodifying labor, alongside corporate benefits and services, in which the wage became a smaller share of total compensation and of personal income, as state benefits and services grew. This strategy tended to produce rigidities and inefficiencies that became unsustain-able as the era of open economies emerged, and it was always paternalistic, giving labor-based security at the price of limited freedom of choice.

Under globalization, there has been a recommodification of labor, with individualized wages, a cut in enterprise and state benefits and services (or a shift to user-paying schemes) and a weakening of protective statutory regulations. The challenge ahead is that while labor is commodified, the worker (labor power) should not be. A basic income could help make that a reality. In short, it could reduce the commodification of people (commodification implying loss of control over the key assets, namely time and security) while allowing for the continued commodification of *labor*. In this it would be compatible with a globalized economic system, while eroding the power of capital over people. It could also be a means of twenty-first-century Keynesianism, since it would provide a means of stabilizing aggregate demand.

THE DILEMMAS WITH COAG

A COAG would be a one-off grant given to 21-year-olds, or spread over several years in certain circumstances, and given to all those who had graduated from secondary school, excluding drop-outs and those who have foolishly criminalized themselves before they reached that age. The UK "baby bond" scheme would not apply such conditions, apparently.

By contrast, a CIG would provide *basic* economic security, in which to avoid the worst excesses of labor commodification, and it would do so in an essentially non-moralistic way. It would not make a judgment on *when* a person deserves a blast of security, and would not make any moralistic judgment about who should receive it and who should be excluded. A COAG seems to fail on both these scores. Giving a 21-year-old a huge lump sum offends the idea of *basic* security. It is also arbitrary because the age of 21 is not necessarily ideal or optimal; people mature at widely different ages, and their capabilities develop differently. The development of a capacity to make rational choices will vary across individuals and groups and communities. And excluding those 21-year-olds who have been *criminalized* or who have dropped out from, or failed to complete, high school seems both moralistic and arbitrary, as well as inegalitarian.[14] A COAG offers enhanced security, wealth and future income for the more secure (the middle class) relative to the least-secure groups in society. It thereby offends the Security Difference Principle.

A COAG is also not neutral in terms of what type of behavior it encourages and rewards. It offers to benefit the commercially astute over those who have no commercial acumen. In what way is that fair? A COAG would give to those with relatively good talents (high-school graduates without criminal records) the opportunity to become Winners in a winners-take-all, losers-lose-all market society.

Both a COAG and a CIG would be given to individuals. A danger is that schemes for *individuals* can be depicted as *individualistic*, i.e. encouraging and facilitating selfish and opportunistic behavior and attitudes. Surely a Good Society could not come about if policies and institutions were to promote individualistic behaviour in the absence of policies to facilitate *social solidarity* (of some sort). One of the concerns about a block grant such as a COAG is that it would indeed foster the ethos of competitive individualism, while further eroding the already weak sense of social solidarity in most industrialized societies. It is definitely not neutral in that respect.

In the last quarter of the twentieth century, as globalization gathered strength, governments all over the world moved to cut back on policies that were mechanisms of social solidarity and to create more individualistic systems, limiting protective regulations, putting controls on unions, and cutting back on redistributive direct taxation. These trends accelerated the growth of more fragmented labor markets and social structures. How would a COAG affect this? It might give more meaning to *equality of opportunity*. But it would be equalizing the opportunity to become more unequal. It would not affect the societal fragmentation or resultant inequalities in a direct way. By contrast, a CIG would strengthen the income security (albeit modestly) of what we have called *outsiders*, and would increase the bargaining position of flexiworkers, simply because increasing basic security usually strengthens backbones. Presuming that increased bargaining capacity would result in their obtaining higher incomes, which would thereby help to reduce intra-class income differentiation.

What about the impact of a COAG and a CIG on the so-called "self-employed," a poorly named group that includes a lot of people working on contract or on a piece-work basis? On the face of it, both a COAG and a CIG would boost the *supply* of self-employed, including the number of petty capitalists (all those small-is-beautiful enterprises), for which a grant would help in dealing with set-up costs whereas a CIG would make risk-taking less daunting. But one cannot be so confident about the positive impact on *demand* for the self-employed goods and services, which might be such that average net incomes would fall among the "self-employed," even widening the *income* differential between those involved and those in (core) wage labor. This is an empirical issue.

The COAG seems more clearly problematical in that, by targeting on young labor force entrants, it is in effect a subsidy to the young that gives them an advantage over older workers.[15] As such, it suffers from the defects of any selective subsidy. It would enable the young to accept a lower wages and thus help them displace older, more experienced workers. This could, on certain assumptions, actually lower the overall productivity, and even output, of the self-employed as a group. It might also have negative effects on the skill reproduction propensities of older workers, discouraging them from trying to update or broaden their skills because they would face a double competitive disadvantage (being older *per se*, and facing a subsidised competitor group in the labor market).

By contrast, a CIG does not give one group an inbuilt advantage, and if anything would help to reduce segregation. This is an advantage of a universal income scheme.

Finally, in thinking of a COAG on its own terms, one must allow that such a concentrated influx of money targeted on one narrowly defined age group is almost certain to raise the price of goods and services consumed by that age group – good news for surf-board makers, bad news for 30-year-old new surfers. And interest rates for loans to this age group will tend to rise. The outcome could be that much of the transfer would go to other groups, leaving youth little better off.

A COAG VERSUS A COG

A more general concern with COAG is that it offers to fill the space where another variant of a capital grant could fulfil both the objectives of its proponents and the dictates of a Good Society, without its behavioral and distributional drawbacks. What are the *ideal* properties of a Utopian capital grant scheme? This big question is not asked or answered in the chapters of this book. Before considering that, consider the semantics.

What attracts us to the underlying idea of a Capital or Stakeholding Grant is that it suggests a capital *sharing* device, coupled with a *participatory* component and a *redistributive* capacity. The principal proponents of the COAG use the term Stakeholding Grant, which has these connotations. However, in fact they are liberals and are primarily concerned with what they believe are the scheme's *freedom-enhancing* characteristics, rather than its redistributive egalitarian properties (which are not too hot). One does not doubt the laudable motives, but the term is misleading. And in using the term "stakeholding" they tend to block consideration of genuinely more Utopian capital-sharing or stakeholding ideas.

Now let us consider the big question. If what is attractive about the idea of stakeholding and capital grant is a complex image of sharing, redistribution, participation and freedom-enhancement, then we could say that the *optimum* design of a (Real Utopian) scheme is that it should (1) encourage, or at least not discourage, investment, (2) encourage investment that is more ecologically and socially responsible, (3) redistribute income to the most insecure and disadvantaged groups in society, (4) promote participation in economic and social activities, (5) strengthen (or at least not weaken) a sense of *social solidarity*, (6) strengthen real democracy, (7) promote good "corporate governance," and (8) limit economic opportunism.

No scheme could do well on all these counts. And, of course, neither the CIG nor the COAG addresses most of these issues and are not intended to do so. However, unlike a CIG, a COAG might be seen as occupying the space for a more progressive stakeholding grant.

In this respect, there is surely more to be gained by promoting moves towards *economic democracy through collective forms of profit-sharing*. This brings to mind something like the early version of the Swedish *wage-earner funds*, as proposed by Rudolf Meidner, and even the Alaska Permanent Fund. We may call the ideal a COG (Community Capital Grant). It should contain three elements that reflect the emerging character of the productive system and the distributive system emanating from it.

A COG is close to what seemed to be at the heart of the "stakeholder capitalism" debates that emerged in the late 1980s and early 1990s, when stakeholding was primarily seen as a quasi-Keynesian method of promoting growth and employment. The emphasis was on *profit-related pay*, but many economists also touted collective profit sharing for incentive and capital-sharing reasons. Most crucially, any desirable COG scheme must be at least partly *collective*, must go beyond the firm as a unit, and must allow for workers and their representatives to have a Voice in decisions over the use of the resultant funds. The democratic governance is crucial. The main difficulties with a purely company-oriented approach to stakeholding is that it would exclude the "flexiworkers" (casual workers, contract workers, agency workers, etc.) on the edge of companies and it would be a scheme that would widen inequalities between workers in high-tech, high-profit, tradable firms relative to those working in or for low-tech, non-profit-oriented and non-tradable firms and organizations, including those working in public social services.

This is why an ideal model of capital sharing or stakeholding should have a broader *community* element, which might take the form of a *social investment fund*, by which a percentage share of profits would go into a fund that would be governed democratically, as a means of social infrastructural and skill development. Such a fund could be broken into one component for re-investment inside the firm and another that would be for the community outside the firm, which would facilitate redistribution to people other than outside the privileged insiders.[16]

If properly designed, a COG could limit the leakage of capital from the national and local economy, because a key point of the system should be a restructuring of corporate governance, with the social investment funds having voting rights on the firm's investment strategies as stakeholders in their own right.[17] This contrasts with the classic so-called Anglo-American model of shareholder capitalism, because in the latter the *principals* (shareholding elites, including nominal salaried employees) are only interested in their income, which comes mainly from shares.[18]

As such, there are good reasons for thinking that a COG could combat the biggest threat to the emergence of a moderately egalitarian capitalism, by providing a capital-sharing scheme with inbuilt mechanisms to limit leakage in capital flight. Whether or not companies *report* that tax rates on corporate profits and capital are influential in determining their location and marginal investment decisions, the fact is that, over the past 20 years, country after country has reduced or abolished taxes on capital. A sensibly constructed COG could check capital flight and encourage high and socially responsible investment in the local economy. It would also make for a greater degree of participation in corporate and communal decision-making and so encourage *economic democracy*. This is what *stakeholding should be all about*.

The proponents of COAG have sold it as a *stakeholder grant*, and have claimed that it would be "democratic." Yet it is neither an extension of democracy nor a reflection of stakeholding in the production process. By contrast, a COG would be an extension of real democracy – economic democracy – and would be real capital sharing.

Almost incidentally, a COG would also have the potential to improve the way people live and work (unlike the commercialized individualistic frenzy that would be opened up by a generous COAG). By giving workers and working communities a greater Voice inside firms *and* inside the surrounding communities, a COG would tend to give workers a means of altering labor relations and workplace organization, so taking the place of the weakening Voice of old-style trade unionism.

CONCLUDING REMARKS

What is remarkable is the timidity of those talking about Stake-holding Grants. A COAG is fundamentally a populist measure, in the proper sense of that emotive term. It is likely to appeal most to those who do not have a stake in the system, but it does not touch the basic *structure* of capitalism. In that sense, it is profoundly un-Utopian. One could imagine TV chat shows and tabloids having endless items on "how Jane splurged her $80,000," and another patting Jim on his broadening shoulders for having been an exemplary young adult.[19] There would be a splurge of sentimentality. If anything it would help legitimize the unequal society by encouraging people to adopt a casino-type set of attitudes.[20]

By contrast, a CIG is a low-key measure that could reduce the extent of frenzied commercialism, facilitating and encouraging a more gentle pace of life, and facilitating the sort of workstyle that is the essence of all Utopias painted throughout the ages: A mix of labor force work, care work, voluntary community work and constructive leisure.[21] It would not discourage work per se, and of course would actually encourage labor compared with the current means-tested social assistance, through weakening poverty traps and unemployment traps.

This brings me to a last point. Freedom and complex egalitarianism – the pillars of the Good Society – require basic security (the prerequisite for real freedom), capital sharing (high inequality being freedom-constraining) and basic Voice representation security (equally strong for all representative interests in society). This is why it is instructive to think of Karl Polanyi, and recognize that for any economic system to be sustainable and stable it must have a main functioning system or scheme of *social protection*, a main system of redistribution and a main system of labor regulation, as well as a public structure for providing those services (merit goods), where the drawbacks of paternalistic provision are outweighed by the drawbacks of private deprivation or market failure. Basic income security, capital sharing and Voice regulation should be the mainstays of a Real Utopia. Without those three elements, the Utopia on offer would not be worth visiting.

NOTES

1 Some of the points and themes indicated in this note are elaborated in a recent book: G. Standing (2002).

2 The terms "employable" and "employability" have been hugely influential in European policymaking circles. The emphasis is always on altering the characteristics of people, including their attitudes and behavior, so as to make them more pliable, adaptable, disciplined and so on. Rarely does one see anything like as much attention being given to making jobs more workable, or whatever the equivalent term might be.

3 See Sen (1999, 293).

4 I use the terms Young and Youth in a broad sense to cover the group in society (15–30?) historically inclined to be most energetic and politically active.

5 It is a major factor in the decline of the progressive vision that membership of political parties of the left has dropped precipitously. In 1988, the French *parti socialiste* had 200,000 members; in 2002, it had only 80,000. In the UK, membership of the Labor Party declined between 1997 and 2001 by almost 100,000, while activism by its members declined even more dramatically – most do not do any work for the Party. *Guardian*, June 18, 2002, 11.

6 These are also lacking for the poor almost everywhere, although some mistakenly portray the poor as having ample time. In reality, because they lack "time-saving" devices and because they have access only to low-productivity activities, they have to spend more time to achieve any given income, and have to spend more time on sheer survival activities.

7 Over 30 years ago, Steffan Linder wrote a book called *The Harried Leisure Class* depicting the increased goods-intensity of non-working time. The problem is more general now.

8 Shortly after this note was written in draft, a major report was published showing that most high-school graduates in the USA did not have even a basic grasp of their country's history, let alone know much about the rest of the world's history.

9 Note the neutral use of euphemisms and acronyms. Who would want a COAG if you could have a COG? Regrettably, the terms one uses are significant aspects of legitimizing reform proposals. In South Africa, we have used the term Solidarity Grant for a CIG. Note also that a "baby bond," the term used in the UK by the government, is merely a COAG with a COA defined as registered date-of-birth. An advantage of the baby bond over the Ackerman–Alstott proposal is that, presumably, no recipient would have a criminal record, so it would be more universal.

10 This theme, drawing on Karl Polanyi's *The Great Transformation*, is developed at length in my recent book. Standing (2002).

11 Standing (2002) ch. 9.

12   Across Europe and other industrialized countries there are thousands of variants. Thus, only if You, as an unemployed youth, look for a job three times a week and have written evidence to show you are prepared to travel to work 20 miles from home are you entitled to a benefit. Only if You, a disabled elderly person, have less than 2,000 pounds (or Euros) in savings can you be entitled to a grant to pay for care services. Of course, we exaggerate. But we all have our favorites.

13   Some advocates, including Philippe Van Parijs, have in mind a larger amount. Most envisage a modest amount, just enough to cover the basics in life. It is possible that a lot of confusion in the debate arises from different images of what level of basic income is envisaged.

14   It would also seem to offend a basic principle of justice, that a person should not be punished twice for the same offence. One senses that the proposal to exclude those who have fallen foul of the justice system is merely a sop to gain middle-class political support for the COAG.

15   Also, of course, it would worsen the relative and absolute position of the youth who have been criminalized or who have dropped out of school. This is an inegalitarian feature of the COAG. Another distorting aspect is that it would alter inter-generational relations, notably inside families. A COAG would give teenagers or 21-year-olds financial freedom from their parents, compromising parental guidance and potentially severing inter-generational ties. One may or may not like that prospect; one should not ignore it.

16   Of course, deciding what is "the community" is a political and adminis-trative matter. Although it had earlier antecedents, the modern thrust to this way of thinking was Rudolf Meidner's original version of "wage-earner funds" in Sweden in the mid-1970s. This was partly stimulated by the strains in the Swedish *solidaristic wage policy*, and in particular by the way Volvo was bypassing the wage policy by introducing individual profit-sharing pay, thereby increasing wage inequality.

17   The *agents* would become part-*principals*, just as many managers and chief executives have become largely *principals* (receiving most of their income from capital).

18   The Enron implosion is indicative of the danger of having elite *principals* divorced from the *agents*, which management is expected to be in shareholder capitalism. If corporate executives receive most of their income from share options rather than from their salary, they will not have the interest of their workforce very high on their priority list.

19   Hissing and loud clapping in the studio would be amplified, with appro-priate music.

20   I recall visiting lower "middle-class" families in small-town Pennsylvania who were living from state lottery to state lottery, all their hopes crystallized in the monthly set of numbers. Is this freedom?

21 A CIG would also reduce the widespread tendency, induced by flexible labor markets and the international drift to conditionality and means-tested state benefits, for much labor to drift into the grey or illegal economy, evading taxes and contributions, and thereby contributing to pervasive disentitlement. For instance, a CIG would do away with the arbitrary conditionality of unemployment insurance benefits, which have long been a misnomer.

REFERENCES

Sen, Amartya. 1999. *Development as Freedom*. New York: Knopf.
Standing, Guy. 2002. *Beyond the New Paternalism: Basic Security as Equality*. London: Verso.

PART III

Responses

Basic Income versus Stakeholder Grants: Some afterthoughts on how best to redesign distribution

*Philippe Van Parijs**

TWIN IDEAS?

I have always liked the idea of a universal basic endowment or, as Bruce Ackerman and Anne Alstott prefer to call it, a stakeholder grant. But I have never regarded it as belonging in quite the same league, in terms of either feasibility or transformative power, as that of a universal basic income: Either it is feasible but does not change much, or it would change a lot but then it is not feasible, and rightly so. Let me explain.

There is, of course, an intimate conceptual link between the two ideas. So close that, after Hillel Steiner first drew my attention to Thomas Paine's *Agrarian Justice* (1796), the first known formulation of a basic endowment proposal, I regretted for a while having baptised "Collectif Charles Fourier," rather than "Collectif Thomas Paine," the group with which I launched the European discussion on basic income in the mid-1980s.[1] Only for a while, though, for although Fourier's (1836) authority could only be invoked to justify a work-unconditional but means-tested form of minimum income, the two earliest formulations of a genuine universal basic income I subsequently discovered – in Joseph Charlier's *Solution du problème social* (1848), and in the 1849 edition of Mill's *Principles of Political Economy* – were explicitly in Fourier's lineage.[2]

---

* These afterthoughts have been largely fed by stimulating discussions at the workshop Rethinking Redistribution (Madison, WI, 3–5 May 2002). On the pros and cons of basic income and stakeholder grants, see now also Dowding, De Wispelaere and White, eds (2003).

Nevertheless, between grants given unconditionally and equally once in a lifetime, once every decade, once every year, once every month and once every week, there does not seem to be a fundamental difference in a world in which one can borrow and save, and certainly not so deep a difference that the effects would diverge markedly and that very different justifications would be required. So, why do I find one of the two ideas so much more promising than the other?

COMPARING THE COMPARABLE

To answer this question, it is important to first reflect on what would constitute comparable versions of the two ideas. Universal basic endowments in cash already exist in a number of countries. For example, every newborn Belgian baby, boy or girl, rich or poor, is given a non-taxable "birth premium" (*prime de naissance*) of about US$860.[3] The parents are at liberty to put this money aside for when the child will reach adulthood, or to use it (sensibly, no doubt, in most cases) for some more immediate purposes. But even if they had the obligation to save this amount until the child reaches majority, the amount this would represent pales in relationship to the amount currently distributed in the form of (practically) universal monthly child benefits, which average over US$25,000 per child over a period of entitlement that varies from 18 to 25 years, depending on how long a child studies. And it would obviously be even less of a match to even a very modest basic income paid throughout each person's life. Other existing universal endowment schemes, most recently the much publicized "baby bond" introduced in the UK in April 2003, are even less significant.[4]

To make a meaningful comparison of the pros and cons of one-off endowments versus regular basic incomes, it is therefore essential to choose levels of the endowment and of the regular (say, monthly) income that would be, in some sense, equivalent. Bruce Ackerman and Anne Alstott (henceforth A&A) are aware of this. They suggest that their proposed grant of US$80,000, possibly handed out in four instalments of US$20,000 can be regarded approximately equivalent to a basic income of US$400 per month from the ages of 21 to 65. The sum of the corresponding 528 monthly instalments of US$400 obviously comes to considerably more than their grant, namely $211,200, owing to a small extent to some people never reaching the age of 65 but above all to an interest rate which I understand they assumed (very generously) to be 5 per cent p.a. in real terms. After the age of 65, A&A's full reform package includes, like Thomas Paine's, an unconditional regular pension given to all, irrespective of other income and past career, and I shall therefore take for granted in what follows that there is no difference between basic income and their proposal beyond the age of 65. Let us instead scrutinize the claimed equivalence between US$80,000 at 21 and US$400 every month between 21 and 65.

One important feature of the A&A proposal which needs bringing in at this stage is the claw-back of the stakeholder grant at the end of each person's life. If the grant is supposed to be returned to society with the interest it could have generated over this period if invested safely (which is, I believe, A&A's own preferred interpretation of this requirement), it is clear that the best thing to do for any dutiful bene-ficiary is precisely to invest it safely – unless she belongs to the small minority of those who can rightly feel pretty sure of using the money so as to yield a higher-than-average rate of return. Under this inter-pretation, the stakeholder's grant is not really an endowment at all, but rather a loan, and its equivalent in terms of a monthly basic income is not US$400 but zero.

On a milder, and perhaps more sensible construal of the claw-back clause, what needs to be returned to society is not the capital plus interest, but only the capital. In this case, the "equivalent" basic income simply corresponds to the "social dividend" yielded by a person's personal share of society's capital. Under A&A's optimistic assessment of the interest rate, this means 5 percent of US$80,000 or US$4,000 annually and US$333 every month. Owing to the high interest rate, this is not far below the US$400 mentioned by A&A for the case in which both interest and capital are consumable by the ben-eficiary. Under what would seem today a more realistic long-term estimate of the real interest rate, however, this amount should easily be more than halved, and hence be of the same order of magnitude as the dividend paid to every Alaskan resident by Alaska's Permanent Fund (about US$2,000 in 2000, though only US$1,540 in 2002, or about US$130 per month).

Thinking about "equivalent" basic income schemes by bringing in the claw-back, however, takes for granted that the basic income would be introduced cohort by cohort, starting with the one reaching the age of 21 in the current year. This would mean that the first basic income cohort would, unlike the older ones, enjoy a basic income throughout its life, just as, in A&A's proposal, the first cohort of stakeholders will get the full stake without older cohorts receiving anything. But there is another, no less natural (and, for a number of reasons, less problematic) way of thinking about the equivalence. The "equivalent" basic income scheme would then be obtained, not by spreading the grants A&A propose to concentrate on one year of one cohort equally over the 45 years of life of that cohort, but by spreading them equally this year over the forty-five cohorts aged 21 to 65. How much this amounts to per capita obviously depends on the age pyramid. A glimpse at recent demographic figures for the US suggests that the youngest cohort makes up somewhat less than 1/42 of the total population aged 21 to 65, and hence that the basic income equivalent to A&A's US$80,000 would be around US$1,900, or US$160 per month.

There is no need to quibble about the fine details of the simple reasonings leading up to these two estimates. The basic message should be clear. If one has in mind a basic income at the sort of level granted to single people by Europe's existing guaranteed income schemes (at least US$600 per month), then the "equivalent" amount of A&A's grant should be in the order of US$300,000 per capita rather than 80,000. If instead we need to take the latter figure as the relevant reference amount, the "equivalent" basic income is a low "partial" basic income of about US$160 per month for every person aged 21 to 65. A sensible discussion of pros and cons would be best served, it seems, by using these orders of magnitude.

This is by no means the end of the story, however, as part of the funding of the SG may come from a reduction of public expenditure (higher education, mortgage relief, etc.), which would be less naturally coupled with a basic income. In that case, only the "fresh money" component in the funding would be meaningfully available for funding the BI, whose "equivalent" amount would need to be correspondingly reduced. The choice would then be: Either a SG of US$80,000 without mortgage tax relief nor subsidised higher education or a BI of, say, 100, with unchanged mortgage tax relief and subsidies to higher education.

But this again is too simple, because BI too would be naturally combined with (and partly funded by) a restructuring of tax-and-transfer systems, in particular the transformation of existing general income tax exemptions and of the bottom part of existing welfare and social insurance benefits into a basic income for the people involved. Hence, it would be naive to spread evenly into a basic income of, say, US$100 the "fresh money" component in the funding of a SG that is available for funding an "equivalent" basic income scheme. It would make far more sense to concentrate that money on people with low benefits and tax exemptions or none whatever, and to combine it with the money freed by the redefining of the bottom part of existing tax-and-benefit systems to fund a much higher basic income. The real choice would then rather be something like: Either a SG of US$80,000 without current mortgage relief and higher education funding, or a BI of, say, US$300 without some of the existing means-tested benefits and income tax exemptions.

The comparison thus becomes more complex, no doubt, but these complexities are essential for a meaningful comparison between actual reform proposals. To keep a sharp focus on the principled differences that may emerge, however, I shall assume in what follows that one is comparing a SG of US$ 80.000 to an "equivalent" BI of about US$ 160 a month, both funded out of the same amount of new fiscal resources without any substitution of existing schemes.

THE EQUALISATION OF OPPORTUNITIES

SG and BI have much in common. They are given on an individual basis, without means test or work requirement. Yet, they seem to belong to very different perspectives. SG is evidently intended to make opportunities more equal, whereas basic income is no less evidently intended to provide basic economic security more effectively than conditional schemes. However, while it is true that basic income does, and is intended to, contribute to security, it can and does also make sense from the standpoint of the "radical rhetoric of redefining inheritance," and hence of equalizing opportunities. Both stakeholder grants and basic income can be said to make the citizen's opportunities less unequal over their life courses by distributing part of our common inheritance "equally" to all. What this "equally" means is different in the two proposals: The same amount to all those who reach the age of 21 versus the same amount each month to all those who are adult citizens (aged 21 to 65) alive that month.

In the most superficial sense, SG is the more egalitarian variant, since those dying, say, at 25 will have received the full amount. But this is a misleading appearance. First, given that the end of life is generally unforeseen, this hardly makes a difference to the "injustice" stemming from the inequality in the length of (the healthy part of) people's lives: The person dying at 25 may have turned it into an annuity most of which will be left unconsumed or, worse still, devoted it entirely to an investment which has not yet started to bear fruit.

Second, and crucially, SG opens up the possibility of "stake blowing," whether deliberately for consumption purposes or involuntarily through bad investments (wrong house, wrong training, wrong business). This is bound to make SG far less opportunity-egalitarian than BI. Why? Lifetime opportunities are of course determined only to a very limited extent by the stake received at 21. They are powerfully affected by intellectual abilities, parental attention, school quality, social networks of various sorts, and so on. On average, those young people who are already favored along these various dimensions are precisely those who are most likely to make the best possible use of their stake. The real value of a stake of the same nominal amount will therefore be considerably less for those who lack the intelligence, guidance, education, connections, etc. that would enable them to competently select, in the light of what they care about on reflection, what is best for themselves.

This huge egalitarian advantage of a BI over a pure SG scheme is significantly reduced, though far from abolished, relative to A&A's actual proposal because of two important restrictions they impose. One is that they advocate a basic pension for the elderly, which amounts to preventing the young from blowing the part of their stake that is needed to secure them a minimum standard of living if and when they reach old age. The other is that they compel those who fail to complete high school to turn their stake into an annuity: BI as a consolation prize for the school drop-outs. However, even with the stakes reduced to the 21–65 stretch and with the set of potential stake-blowers shrunk to the 80 per cent of each cohort who complete high school, the room for an inequality-amplifying effect remains considerable.

BI, on the other hand, is assumed to be non-mortgageable, as is in most countries the lowest layer of any household's income. Hence it denies young people the freedom to blow their life-long stake in one go. However, especially for the less well endowed among them, it improves the real freedom to make sensible long-term investments. As Bart Nooteboom (1986), James Meade (1989) and many others have emphasized, an unconditional life-long security gives less wealthy people the confidence and endurance to make investments and take risks, while also making potential (private and public) lenders more willing to make the loans that will enable them to acquire qualifications or go into business. Unlike the freedom to make choices that jeopardize later freedom, therefore, the freedom to make choices that enhance it is far less affected by the difference between SG and BI. Hence, while it is clear that a BI does better than an "equivalent" SG in terms of security, it is by no means evident that a SG does better than an "equivalent" BI in terms of equalizing opportunities – quite the contrary.

WEALTH EQUALIZATION

Sensible SG advocates may concede that SG is worse than BI in terms of equalizing opportunities as soon they realize, on the basis of considerations of the sort just sketched, that the opportunity space is enlarged to very different extents by a given SG depending on the genetic and social equipment of its beneficiary. But they may still feel confident that a SG funded by a wealth tax, as proposed by A&A, is more wealth-equalizing than a BI financed by an income tax (be it in the form of a consumption tax or energy tax or value-added tax), as proposed by most BI supporters. To shake this confidence, I invite them to pay some attention to the notion of wealth.

First, economists soundly regard a working person's current entitlement to a future retirement pension as a component of her present wealth, on a par with her savings. A secure future flow of basic income is no different. This broad sense of wealth is routinely used by economists – in his efficiency wage models, Edmund Phelps (1994, 1997), for example, uses the expression "social wealth" to refer to the bundle of work-independent rights to an income. On the benefit side, therefore, BI constitutes no less than SG a form of wealth redistribution. Moreover, given what has just been said about the non-random inegalitarian distribution of stakeblowing, there is even no doubt – as far as the benefit side is concerned – that this wealth redistribution is more egalitarian with BI than it is with SG.

As we turn next to the tax side, it must first be noted that BI could in principle be financed, be it partly, as it is in some proposals (including the very first one I made myself, back in 1982), by a wealth or inheritance tax. Note, moreover, that even a pure tax on labor income can be largely viewed as a tax on the return to human capital. If a person's human capital is understood, as is again sensible, as part of her wealth, its assessed value is bound to be negatively affected by the taxation of its return. Consequently, it cannot be said a priori whether a conventional wealth tax or an income tax is more wealth-equalizing in this broad sense of wealth (which we have every reason to find more ethically relevant than the narrower concept). Much would depend, for example, on the correlation between income and human capital, and on how high and how progressive the income tax and the wealth tax are.

DECOMMODIFICATION

A final remark on the decommodification of human beings. There is an obvious sense in which both BI and SG contribute to it. A substantial and universal individual cash entitlement entirely independent of one's selling or being prepared to sell one's labor power amounts to conferring a radically decommodified economic status onto each person.

There is, however, a sense in which SG is, on the contrary, meant to produce a "commodifying" effect. A&A like to point out that their scheme would tend to foster a conversation among the young, and between the young and their parents, about how to use most profitably the stakeholder grant. They will devote time to discussing whether it should be used as an investment in the beneficiary's human capital, or as the capital base for some business venture, or as a more or less secure form of saving. All this, it is argued, will effectively foster a market-oriented frame of mind. This is certainly no part of the typical pro-BI rhetoric. Quite the contrary: one argument frequently used is precisely that there will be less need to speak about money, owing to the security offered by the scheme, and hence, it is sometimes argued, more time to think about and experience what really matters: God, women, men, children, the natural world and other hopefully not too commodified entities.

There is, however, a distinct sense in which BI can also be said to contribute to commodification. For BI's stated purpose of fighting exclusion from paid work can be re-described in terms of a re-commodification of the skills of the excluded. This is supposed to be achieved through two mechanisms. First, a BI is not only unconditional as regards (willingness to) work, but also as regards earned income, which amounts to making it an implicit subsidy for low-paid work and hence (relative to means-tested guaranteed income schemes) a means of helping more people into a job without lowering their standard of living. Second, by making it possible, or cheaper, to reduce working time or interrupt one's career at a time that best suits the person concerned, BI works as a mechanism for sharing jobs between more people (the jobs one frees on a part-time or temporary basis can be taken up by others) and spreading paid employment over a longer stretch of one's life (taking time off to look after one's young children and to retrain before it is too late makes it less likely that one will have to retire early as a result of deskilling or burnout). Consequently, BI can be said to increase the commodification of people, in the sense that it fosters participation in the labor market for a greater proportion of people and a longer portion of their lives, while at the same time decreasing the commodification of people by making them less dependent on the labor market for their subsistence.

This is a paradox, not a contradiction. Indeed, the fundamental reason why I find BI such a good proposal is precisely that it contributes to commodification in the former sense while contributing to decommodification in the latter. And the fundamental reason why I find BI so much better than a comparable SG is precisely that BI plausibly promises to do both these things both more powerfully and more equally than SG.

NOTES

1 See Collectif Charles Fourier (1984).

2 My attention was drawn to Charlier by John Cunliffe and Guido Erreygers (2001, 2003a, 2003b) and to Mill's section on Fourierism by George D.H. Cole (1953) via Walter Van Trier (1995).

3 In 2002, the *prime de naissance* was EUR983.68 (or about US$1,150) for every first child, or twin, or triplet, etc., EUR740,10 (or about US$860) for each other child. To be entitled, it suffices that at least one of the parents should belong to a "family benefit fund" (*caisse d'allocations familiales*) by virtue of being employed, or officially unemployed, or a student, or retired, etc.

4 The Blair government's "baby bond," whose introduction was announced in April 2003 by Chancellor Gordon Brown, has been fixed at £250 (about US$400, and hence less than half Belgium's universal "birth premium"), for every newborn child. It rises to £500 for the children of the poorest third of households (*Financial Times*, 10 April 2003).

REFERENCES

Ackerman, Bruce and Alstott, Anne. 1999. *The Stakeholder Society*. New Haven, CT: Yale University Press.

Charlier, Joseph. 1848. *Solution du problème social*. Brussels: Chez tous les libraires du Royaume.

Cole, George D.H. 1953. *History of Socialist Thought*. Basingstoke: Palgrave Macmillan, 2003.

Collectif Charles Fourier 1984. "L'allocation universelle", *Le Travail dans l'Avenir*, Bruxelles: Fondation Roi Baudouin, 9–16. (Reprinted in *La Revue nouvelle* 81, 1985, 345–351. English translation in *Resurgence* 110, 1985, 13–14.)

Cunliffe, John and Erreygers, Guido. 2001. "The enigmatic legacy of Fourier: Joseph Charlier and basic income," *History of Political Economy* 33 (3), 459–84.

— 2003. "Basic Income? Basic Capital! Origins and Issues of a Debate," *Journal of Political Philosophy* 11 (1), 89–110.

Cunliffe, John, Erreygers, Guido and Van Trier, Walter. 2003. "Basic Income: Pedigree and Problems," in *Real Libertarianism Assessed*.

Political Theory after Van Parijs (A. Reeve and A. Williams, eds), Basingstoke: Palgrave Macmillan, pp. 15–28.

Dowding, Keith, De Wispelaere, Jurgen and White, Stuart eds. 2003. *The Ethics of Stakeholding*. Basingstoke: Palgrave Macmillan.

Fourier, Charles. 1836. *La Fausse Industrie, morcelée, répugnante, mensongère, et l'antidote, l'industrie naturelle, combinée, attrayante, véridique, donnant quadruple produit et perfection extrême en toutes qualités*, Paris: Anthropos. 1967.

Meade, James E. 1989. *Agathotopia: The Economics of Partnership*. Aberdeen: University Press, David Hume Institute.

Mill, John Stuart. 1849. *Principles of Political Economy*, 2nd edn. New York: Augustus Kelley, 1987.

Nooteboom, Bart. 1986. "Basic Income as a Basis for Small Business," *International Small Business Journal* 5 (3), 10–8.

Phelps, Edmund S. 1994. "Low-wage Employment Subsidies versus the Welfare State," *American Economic Review. Papers and Proceedings* 84 (2), 54–58.

— 1997. *Rewarding Work*. Cambridge, MA: Harvard University Press.

Van Trier, Walter. 1995. "Everyone a King. An Investigation into the Meaning and Significance of the Debate on Basic Incomes with Special Reference to Three Episodes from the British Inter-War Experience." Katholieke Universiteit Leuven: Fakulteit politieke en sociale wetenschappen, PhD thesis.

Macro-Freedom

Bruce Ackerman and Anne Alstott

Current social policy divides each life into three broad phases – childhood, adulthood, old age – and treats each very differently. For example, children get education, the elderly get pensions, and adults get help when they need it most. Within this three-part framework, basic income and stakeholding join in a shared critique of the status quo: They both challenge the need-based approach to the adult phase of life.

But as suggested in Chapter 2, we also seek to raise a deeper question that eludes the partisans of basic income. We mean to challenge the now-conventional tripartite division of the course of life and to urge social recognition for a distinctive fourth phase. Call it *early maturity*.

Stakeholding is designed to confront the distinctive life-shaping opportunities that are open at this stage of life. The debate in this volume has, to our mind, insufficiently attended to this point, and for the best of reasons: We did not spell out this distinctive rationale sufficiently. We hope that this chapter will compensate for our deficiency and help clarify the next round of discussion.

Consider the problems of early maturity a bit more elaborately. For upwardly mobile men or women, early maturity begins when they leave secondary school and look forward to a few years in university; for the downwardly mobile, it begins when they are thrown onto the labor market after completing formal schooling – which is always shorter than, and usually inferior to, that provided their upwardly mobile peers.

All these young adults have much in common.[1] They are physically and sexually mature, and capable of forming lasting emotional

relationships. Their socialization and education enable them to nego-
tiate the ordinary tasks and small pleasures of life – going to the
supermarket, taking in a movie. Day in and day out, they are making
many small choices and taking responsibility for their decisions.
Whether they are moving up or down on the escalator of life, they all
experience the joys and frustrations of freedom on a day-to-day basis.
Micro-freedom, as it were.

The big difference comes when they try to take the measure of their
life as a whole. For the college-bound, life is full of life-shaping
choices. Should they prepare for a practical profession, or embark on
a more idealistic life? Do they care most about building a business,
exploring the arts, or protecting the environment? To be sure, no
one's options are unlimited: Ability and economic reality are very real
constraints, and woe to the person who refuses to recognize them.
Nevertheless, typical university students have a sense that they are
taking an active role in determining the overall shape of their lives.
They enjoy macro-freedom, not only micro-.

This isn't true for most other young adults. For them, early
maturity is a time of pervasive economic subordination. They come
to the labor market with no property and few skills. The challenge is
to put some bread on the table and pay the rent – not to fantasize
about the shape of their lives as a whole, but to make ends meet in the
here-and-now. Macro-freedom is a luxury that is simply beyond their
means. Perhaps they can steal a weekend away from their ordinary
life, and have a great time with their friends, families, or lovers; but
escapism isn't quite the same thing as macro-freedom.

Nevertheless, it is the best that most people can afford in the real
world. They can't experiment with a variety of occupations; nor can
they take some time off and invest in training for one or another skill.
They may be reluctant to move to a more prosperous city or quit a
half-decent job even if their boss is an oppressive martinet. These
early years of subordination can profoundly shape self-understanding
– rather than seeing themselves as actively engaged in the construction
of their lives, they see themselves almost entirely as passive agents of
economic necessity.

This great macro-freedom divide is not based on some great natural
fact. It is the consequence of the three-part division that social policy
now imposes on the course of human life. Since early maturity is not
marked out as a distinct phase, social policy sorts 18-year-olds into
the two remaining categories – either they are "very old children" or
"very young adults." Or – the worst conceptual option – some are
stuffed into one category; some into the other.

Broadly speaking, welfare states in both America and Europe have been pursuing the worst conceptual option in the worst possible way. Upwardly mobile 18-year-olds are treated as if they were "very old children" during their university years – they receive free, or heavily subsidized, schooling, just as they did during their childhood. But their downwardly mobile peers are treated as "very young adults" – once they leave school, they are on their own, except when they suffer unemployment, serious disability, or some other special need.

The result is a profound injustice. If anything, university students deserve smaller subsidies. Their symbol-using skills will put them on the high road to high income for the rest of their lives. In contrast, a generous stake provides the rest of their fellow citizens with the only opportunity they will get, as young adults, to hold their head up high and act affirmatively to shape their own economic future.

The partisans of basic income are blind to this disparity, since they fail to reflect on the distinctive predicaments of early maturity. They propose to pay out a specified sum to all adults of all ages – regardless of the extent to which they have had a genuine chance to enjoy the benefits and burdens of macro-freedom as they reach early maturity.

Stakeholding is different. We selected $80,000 as our stake because this is the amount it costs to attend a good four-year college in the United States. Young adults who take advantage of this educational opportunity will largely spend the money on tuition and living expenses, exchanging their stake for a university degree. While the stakeholding grant may well give them greater flexibility in choosing academic programs, it will not radically transform their lives. They already have macro-freedom, and the stake will only help them exercise their life-shaping powers in better ways.

Not so for the broad middle of the population. Many people simply aren't very good at the symbolic manipulations required by university education. But they are perfectly capable of the responsible exercise of macro-freedom if they were given a stake. With $80,000 in the bank, they too could ponder their life choices, taking account of their abilities and economic realities, in a spirit similar to that of their upwardly mobile peers. Perhaps more men and women might now find it economically plausible to combine their $80,000 together and take on the responsibilities of marriage and child-rearing; perhaps stakeholders might chip in a part of their stakes to form a small business; perhaps it makes most sense for some to put the $80,000 in a bank, and use the interest as a monthly basic income – at least until some more fundamental life-shaping opportunity comes along ...

Or perhaps, says the skeptic, they will simply blow the money away on something frivolous?

Nobody ever seems to ask this skeptical question about the college-bound. We are lucky enough to teach at one of America's great universities, which imposes very meritocratic standards on those who seek admission. And yet there are a sizeable number of Yalies who spend most of their "bright college years" carousing at parties while cramming bits of useless information into their brains before final examinations. Undoubtedly, university authorities should do more to make life tougher for these legions of goof-offs. But even the toughest administrator recognizes that a significant number of his students will manage to manipulate the system, emerging with passing grades but little genuine understanding. We have long since accepted this great waste of resources as part of the price we must pay for a system enabling millions of university students to use their macro-freedom in a thoughtful and responsible fashion.

We call for similar tolerance when it comes to stakeholding. Just as some university students use their macro-freedom to booze it up, so will some of the newly empowered members of the stakeholding class. But the abuse by some should not destroy the claim of millions of others to gain the power actively to shape the contours of their lives.

To minimize the dangers of abuse, we would postpone the age of stakeholding for those who don't use the money for higher education. We urge the Blair government to rethink its decision to distribute "baby bonds" to all citizens when they reach the age of 18, especially if future funding increases enrich these capital grants beyond their present modest size. Young adults should spend some time in the "school of hard knocks" to gain the maturity required to use their stakes responsibly. But at that point, we think that the broad middle class, no less than the symbol-using class, are entitled to the resources necessary for the effective exercise of macro-freedom.

Indeed, the recurrent emphasis on stakeblowing may tell us more about the anxieties of our critics than the likely conduct of stake-holders. After all, our critics come from the symbol-using classes, enjoy comfortable lives, and, quite naturally, insulate their own children from the rigors of economic necessity. When these children rise to early maturity, some of them may not have been taught the value of money, and so might blow their stakes – unless their parents make it clear that prodigal sons and daughters can't expect further unconditional assistance if they fritter away their $80,000. But the overwhelming majority of stakeholders – especially those who steer clear of university – won't come from such pampered backgrounds.

From their early childhood, they will understand the value of money. When they finally gain their capital grants in their early twenties, they will overwhelmingly see the stake for what it is: A precious resource for taking control of their lives, a once-in-a-lifetime opportunity.

To be sure, many may lack financial sophistication equal to that achieved by young adults from the symbol-using classes. Although this gap can't be entirely eliminated, it can certainly be ameliorated by the school system: "How to Manage Your Stake" should be made a mandatory subject in all secondary schools, serving as a practical introduction to economics – a subject too often ignored in our curricula. And given their prospective stakes, students will have a unique motivation to master the material!

We don't deny the obvious. There *are* some people who lack the cognitive and emotional capacities required to engage actively in shaping their lives. We propose a crude sociological test to identify these people. About 20 percent of Americans, for example, fail to obtain a high school diploma. Some of these people can't cope with the daily challenges of life, and require intrusive custodial management, and generous assistance, before they can lead half-decent lives. But others can operate effectively on a day-to-day basis even though they lack the discipline required to stay in school and graduate.

We would deny these drop-outs full access to their stakes, even though we will be doing some of them an injustice. Despite their failure to gain a high school diploma, some may well have the practical intelligence needed to handle the responsibilities of stakeholding. Nevertheless, many won't use their macro-freedom responsibly, and given this likelihood, it seems prudent to deny them access to a sum as large as $80,000. Instead, they should be provided with a basic income of $400 to $500 a month – representing the annuitized value of the underlying stake. While high school drop-outs should always be encouraged to gain their full stakeholding privileges by passing an appropriate examination, they should only receive a basic income until they manage to leap over this hurdle (or some other one that may be better designed to test for the underlying competences).

Our treatment of this group at the bottom illustrates the distinctive values that inform the contrast between stakeholding and basic income. By hypothesis, this group does possess the day-to-day skills needed to manage their micro-freedom in a minimally responsible fashion; but they lack the larger set of competences required to play an active role in shaping the overall contours of their lives. Since this is the distinctive interest supporting stakeholding, we are willing to endorse basic income when the exercise of macro-freedom no longer seems a realistic option.

Stakeholding represents a new collective commitment to macro-freedom for all who have a realistic chance to exercise it responsibly. We believe that this is an enormously attractive ideal for progressive politics in the twenty-first century, and we are greatly encouraged that Tony Blair has given it his backing – first by making it his Big Idea during his successful re-election campaign, and then by following through with a first, very small, down payment in his budget for 2003.

But if the program gains political traction, it will involve very large transfers over time. If our own $80,000 proposal were implemented in America, there would be an annual transfer of $250 billion to the rising younger generation from those, mostly over 55, who hold the lion's share of the nation's wealth. This large sum is enough to stagger defenders of the needs-based welfare state of the twentieth century, who are well-represented in this volume. So far as they are concerned, a large commitment to stakeholding will drain resources desperately required for the truly needy.

Technocratic analyses demonstrating this point invariably assume that the larger political commitment to the existing welfare state will remain roughly constant. We respectfully disagree. Without new ideals that inspire political commitment from the majority, traditional programs for the needy will wither. Progressives must work to reattach the interests of the broad majority to the interests of the truly needy. Otherwise, the middle classes will join an anti-tax coalition with the wealthy that restricts funds flowing to the bottom. Stakeholding is just the sort of program that can convince the middle that it has everything to gain from rejoining a coalition in support of distributive justice. Such a coalition will make it more likely that the claims of the truly needy will be given substantial recognition.

Of course, there is a risk that stakeholding might be used as an excuse to cut off other forms of legitimate assistance. But there is no politics without risk. And those welfare-staters who refuse to innovate strike us as embarking on a very high-risk strategy indeed.

Putting politics to one side, there are many ways of financing the stake – some better than others. This is true of basic income as well. When comparing the two initiatives, analysts should insist on a level playing field – since our program carries a $250 billion tax bill, one should compare it with a $250 billion program for basic income. If one chooses to finance basic income with a substantial increase in the progressive income tax (as does Philippe Van Parijs), one should use the same financing method in assessing a comparable stakeholding program.

We have our own favorite financing scheme. But it is important to keep the tax side of the issue distinct from the benefit side. Arguments about financing are secondary to arguments about the merits of stakeholding. The key question is whether the macro-freedom advantages of stakeholding are offset by countervailing advantages of basic income. If stakeholding comes out on top in this assessment, we would be happy to join any plausible financing scheme that gains general favor amongst analysts and politicians.

With this caveat, allow us a few parting words on behalf of our favorite financing devices. We conceive of stakeholding as a form of citizen inheritance that deserves recognition as an appropriate complement to the traditional system of private inheritance. A young adult's share of the wealth should not so heavily depend on whether her parents have done well in the marketplace and whether they die early or late in life. Her status as a citizen should also entitle her to a stake based on the great contributions of previous generations of citizens to the commonwealth.

This understanding of stakeholding provides a normative focus to our choice of tax base. Since we are funding a system of citizen inheritance, it seems particularly appropriate to get the money out of taxes on private inheritances. In contrast to the libertarian views voiced by the Republican Party of George W. Bush, we regard inheritance taxes as the fairest tax of all. [2] Children of rich parents didn't choose their parents, nor did they earn their wealth through their own efforts. It is entirely proper to tax their inheritance at high progressive rates and funnel the money into a much fairer system of citizen inheritance.

Given the ease with which inheritance taxes may be evaded, we propose a wealth tax as a prophylactic measure. Rather than waiting for rich people to die, we would require Americans to pay a flat 2 percent annual tax on all assets over a generous exemption of $230,000. Using 1998 data, this means that about 85 percent of households will be completely exempt from the tax, with the top one percent paying about 40 percent of the total. This will be more than enough to fund an $80,000 stakeholding program. [3]

Over the long run, we envision a second funding source. When the first generation of stakeholders die, they should contribute to the stakeholding fund for the next generation. They should not be permitted to bequeath large sums to their own children before paying back their initial stake, with interest, to the stakeholding fund. We conceive this payback as another form of inheritance taxation, but with even greater ideological appeal: If somebody parlays his initial $80,000 into a large capital stock, it seems hard for even the most libertarian folks to protest when he is required to return his stake to the fund which gave him his head start in life. But we only expect market winners to make this payment. For the overwhelming majority, the initial stake will not be a lifetime loan, but a lifetime grant.

If we stand back from the details, the two sides of our program cumulate into a larger whole. As the younger generation rises to early maturity, their claim to citizenship is redeemed by the reality of macro-freedom for all who can responsibly use it. As the older generation declines toward death, those who have been successful in the marketplace recognize their debt to the polity by providing the resources needed to assure macro-freedom for their successors.

Symbolically, this whole seems to be larger than the sum of its parts. We think it constitutes as a compelling idea that might serve as the foundation for a new progressive politics in the twenty-first century. But we are more than willing to accept half a loaf, and accept any plausible tax scheme that generates significant stakeholding for the next generation. Macro-freedom is a precious good, which should be available to all citizens capable of actively shaping their own lives. It should no longer be treated as a luxury enjoyed only by the upwardly mobile university crowd.

NOTES

1 There are a substantial number of young adults whose physical and social development does not allow them to function in the way contemplated by this paragraph. We defer our discussion of this group to a later point.

2 See Bruce Ackerman (1980), ch. 7.

3 Mark Wilhelm (2001).

REFERENCES

Ackerman, Bruce. 1980. *Social Justice in the Liberal State*. New Haven, CT: Yale University Press.

Wilhelm, Mark. "A Proposed Wealth Tax: Revenue Estimates and Distributed Analysis Using the 1998 Survey of Consumer Finances," April 2001 (unpublished paper on file with authors).

List of Contributors

Bruce Ackerman
Sterling Professor of Law and Political Science, Yale Law School
http://www.law.yale.edu/outside/html/faculty/baa27/profile.htm

Anne Alstott
Jacquin D. Bierman Professor of Taxation, Yale Law School
http://www.law.yale.edu/outside/html/faculty/ala23/profile.htm

Philippe Van Parijs
Professor at the Faculty of economic, social and political sciences of
the Catholic University of Louvain (UCL)
http://www.etes.ucl.ac.be/PVP/VanParijshomepageEN.htm

Barbara R. Bergmann
Distinguished Professor of Economics, American University
(Retired)

Irwin Garfinkel
Mitchell I. Ginsberg Professor of Contemporary Urban Problems,
Columbia University School of Social Work
http://www.columbia.edu/cu/ssw/faculty/profiles/garfinkel.html

Chien-Chung Huang
Assistant Professor Social Work, Rutgers' School of Social Work.
http://www.rci.rutgers.edu/~huangc/

Wendy Naidich
Doctoral Candidate, Columbia University School of Social Work
http://www.columbia.edu/cu/ssw/phdprogram/onthemarket/phds_on_
market/NaidichCV.pdf

Julian Le Grand
Richard Titmuss Professor of Social Policy, London School of
Economics
http://www.lse.ac.uk/people/j.legrand@lse.ac.uk

Carole Pateman
Professor of Political Science, University of California, Los Angeles
http://www.polisci.ucla.edu/menu/people/faculty/carole_pateman.php

Guy Standing
Director, ILO Programme on Socio-Economic Security

Stuart White
Fellow and Tutor in Politics, Jesus College, University of Oxford.
http://www.politics.ox.ac.uk/about/stafflist.asp?action=show&person
=44

Acknowledgements

This book grew out of a *Real Utopias Project* conference, "Rethinking Redistribution," held in May, 2002, at the University of Wisconsin - Madison. We would like to thank the Vilas Trust of the University of Wisconsin, the editorial board of *Politics & Society*, and the Macarthur Foundation Research Network on Equality and Economic Performance for their generous funding of the conference. The staff of the A.E. Havens Center – Patrick Barrett, Shamus Khan, and Grace Livingston – provided invaluable help in organizing the conference.

Earlier versions of a number of the paper in this volume were previously published in a special issue of *Politics & Society*, copyright Sage Publications, Inc., March 2004, Volume 32, Number 1, and are reproduced here with permission. They are:

Erik Olin Wright, "Introduction", pp. 3–6.

Philippe van Parijs, "Basic Income: a simple and powerful idea for the twenty-first century", pp. 7–40.

Bruce Ackerman and Anne Alstott, "Why Stakeholding?" pp. 41–60.

Stuart White, "The Citizen's stake and Paternalism" pp. 61–78.

Erik Olin Wright, "Basic Income, Stakeholder Grants and Class Analysis" pp. 79–88.

Carole Pateman, "Democratizing Citizenship: some advantages of a basic income" pp. 89–106.

Barbara Bergman, "A Swedish-style welfare state or basic income: which should have priority" pp. 107–118.

Index